www.lakeforestlibrary.org

THE HISTORY OF PAKISTAN

ADVISORY BOARD

John T. Alexander
Professor of History and Russian and European Studies, University of Kansas

Robert A. Divine
George W. Littlefield Professor in American History Emeritus, University of Texas at Austin

John V. Lombardi
Professor of History, University of Florida

THE HISTORY OF PAKISTAN

Iftikhar H. Malik

The Greenwood Histories of the Modern Nations
Frank W. Thackeray and John E. Findling, Series Editors

Greenwood Press
Westport, Connecticut • London

Library of Congress Cataloging-in-Publication Data

Malik, Iftikhar Haider, 1949–
The history of Pakistan / Iftikhar H. Malik.
p. cm. — (The Greenwood histories of the modern nations, ISSN 1096–2905)
Includes bibliographical references and index.
ISBN-13: 978–0–313–34137–3 (alk. paper)
1. Pakistan—History. 2. India—History. 3. Indus civilization. I. Title.
II. Series.
DS384.M2716 2008
954.91—dc22 2008012989

British Library Cataloguing in Publication Data is available.

Copyright © 2008 by Iftikhar H. Malik

All rights reserved. No portion of this book may be reproduced, by any process or technique, without the express written consent of the publisher.

Library of Congress Catalog Card Number: 2008012989
ISBN-13: 978–0–313–34137–3
ISSN: 1096–2905

First published in 2008

Greenwood Press, 88 Post Road West, Westport, CT 06881
An imprint of Greenwood Publishing Group, Inc.
www.greenwood.com

Printed in the United States of America

The paper used in this book complies with the Permanent Paper Standard issued by the National Information Standards Organization (Z39.48–1984).

10 9 8 7 6 5 4 3 2 1

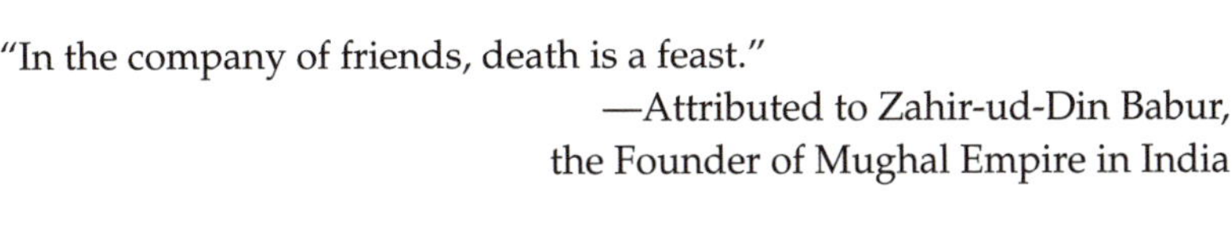

"In the company of friends, death is a feast."

—Attributed to Zahir-ud-Din Babur,
the Founder of Mughal Empire in India

Contents

Series Foreword

The Greenwood Histories of the Modern Nations series is intended to provide students and interested laypeople with up-to-date, concise, and analytical histories of many of the nations of the contemporary world. Not since the 1960s has there been a systematic attempt to publish a series of national histories, and, as editors, we believe that this series will prove to be a valuable contribution to our understanding of other countries in our increasingly interdependent world.

Over thirty years ago, at the end of the 1960s, the Cold War was an accepted reality of global politics, the process of decolonization was still in progress, the idea of a unified Europe with a single currency was unheard of, the United States was mired in a war in Vietnam, and the economic boom of Asia was still years in the future. Richard Nixon was president of the United States, Mao Tse-tung (not yet Mao Zedong) ruled China, Leonid Brezhnev guided the Soviet Union, and Harold Wilson was prime minister of the United Kingdom. Authoritarian dictators still ruled most of Latin America, the Middle East was reeling in the wake of the Six-Day War, and Shah Reza Pahlavi was at the height of his power in Iran. Clearly, the past 30 years have been witness to a great deal of historical change, and it is to this change that this series is primarily addressed.

With the help of a distinguished advisory board, we have selected nations whose political, economic, and social affairs mark them as among the most important in the waning years of the twentieth century, and for each nation we have found an author who is recognized as a specialist in the history of that nation. These authors have worked most cooperatively with us and with Greenwood Press to produce volumes that reflect current research on their nations and that are interesting and informative to their prospective readers.

The importance of a series such as this cannot be underestimated. As a superpower whose influence is felt all over the world, the United States can claim a "special" relationship with almost every other nation. Yet many Americans know very little about the histories of the nations with which the United States relates. How did they get to be the way they are? What kind of political systems have evolved there? What kind of influence do they have in their own region? What are the dominant political, religious, and cultural forces that move their leaders? These and many other questions are answered in the volumes of this series.

The authors who have contributed to this series have written comprehensive histories of their nations, dating back to prehistoric times in some cases. Each of them, however, has devoted a significant portion of the book to events of the last thirty years, because the modern era has contributed the most to contemporary issues that have an impact on U.S. policy. Authors have made an effort to be as up-to-date as possible so that readers can benefit from the most recent scholarship and a narrative that includes very recent events.

In addition to the historical narrative, each volume in this series contains an introductory overview of the country's geography, political institutions, economic structure, and cultural attributes. This is designed to give readers a picture of the nation as it exists in the contemporary world. Each volume also contains additional chapters that add interesting and useful detail to the historical narrative. One chapter is a thorough chronology of important historical events, making it easy for readers to follow the flow of a particular nation's history. Another chapter features biographical sketches of the nation's most important figures in order to humanize some of the individuals who have contributed to the historical development of their nation. Each volume also contains a comprehensive bibliography, so that those readers whose interest has been sparked may find out more about the nation and its history. Finally, there is a carefully prepared topic and person index.

Readers of these volumes will find them fascinating to read and useful in understanding the contemporary world and the nations that comprise it. As series editors, it is our hope that this series will contribute to a heightened sense of global understanding as we embark on a new century.

Frank W. Thackeray and John E. Findling
Indiana University Southeast

Preface

Pakistan may be a new name but Pakistanis comprise an ancient society whose ancestors lived in the historic Indus Valley and interacted with the conquerors, scholars, visitors, preachers, Sufis, and immigrants from western and central Asia. Featuring some of the tallest mountains, vast alluvial plains, and arid deserts, this predominantly Muslim country lies at the crossroads of history and shares several characteristics with its neighbours. Our study of this country begins with a lesser known Dravidian past, when the valley experienced the development of agriculture under the priest kings, until the advent of the Aryans, when Brahmanism and Hinduism evolved as two powerful religious forces. Buddhism, Jainism, and Zoroastrianism flourished in ancient Pakistan, which, for a time, was an important part of the Persian Empire that Alexander was able to conquer after extensive military campaigns. The revival of Hindu empires, advent of early Christian communities in the historic city of Taxila, and a series of invasions from the northwest featured in this early history until the arrival of Islam through Sufis and invading Arab armies. Evolution of the Turkic Muslim dynasties, also known as the Delhi Sultanate, ushered in the era of a splendid Indo-Islamic culture, with Persian assuming center stage in the entire subcontinent. The Mughal Era is well known for its political, economic, and cultural contributions at a time when Europeans began to reach Indian coastal towns. Evolution of the British rule from the mid-eighteenth century coincided with the Mughal decline, and after the Rebellion of 1857, divergent responses characterized south Asian Muslim interaction in a pluralistic subcontinent. This book describes the formation of Pakistan in 1947, following a protracted political movement, and efforts to establish a consensual national ethos. It is hoped that the volume will be equally helpful to a student and a lay person in coming to grips with the realities of this rich and pluralistic historical heritage.

Several institutions including the British Library, Bodleian Library, Bath Spa University, Wolfson College, and numerous individuals across Pakistan, the subcontinent, and North Atlantic regions have helped me form my views on this vast subject. Sustained interaction with colleagues, students, and friends in Oxford, Bath, and London kept me on the right path, and my family provided energy and humor when I needed them the most. Nighat, Sidra, Kiran, and Farooq merit special thanks; I hope that millions of capable and well-meaning Pakistanis like them will be able to take this country to its deserved place. I acknowledge the support from Greenwood Press for commissioning me to undertake this second volume after the publication of *Culture and Customs of Pakistan.* Special thanks are due to Kaitlin Ciarmiello for her professional camaraderie. I hope that this book will lead its readers on a more comprehensive journey across the further challenging labyrinths of south Asian history and Islam in the Indus regions.

Oxford
March 23, 2008

Acronyms

AIML	All-India Muslim League
AJK	Azad Jammu and Kashmir (Azad Kashmir)
AL	Awami League
ANP	Awami National Party (NAP)
APWA	All-Pakistan Women's Association
BJP	Bharatiya Janata Party
CENTO	Central Treaty Organisation (formerly the Baghdad Pact)
COP	Combined Opposition Parties
FANA	Federally Administered Northern Areas
FATA	Federally Administered Tribal Areas
HRCP	Human Rights Commission of Pakistan
IDA/IJI	Islamic Democratic Alliance
IMF	International Monetary Fund

INC	Indian National Congress
ISI	Inter-Services Intelligence
JI	Jamaat-i-Islami
JUI	Jamiat-i-Ulama-i-Islam
JUP	Jamiat-i-Ulama-i-Pakistan
LFO	Legal Framework Order
KKH	Karakoram Highway
MMA	Muttahida Majlis-i-Ammal (United Action Forum)
MNA	Member, National Assembly
MPA	Member, Provincial Assembly
MQM	Muhajir/Muttahida Qaumi Movement
MQM (A)	MQM (Altaf Hussain Group)
MQM (Haqiqi)	MQM (Anti-Altaf Group)
MRD	Movement for the Restoration of Democracy (founded in 1981)
NAP	National Awami Party (renamed as ANP)
NWFP	North-West Frontier Province
PDA	Pakistan Democratic Alliance
PIF	Pakistan Islamic Front
PML	Pakistan Muslim League
PML (N)	Pakistan Muslim League (Nawaz Sharif Group)
PML (Q)	Pakistan Muslim League (pro-Musharraf, Quaid-i-Azam group)
PNA	Pakistan National Alliance
PPP	Pakistan People's Party
SAARC	South Asian Association for Regional Cooperation
SEATO	South East Asian Treaty Organisation
WAF	Women's Action Forum

Timeline of Historical Events

B.C.E.

c. 2500	The Harappan culture: Ancient Indus Valley era
c. 1500	Migration of the Aryans into the subcontinent
c. 519	Cyrus, the Persian Emperor, conquers the Indus Valley
486	Death of Buddha
c. 468	Death of Mahavira, the founder of Jainism
327–325	Alexander conquers the Indus Valley
321	Accession of Chandragupta, the founder of the Mauryan Dynasty
268–231	Reign of Emperor Ashoka

C.E.

c. 50	Mission of St. Thomas to Taxila
c. 78	Accession of Kanishka, the Kushan king

319–320	Accession of Chandra Gupta I
405–411	Visit of Fa-Hsien, the Chinese scholar
c. 500	Invasion by Huns
606–647	Reign of Emperor Hersha
712	Ibn Qasim conquers Sindh
997–1030	Mahmud of Ghazna's invasions of the subcontinent
1206	Establishment of the Slave dynasty under Qutb-ud-Din Aibak in Delhi
1206–1525	Various Muslim Sultan dynasties (Delhi Sultanate)
1288, 1293	Marco Polo's visits to southern India
1325–1351	Ibn Battutah visits India
1336	Founding of Kingdom of Vijaynagar
1345	Founding of Bahmini kingdom in Deccan
1469–1539	Baba Guru Nanak, the founder of Sikhism in Punjab
1526	Babur, the Mughal king, defeats Delhi sultan at Panipat
1600	East India Company established in London
1707	Aurengzeb, the last great Mughal emperor, dies
1757	British Company defeats the nawab of Bengal
1799	Sultan Tipu killed in Mysore
1857	Rebellion against the East India Company
1858	British Crown takes over India
1885	Indian National Congress established in Bombay
1906	All-India Muslim League founded in Dhaka
1913	Jinnah joins the Muslim League
1930	Muhammad Iqbal's address at Allahabad
1940	Lahore Resolution of the Muslim League
1947	Independence of India and Pakistan
1948	Jinnah dies; Indo-Pakistani war over Kashmir

1958	General Ayub Khan's coup
1965	Second Indo-Pakistani war
1969	General Yahya Khan's coup
1971	Indo-Pakistani War and the separation of East Pakistan (Bangladesh)
1973	Pakistan's constitution approved
1977	Zulfikar Ali Bhutto overthrown by General Zia-ul-Haq
1988	General Zia-ul-Haq killed in an air crash
1988–1999	Elected regimes of Benazir Bhutto and Nawaz Sharif
1998	India and Pakistan hold nuclear tests
1999	General Pervez Musharraf stages military coup
2002	Elections in Pakistan; Musharraf becomes president
2005	Earthquake in northern Pakistan and Azad Kashmir
2007	Musharraf's problems with the chief justice and civil society
October 18	Benazir Bhutto returns to Pakistan from exile
November 3	Musharraf imposes emergency and assumes more powers by amending the constitution
December 27	Benazir Bhutto killed at an election rally in Rawalpindi
	Bilawal Bhutto-Zardari, the 19-year-old son of the late Benazir Bhutto, is appointed as the chairperson of the Pakistan Peoples Party (PPP)
2008 January	Musharraf visits Brussels, Paris, and London for public relations
February 18	Elections held
March 25	Syed Yusuf Raza Gilani is sworn in as Prime Minister

Map of Pakistan. Cartography by Bookcomp, Inc.

1

The Indus Heartland and Karakoram Country

Pakistan, once the largest and most populated Muslim country in the world, still remains a significant actor in regional and global affairs. Formed in 1947 from what used to be called British India, Pakistan was idealized by south Asian Muslims to be a state where the forces of tradition and modernity would unite, offering economic welfare and peaceful coexistence to its inhabitants. Achieved through a constitutional struggle led by Muhammad Ali Jinnah (1876–1948) under the banner of the All-India Muslim League (AIML), *Pakistan* was the term coined by some Muslim students at the University of Cambridge in 1933. Inclusive of areas like Punjab, the Frontier (identified as *Afghania*), Kashmir, Sindh, and Balochistan, it was visualized as the heartland of the Indus Valley, which has been the home of some of the oldest cultures in this part of the subcontinent.[1] Sought as a political dispensation for various ethnic communities living across the Indus regions, *Pakistan* was not only perceived as a neutral term among all these regional identities, but was also seen as a utopia where rural, tribal, and urban population groups would have equal opportunities and unalienable citizenry irrespective of their religious and ideological diversities. Although Pakistan was established as a Muslim state (owing to Islam as the common denominator for most of the inhabitants in the Indus Valley and likewise in the lower Gangetic Bengal delta),

Jinnah and his associates were emphatic with regard to equal rights and opportunities for all Pakistanis. Even today, despite Muslims being an absolute majority, around 10 percent of Pakistanis belong to various other religious traditions, although further Islamization of the country has never been too far away from the public discourse and the agenda of religiopolitical parties.[2] Pakistan, like several other countries, is a pluralistic society, although Islam and Urdu are two of its main national characteristics. From its history to its population and from its topography to its climate, however, the country is quite diverse. Various epochs in its history offer a greater sense of antiquity and continuity to an otherwise young state. Although it is defined as a recent state, Pakistan is, in fact, the inheritor of the Indus Valley civilization, viewed as one of the oldest continuing cultures in the world. This civilization is reflected in Pakistan's history through its various political, religious, and territorial identifications. In that sense, Pakistan is privileged to be the successor of a continuum of cultural and historical traditions all the way from its ancient Dravidian, Aryan, Hindu, Persian, Greek, and Buddhist past to its 13-centuries-old Islamic heritage as bequeathed by the Arab, central Asian, and Indian influences.

GEOGRAPHY: KARAKORAMS TO KALAT

Comprised of 310,000 square miles, with 16,000 square miles covered with water, Pakistan is slightly smaller that twice the size of California and overall about a twelfth the size of the United States. Three times as large as Britain, it is inhabited by 160 million people. To its north, the People's Republic of China shares Pakistan's immensely majestic and scenic Kararkorams, and the Sino-Pakistani borders run for 330 miles through the glacial mountains. To the west, Afghanistan neighbors Pakistan for 1,600 miles across a predominantly mountainous region extending from the peaks of the Hindu-Kush in the north toward the borders with Iran farther south. Demarcated by the British in the closing years of the nineteenth century and often called the Durand Line, this borderland retains the world's oldest and still intact tribal heritage, where traditional values like hospitality, resistance against alien influences and control, and a greater devotion to one's own family, land, religion, and language supersede everything else. Iran, located to the west of Pakistan, shares a 570-mile border; Pakistan's southern frontiers are in fact demarcated by 660 miles of the coastline on the Arabian Sea, which brings it quite close to the vital Straits of Hormuz in the west. Toward the east, coastal Pakistan extends well into the marshes of Kuchh. India is Pakistan's only neighbor in the east; they share 1,835 miles of borders, mostly characterized by the plains of Punjab and the deserts of Sindh and Rajasthan. The disputed territory of Jammu and Kashmir—equal to the size of the United Kingdom—is wedged between China, Pakistan, and India, with all three states controlling parts of it. Here the

Line of Control (LOC), demarcated after the Indo-Pakistani wars of 1948 and 1971, keeps these two rivals apart, although in recent years their often tense relations have greatly thawed, allowing some restrictive movements of relatives and goods across the borders.[3]

Pakistan's location might pose serious geopolitical challenges to its rulers, but it also accounts for its regional and extraregional significance, allowing the country a rather larger-than-life profile in foreign relations. Pakistan's northern regions proximate it with central Asia and the historic Silk Road; its northwestern territories have been geographically and culturally linked with Afghanistan and the Turkic regions farther north, which, for centuries, fashioned the sociopolitical life in the Indian subcontinent. Pakistan's shared history with Iran and other west Asian regions over the centuries played an important role in the evolution of a unique Perso-Islamic culture, sometimes referred to as Persianate, or the Indo-Islamic heritage. Pakistan's multiple relations with the Gangetic valleys and areas farther south forming the present-day Indian Union allowed it a vanguard role in the expansion of the Indus Valley civilization. Future waves of immigrants and invaders played

Provinces and regions of Pakistan. Iftikhar Malik, *State and Civil Society in Pakistan: Politics of Authority, Ideology, and Ethnicity*, 1997, Palgrave Macmillan. Reproduced with permission of Palgrave Macmillan. Reproduced by Bookcomp, Inc.

a crucial role in the evolution of Hinduism and the formation of ancient Persian and Greek empires during the classical era. In the same vein, the arrival of Islam, although initially only on the coast, has been largely through the mountain passes opening into western and central Asian regions. The arrival of Islam provided enduring Sufi, artistic, literary, philosophical, and other influences, infusing the subcontinent with newer and dynamic ideas and institutions. Concurrently, it is vital to note that these Pakistani regions also operated as the bridgeheads for south Asian influences such as Buddhism, which then flourished into the interiors of the Asian continent.

Pakistan's geographical features have certainly played a pivotal role in the historical, political, and ecological realms. Here, other than ongoing geological changes, mountains, glaciers, rivers, alluvial plains, deserts, and other topographical features retain their own imprints. Pakistan has the distinction of being home to some of the world's tallest mountains, which are concentrated in its northern regions. Although they serve as a lifeline for millions in south Asia by harboring vital river and climate systems, they can also usher frequent and even destabilizing geological events in the forms of earthquakes, floods, landslides, and avalanches. The large-scale deaths and devastation brought about in Pakistani Kashmir and the adjoining regions on September 8, 2005 is proof of the invincibility of the powerful forces of nature manifesting themselves through ongoing tectonic movements in an area where the Himalayas, Karakorams, and Hindu Kush converge. This earthquake affected most of Azad Kashmir, in addition to the neighboring districts of Pakistan in the Frontier province, with the death toll reaching almost 100,000.[4] In addition, hundreds of thousands of people were severely injured as a result of falling buildings and massive rockslides in busy urban centers such as Balakot, Batrasi, Shinkiari, Muzaffarabad, Bagh, and Rawlakot.[5]

Pakistan's northernmost regions of Chitral, Gilgit, Hunza, Chilas, and Baltistan are popular for trekkers and mountaineers and, within a rather small area, offer some of the most daunting and equally captivating scenes featuring valleys, cliffs, snowbound peaks, and certainly some of the largest glaciers in the world. Closer to Afghanistan lies Pakistan's northwestern district of Chitral, which, among other features, is known for its historic Kalasha community living in the three adjacent valleys of the Hindu Kush. Lying at about 5,000 feet above sea level, the district is not too hot in summer and is snowbound during most of the winter months. The district is accessible only through the Lowari Pass, which is at the altitude of 10,500 feet, or via air travel. At the other end of the district is a unique mountain peak known as Tirichmir.[6] With an altitude of 25,230 feet, this is the highest peak in the Hindu Kush and is often covered in a thin film of clouds. According to the local traditions, the peak, known for sudden icefalls, is defended by fairies who welcome mountaineers with bowls of milk or blood, stipulating happiness or grief. Farther south one finds quite a few natural hot springs and the region retains its own distinct ethnocultural features.

More popular than Tirichmir is Nanga Parbat situated between the Kaghan Valley and the Indus that has attracted attention from the mountaineers and writers, as it lies close to the flight route on the way to Gilgit. Deriving its name from Sanskrit and meaning "naked mountain," this 26,660-feet peak is the loftiest amongst its other Himalayan counterparts in Pakistan. Some of its slopes are bare of snow or any greenery and are quite sharp and steep. Nanga Parbat is the westernmost peak in the Himalayas and is made of several successive ridges. No other peak within the radius of 60 miles comes close to its gigantic size. On its southern side is one of the world's greatest precipices at a drop of 16,000 feet, which is also the starting point for Kashmir.[7] To the west of Nanga Parbat lie the valleys of Astor and Buner; the Indus, coming in from the Karakorams, flows to its north. The area in between is characterized by massive slopes rather than sheer precipices.[8]

Although the Hindu Kush and Western Himalayas retain their higher peaks in Chitral and Kaghan, it would not be wrong to describe Pakistan as "the Karakoram country," given that it houses the K-2 and several other higher peaks and large glacial systems in its extreme northeastern region, administratively grouped as the Federally Administered Northern Areas (FANA). Siachin, Baltoro, Godwin-Austen, Concordia, Biafo, Kaberi, and Hispar are the gigantic glaciers lying on this side of the K-2 and are situated in Baltistan, which neighbors China and Indian-controlled Kashmir. These glaciers source several rivers such as the Shyok, Saltoro, and Shigar, which join the Indus on its fresh entry from Tibet, along with several lakes dotting the entire mountainous regions that are often identified as the mythical Shangri La, or Little Tibet.[9] K-2 reaches an altitude of 28,253 feet and is often viewed as the highest mountain in the world. Compared to Mount Everest, it is quite formidable. It was first successfully climbed in 1954 and is visible only from certain points in the region owing to its distance and to the fact that it is surrounded by some of the world's tallest mountains. In fact, within 15 miles around the icy Baltoro Glacier are 10 of the world's 30 highest peaks, which seem to be protecting K-2 from all encroachments. Other peaks include Gasherbrum I at an altitude of 26,470 feet, Broad Peak at 26,400 feet, and Mashebrum at 25,660 feet.

Farther west and adjacent to Baltistan lie the Karakoram regions of Gilgit and Hunza, which have become more accessible since the opening of the Karakoram Highway (KKH), a road connecting Pakistan to China. It passes through these majestic mountains and breathtaking scenery until it reaches the Khunjerab border post at an altitude of 15,000 feet. Here the valleys of Gilgit, Hunza, and Nagar are watered by the Gilgit, Khunjerab, and Hunza rivers that originate from glaciers such as Passu, Hispar, and Hoper. Among the known peaks in and around Hunza, the Lady's Finger, Shimshal Cones, and Rakapohsi are quite preeminent. The Rakaposhi is visible from many points in and around these valleys and, in fact, the KKH itself has been built on its northernmost reaches.[10] The peak is 25,550 feet high and remains the most photographic of all the Karakorams. It appears to be more accessible given its location near Hunza, which is the center of northern Pakistan's cultural and recreational activities. From Gilgit and Hunza, the Shandur Pass is the entry point into the neighboring Chitral. Lying at an altitude of 12,250 feet, it is the birthplace of the sport of polo, which is played even today with much fanfare.

Pakistan's Koshistan and Hazara regions, like other border districts located in the North-West Frontier Province (NWFP), are predominantly mountainous, with valleys and passes allowing human habitation and movement. In the same way, western and coastal regions of Balochistan and those of northern Punjab feature low-lying mountains. Unlike the Suleiman Mountains, situated to the west of the Indus, the Salt Range hills are the final eastern frontier for Pothowar Plateau and give way to the great plains of Punjab that extend all the way to Bangladesh. These plains are fed by five rivers called the Indus River system, which itself is formed by the mountains and glaciers discussed previously. Since the canalization dating from the 1870s and 1880s, Punjab—the land of five rivers—has been the breadbasket for the subcontinent. Emerging through the Salt Range, the Indus at Kalabagh finally enters the plains of Punjab; the Jhelum, Chenab, Ravi, and Sutlej join its waters until the former reaches the plains of Sindh before emptying itself into the Arabian Sea. Rivers such as the Kabul, Swat, Chitral, Kunhar, and Kurram flow through the NWFP and eventually merge with the Indus; but Balochistan is largely arid and lacks any major rivers, although occasional monsoon rains cause some flash floods in low-lying areas. Since the evolution of canals and barrages in the early twentieth century, Sindh has become quite fertile, although the demands for water for power and irrigation purposes create serious friction among the four constituent provinces of Pakistan. The distribution of scarce water resources in the subcontinent led to Indo-Pakistani tensions soon after independence in 1947. The complex issue was largely resolved with the intervention by the World Bank in 1959, but as both countries seek to generate more power and water storage for irrigation, they have often contested the construction of newer upstream dams and barrages.

Sindh still includes some areas in the interior and farther east that feature sandy deserts. Closer to the sea its soil is more fertile. On the other hand, Balochistan, which accounts for 43 percent of Pakistan's territory but only 5 percent of its population, shares topography with some Iranian and Middle Eastern regions where arid land is desert-like but without sand, consisting mostly of pebbles, smaller hills, dunes, and bushes. The coastal areas such as Makran, lying closer to the Arabian Sea, feature some sandy patches that are bordered by the rising hills and plateaus, making it ideal for sheep and goat herding. Compared to the glacial north and tall mountains, southern Pakistan is largely arid and dry. Canals, especially in Sindh, have greatly transformed land features and potentials. Pakistan, like India and several other Asian regions, is a tropical country where summers are long and winters are short and tolerable, at least in the plains. Temperatures in summer can rise to 120 degrees Farenheit (45 degrees Celsius). Cities such as Jacobabad in Sindh and Sibi in Balochistan are usually identified as the hottest spots on earth. Whereas hills and mountains in and around Murree, Quetta, Hazara, Hunza, Kaghan, Baltistan, Kashmir, Waziristan, and FANA face harsh winter months, it is only during the nights in December and January that temperatures may drop in the plains; however, wintry dawns and dusks are often characterized by a thick fog that covers the entire subcontinental plains for several hours each day. Occasional Siberian weather systems during the winter months may bring in some extra chilly spells as far as Balochistan. Summer lasts from late March to late September, but it usually stays dry and hot until late June, when rainy systems build over the Indian Ocean and are redirected by the Himalayas as showers over Pakistan. July and August bring in relief besides filling up the reservoirs. From September to late November, autumn sets in before the winter takes over. Spring in Pakistan is short-lived. It is characterized by blossoms and harvests and, like autumn, is greatly celebrated in literature and the arts.

PEOPLE AND PLACES

At the time of independence, both East and West Pakistan were predominantly rural and agrarian societies, but after the Green Revolution—marked by increased mechanized agriculture and high yield seeds—and industrialization centered in big cities, rural and tribal people began to flock to the cities. After 1971, despite the separation of its eastern wing as the new state of Bangladesh, Pakistan experienced several new demographic trends including the movement of labor overseas, especially to the Gulf States such as Saudi Arabia, the United Arab Emirates (UAE), Kuwait, and Oman. In the wake of intense urbanization and as a result of geopolitical developments in Afghanistan and Iran during the 1980s, Pakistan received millions of refugees. People could enjoy comparatively better living standards and some improved health facilities. As a consequence, the country's population increased through the 1980s and 1990s. In 1947, the present-day territories of Pakistan had about 37 million inhabitants, including the huge population influx in 1947 from across India. By early 2007, Pakistan's population was estimated at 160 million, resulting in added pressure on land and resources. About 65 percent of these people are young and eager to work and achieve better living standards. Given the limited resources and opportunities, however, they are confronted with serious roadblocks. In addition, the country's major expense has been on a costly defense establishment, resulting in part because of its thorny relationship with India and also because the country has been mostly ruled by the military, preventing any major changes in national budgetary allocations earmarked for the development sector. Greater demand for better education, competition over jobs, professionalization of urban population groups, remittances from expatriates, and a vocal civil society have allowed greater national integration, although ethnoregional and ideological tensions abound and often converge with thorny regional political events. Pakistan has survived through various chasms and crisis in its more than six decades of recent history, and, with a vocal media and alert civic groups seeking peace within and without, its populace might gradually move forward to create a better welfare system.

Pakistanis are, by majority, descendants of the people who have inhabited the Indus Basin for thousands of years. They are certainly an Indo-European stock of people who interacted with other ethnic communities such as Persians, Arabs, Afghans, and Turks and in the process evolved a synthesized identity that combines these pluralistic traditions. Islam has been an important factor in the collective lives of these people for many centuries, especially because of a long period of Muslim rule and demand for Muslim statehood. This religious identification has strengthened Pakistani blood relationship with the west Asian co-religionists. It is true that many of the early ruling and religious Muslim elite came into the northwestern subcontinent from Muslim societies to the north and west, but their interaction with the local south Asian families and cultures underwrote their steady assimilation into a cooperative Indo-Muslim culture. Even though Pakistan received about 8 to 10 million Muslim refugees from India in 1947 while the Hindus and Sikhs left Pakistan for their new home across the borders, these newcomers also shared a common ethnocultural consciousness with the people already living in the young country.

Such religious and national similarities might have worked to help Pakistanis achieve a greater sense of shared belonging, but they still need to override existing regional and ethnic pluralities predating the formation of the country. Although in British India, religion came to operate as the bedrock of collective identities (communities), as Hindus, Muslims, Sikhs, and others, in Pakistan language and territory have both largely defined group-based ethnicity. While the former East Bengalis now defined as East Pakistanis began seeking equity with the West Pakistanis by identifying themselves as Muslim Bengalis and eventually as Bangladeshis, languages such as Sindhi, Balochi, and Pushtu turned into identity markers for the respective communities living in well-defined provinces.[11] In the case of Punjab, such an ethnic identification remained diluted because the province, despite its partition in 1947, turned into the power engine of Pakistan and opted for a larger role. For most of the Punjabis, unlike Sindhis, Balochis, and Pushtuns, Urdu and not Punjabi had been the lingua franca; and Pakistan, not Punjab, defined their territorial nationalism. It is true that over the past several decades, Urdu and English have greatly overshadowed regional languages. An accentuated mobility within the country has allowed more openness toward pluralism, yet a centralized government presiding over weaker participatory institutions has not been helpful in establishing a cohesive federalism.

PUNJAB

The province of Punjab, the most populated and powerful part of the country, is certainly pluralistic given all the barometers of regional and economic diversity. Generally known as Punjabis, its inhabitants account for 60 percent of Pakistan's population. Traditionally the heart of the Indus Valley, Punjabis have been peasants most of their history, although some became soldiers given the location of the province as the gateway to the subcontinent. Descending from the ancient inhabitants of these regions, Punjabis share religious and historical associations with the west Asians, as well as with their counterparts in the subcontinent. Divided between rural and urban communities, Punjabis take pride in their lands and property, and for centuries cities such as Lahore and Multan have been political and cultural centers in northern India. Although second to Karachi in population, Lahore, with its numerous Mughal and British monuments, is viewed as the cultural capital of Pakistan, and its once famous gardens are now hemmed in by ever-increasing posh and exclusive housing developments. With good universities, publishing houses and art galleries, and the National College of Arts—the oldest of its kind in all of south Asia—Lahore is a peaceful, tolerant, and affluent city whose inhabitants, irrespective of their religious traditions, are famous for festivities, fun, and food. Multan, Ucch Sharif, Pakpattan, and Jhang are located in western Punjab and remain known for their age-old Sufi shrines, domed architecture, and folk traditions. Faisalabad, once a hub in the newly developed irrigational systems, is a city of sprawling textile factories and related industries. Sialkot, Wazirabad, and Gujranwala are famous for sports goods, cutlery, leather, furniture, and other manufacturing items. Jhelum, Attock, and certainly Rawalpindi have been garrison towns situated on the open plains lying between the Indus and Jhelum. Some of the prehistoric towns such as Taxila, Rawat, Bhaun, Kattas, and Tillah Jogian are located in this Pothowar Plateau, which, according to some archaeologists, was once an ocean that dried up several millennia back. Such an explanation is offered to understand the rock formation of the Salt Range, which houses the Khewra Salt Mines, the oldest and perhaps the largest of their type on earth. Other than housing Sufi shrines, ornate mosques, and grand Mughal and British buildings, Punjab was the birthplace of Sikhism in the sixteenth century, and several Sikh holy places are located in Lahore, Nankana Sahib, and Hassan Abdal.[12]

Being in a majority and enjoying better economic and professional prospects, Punjabi Muslims are the least ethnic; instead sectarian and kinship/caste-based identities remain more visible. Since this province was divided between India and Pakistan in 1947, it still carries the memories and scars of the communal violence that engulfed all the major religious communities. While Hindus and Sikhs left for India, millions of Muslims came into Punjab from eastern Punjab and wider India, drastically changing the demography of Lahore, Gujranwala, Faisalabad, Sahiwal, Multan, and other cities. Given a higher degree of acceptance for pluralism in view of greater opportunities for all, the refugees from India—both Punjabis and other Muslims—found their new home more tolerant and even supportive. Since the heady days of 1947, Punjab has never experienced ethnic riots or violence of that scale, and this sustained peace has helped Punjabis in assuming the flagship role for the country, which creates jealousy in the other three provinces, where it is not rare to hear complaints of a Punjabi domination.

SINDH

Sindh, the second most populous province in the country, has a more explicit ethnoregional divide, with the Sindhi-speaking inhabitants living mostly in the hinterland and the Urdu-speaking inhabitants settled in cities such as Karachi, Hyderabad, and Sukkur. The former account for 20 percent of the country's population and are believed to be the descendants of Dravidian inhabitants of the ancient Indus Valley. A sizable number claim Arab and Iranian origins. The Urdu-speaking Sindhis prefer to be called Muhajireen[13] and do not like being identified as refugees or settlers, as these terms might trivialize the significance of their exodus from India in 1947. Most of these Muhajireen, accounting for 7 percent of the country's population—were born in Pakistan, however, whereas their forefathers came from a wide variety of Indian regions. Other than migration, Urdu and a shared urban demography underpin their claims for a distinct ethnicity.[14] Rural Sindhis have surely benefited from canalization and irrigation schemes and have often felt squeezed by the arrival of Muhajireen and other Pakistanis into urban areas. Karachi is Pakistan's largest city and its financial capital, besides operating as the only port with its high commercial and defense profile. It remains one of the most pluralistic cities in the country, and its growth from a small fishing town in the

1930s to a megalopolis has occurred in the wake of several urban and demographic challenges.

The ruins of one of the world's oldest cities, Mohenjo Daro, are in rural Sindh. A vast graveyard near Makli is known as an unparalleled necropolis, containing thousands of graves and mausoleums dating from early times and representing various past architectural traditions. These uniquely designed graves, also known as Chaukhandi tombs, are scattered all over the province of Sindh and in the adjoining areas of Balochistan. Sindh is not only the home of the ancient Indus Valley cultures, it is also known as Babul Islam, the Gateway for Islam, as the earliest Muslim community in the subcontinent is known to have evolved in Sindh. Sindh, named after the Indus (*Sindhu*), gave the world Arabic terms such as *Hind, Hindustan* and *Hinduism*, and its English version, Indus, became *India.* All across Sindh are located the shrines of preeminent Sufis, who, in many cases, were the known poets and humanists of their times. The shrines of Shah Latif at Bhit Shah and of Shahbaz Qalandar and Sachal Sarmast at Sehwan Sharif annually attract millions of pilgrims from across Pakistan and Afghanistan, whereas Sindhi folklore (especially in the Thar Desert) retains its own unique place in regional traditions.

BALOCHISTAN

Balochistan, the largest province of Pakistan, lies on the western bank of the Indus, stretching westward and deep into the south. It borders Afghanistan, Iran, and the Arabian Sea. Named after the Baloch ethnic group, northwestern Balochistan is inhabited by Pushtun tribes who share kinship with fellow Pushtun elsewhere. Historic cities include Kalat, Sibi, Chaman, Khuzdar, Gwadar, and Turbat, whereas Balochistan's modern capital is Quetta, which was founded during the British period. The Baloch claim to be non-Semitic people of Indo-Persian origins, and some of them speak Brohi, a uniquely Dravidian language, different from other present-day Indus Valley languages that surround the Brohi-speaking region in central Balochistan. A poor agricultural region because of the paucity of water and fertile soil, Balochistan is immensely rich in natural resources, and its strategic location adds to its geopolitical significance. Pakistan's major natural gas reserves are concentrated in the Bugti tribal regions, often leading to dissention over the amount and distribution of royalty given to the tribal chiefs.

The Baloch tribes are ruled by chieftains called *sardars*, and over time their hold on people seems to be withering away as more and more Baloch migrate to Karachi and the Gulf, seeking better economic prospects and political autonomy. With a total population of 7 million equally divided between the

Baloch and Pushtun tribes, Balochistan accounts for almost half of Pakistan's territory.[15]

NORTHWEST FRONTIER

Northwestern Pakistan, largely inhabited by Pushtuns and some other proto-Punjabi ethnic groups, is known as the NWFP. It is a land of mountains, passes, and valleys that have ensured the sustenance of one of the world's oldest and well-organized tribal systems. Other than Hindko speakers in the urban localities of Peshawar and Abbotabad and some hilly people called Kohistanis, most of its residents are Pushtuns whose tribal belt adjoining Afghanistan is divided into seven semiautonomous agencies. These tribal regions enjoy domestic autonomy and straddle Pakistan-Afghan borders, whereas the Pushtuns in urban centers, such as Peshawar, Mardan, Charsadda, Kohat, and Bannu, are less tribalized and are prominently visible in businesses and other professions. In addition, the former princely Pushtun states of Dir and Swat have been redesignated as regular districts, although the anomalous nature of these tribal agencies is often debated by a growing demand for full integration within the country. Pushtuns are immensely proud of their language, Pushtu, and remain quite attached to their land, where traditional values such as hospitality and revenge reflect preferences for tribal solidarity. After Punjabis and urban Sindhis, urban Pushtuns are now well represented in the country's services. Given the mobility in recent decades, Karachi has become the largest Pushtun city in the country, whereas the NWFP itself accounts for only 13 percent of Pakistan's total population.

Farther north of Dir, on the other side of the Lowari Pass, lies Chitral where the non-Pushtun population originates from their Indo-Persian ancestors. Here the prehistoric communities such as the Kalasha are identified with the ancient Greeks, who, led by Alexander, ruled this area for some time. A former princely state, Chitral is quite pluralistic in its religious composition; southern regions are Sunni and the northern territories are inhabited by Ismaili Shias, also known as the Aga Khanis because of their belief in the constant spiritual leadership of a living *imam*.[16]

The inhabitants of FANA settled in Gilgit, Hunza, and Baltistan. They speak several languages such as Shina and Balti and belong to both Sunni and Shia denominations. The KKH increased trade and tourism, and a greater investment in education and service sector have opened these distant lands to a variety of influences. Over the past two decades, The Aga Khan Support Programme has invested considerably in education and home-based industries, leading to almost universal empowerment and prosperity in Hunza. Other communities in Gilgit, Skardu, and Khaplu are also trying to establish similar institutions.

EDUCATION AND GENDER

Urban Punjabis, Sindhis, and Pushtuns from settled territories have benefited from the economic and educational improvements in Pakistan, but the tribal sections and certain rural areas have been left behind. Here feudal and clerical influences, often in league with bureaucracy, prevail over local affairs. Thus the pace of development has been rather abysmal and will continue to be unless the regimes displace such intermediaries in their efforts to reach out to the grassroots, as well as to women. Urdu is the medium of instruction and official language at various levels, but English continues to carry more status and is the cherished medium of instruction across private schools and institutions of higher learning. Young pupils may speak various mother tongues at home, yet a growing use of Urdu is a familiar phenomenon even in the far-flung areas. On the contrary, urban professionals and younger Pakistanis seek pride in speaking English.[17] Familiarity with multiple languages is a natural response to the Pakistani plural ethos but can be a hurdle to national cohesion. Learning Quran and related Islamic literature in its original Arabic is not controversial, for most Pakistanis and even the hitherto debate over the relationship between one's mother tongue and Urdu or between Urdu and English have given way to a growing pragmatism. Accordingly, more and more Pakistanis, including the ethnic and clerical groups, have come to accept that that these languages can coexist, although English provides the only key in moving higher in worldly affairs.

The abundance of private English-language schools across the country and a substantial growth in technical colleges and multidisciplinary universities are visible phenomena. The tradition of religious seminaries (*madrassas*) also persists as a parallel system of private education. Although these seminaries have often been found wanting in modern disciplines and competent faculty, they have been able to impart basic Islamic learning, as well as shelter many orphans and other disadvantaged groups. The tradition of charity also enables the establishment of more mosques, shrines, and seminaries to keep younger children off the streets and away from drugs.[18] In 1947, only 10 percent of Pakistanis were literate, and the life expectancy was still in the early thirties. In the early twenty-first century, the literacy rate was somewhere in the 50 percent range, although in tribal regions of the NWFP and Balochistan, a vast number of women remained unschooled. Pakistan's avowed preoccupation with security and high defense expenditure is mostly to blame for not spending more on education, along with the pervasive rural poverty and a land-based feudalist system. In a class-based educational system, schools and institutions of higher learning have their own problems, such as low-salaried teachers and inadequate infrastructures.[19] The state-run, elitist, and mosque-based tiered education system, despite its various benefits, offers a formidable challenge for a society where demographically youth abound both in numbers and aspirations. As with any other similar society, Pakistan is challenged by globalization, and Pakistani planners are offered incentives if they can find ways to change the nation's priorities. The solution lies in reformism based on urgent initiatives.

Views about Pakistani women are often unclear or fall victim to generalizations based on assumptions about their inherent inequality, if not sheer inferiority. These assumptions are based on religious strictures and male-dominated socioeconomic structures. There are serious problems of inequities and even of domestic and tribal violence against women, but in a protectionist society like Pakistan, women are not viewed as mere sexual objects. By virtue of being mothers, wives, sisters, and daughters, they are to be protected. To many scholars, the multiple disempowerments of women might reflect a wider malaise by which underprivileged sections, irrespective of their gender or ethnicity, stay vulnerable. The demographic division of the populace into urban, rural, and tribal categories, further criss-crossed by class-based fissures, determines gender realities in the country. A growing middle class may reveal greater professionalization among women and resultant economic and social assertion if not total autonomy, but then, as in North Atlantic regions, it could also spawn more conservative attitudes. Pakistan may have had female prime ministers, ministers, ambassadors, and governors, but most Pakistani women, like their male counterparts, are preoccupied with issues of family survival. Despite the romantic images of nonphysical love celebrated in ballads, folk traditions, and literary compositions, a woman is idealized both as a delicate being and a strong defender of her honor. In addition to some cases of forced marriages, there are periodic reports of honor killing owing to some capricious vendetta. The Human Rights Commission of Pakistan, numerous official and private watchdogs, and an alert media, along with greater awareness and education, offer further hope for tangible safeguards for the rights of women and minorities.[20]

RELIGION AND POLITICS OF IDENTITY

Even a casual mention of Pakistan often strongly evokes images of a Muslim country, with almost everyone believing in the monotheistic religion of Islam and exhibiting some form of intolerance. This may be partly true, as most of its inhabitants are Muslim, but there are several million non-Muslim Pakistanis as well. Muslims themselves include several denominational sects. Campaigned as a predominantly Muslim country during the closing decades of the British control of India, Pakistan certainly has been a self-confessed Muslim state, although the perceptions about the extent and ways of being Muslim or Islamic have varied among sections. Other than geography and the pluralistic ethos of the Indus Valley culture, it is Islam that continues to fashion the perceptions and lifestyles of Pakistanis, and it is equally reflected in official pronouncements on issues such as education, the legal system, and foreign policy. Although many Muslims may define Islam as more than a mere religion, they also differ on its connection to and role vis-à-vis politics. Many of them desire to see their polity transformed into a theocracy through an Islamization of private and public spheres; others posit religion as a private matter and a significant factor in collective lives. Such an ideological polarity is not unique to Pakistan, as the pulls between the sacred and secular are an integral part of recent human history.[21]

Islam, literally meaning peace, is the belief in the unity of God (Allah); prophethood with Muhammad (570–632 C.E.), the last divine messenger; and the Quran as the recent most divine word to guide the community. It shares with Christianity a belief in angels and the Day of Judgment. In addition, a Muslim is required to pursue Quranic teachings and the prophetic traditions while trying to create equilibrium between this existence and the world hereafter. Defining itself as a moderate and tolerant creed over and above racial and ethnonational proclivities, Islam advocates a balance between duties unto Allah and to one's fellow beings. The Prophet Muhammad's role modeling through a diverse career as the Messenger, husband, father, trader, general, and politician is idealized by Muslims and may often blur distinctions between the state and the sacred. The strong emphasis on a collective identity built through daily and weekly congregational prayers and pilgrimage to Makkah stipulates a greater sense of religion-based community (*Ummah*), where camaraderie is idealized over and above local, ethnic, and even national associations. Other than these shared denominators and related practices, Muslims have historically evolved into various sects. The Sunnis account for an overwhelming majority, followed by Shias, who make up 10–15 percent of the total Muslim population. Despite common beliefs and practices with their Sunni co-religionists, Shias allocate the highest status to Ali, whereas Sunnis, despite a great respect for Muhammad's son-in-law, still accord respect to his other companions.[22] These two larger sects further include numerous denominations, given the expansion of Muslim communities amid the ever-growing interpretations of classical Islamic heritage. Most Pakistanis are Sunnis; 20 percent are Shias. Several political groups representing them demand Islamization or implementation of ecclesiastic and legal laws as seen and interpreted by their clerics. Recent developments in a predominantly Shia Iran and overwhelmingly Sunni Saudi Arabia and Afghanistan have also played a crucial role in accentuating divergences between Sunni and Shia Pakistanis, although, curiously, in most cases these two sects often exist even within the same extended family and may not be completely hostile to each other.

Islam in Pakistan certainly has its Middle Eastern roots but maintains a distinct subcontinental personality where local influences appear to unite with core beliefs. Two parallel distinct trends of scripturalism and syncretism characterize Pakistani Islamic experiences and are often described as the Deobandi and Brelvi approaches, named after two seminaries established in British India that articulated these two schools of thought. The former emphasizes a purist approach by shunning any intermediaries in sacred pursuits, whereas the latter acknowledges and even celebrates the spiritual intermediaries called Sufis or Pirs. These Sufis or their descendants are divided into various orders (*silsilahs*) and, over the centuries, have played a vanguard role in establishing bridges with non-Muslim communities and thus heralded the entry of Islam among the underprivileged people in Africa and Asia. The purists are revivalists, seeking their sustenance from the seminary of Deoband where Muslim scholars (*ulama*) felt that over the successive centuries Muslims had diluted pristine Islamic values by co-opting various alien traditions, including seeking intercessions from spiritual mentors. These two main revivalist strands emerged in British India when the contemporary Muslim elite agonized over a general Muslim decline, especially in the wake of a colonial vendetta after the Revolt of 1857 and the disappearance of Muslim political authority from the subcontinent.[23]

Along with these two trends was a third among Muslim intelligentsia. Although asserting Muslimness, they sought a connection with modernity instead of a back-to-roots approach. These modernists established schools and urged Muslims to acquire Western education, unlike some of their successors. For such elements Islam needs to be seen as a civilization open to positive influences from other cultures and communities. Ideological chasms between the revivalists and reformers remain as contentious as they were during the British era, and given the popular recourse to Islam, it has often been difficult for secularists to air their views publicly, as both the purists and syncretists strongly adhere to Islam being the *raison d'être* of Pakistan.

A sizable number of Pakistanis are non-Muslim and practice Hinduism and Christianity. There are about 6 million Hindus, mostly in Sindh, with smaller groups in urban centers; Christians are predominantly concentrated in Punjab, with a visible presence in cities. Their numbers vary between 5 and 6 million, with Catholicism and Protestantism claiming equal followings. The Indus lands were influenced by Christianity in the early era, as St. Thomas is reported to have visited Taxila before going south to Goa. Like Zoroastrianism, Buddhism, and Jainism—the other three contemporary religious traditions—Christianity disappeared when an assimilationist Hinduism reestablished its dominance over these regions.

Hinduism was further strengthened with the establishment of Hindu kingdoms during the classical era until Islam made its entry in the Indus Valley.

With the passage of time, the regions west of the Indus became overwhelmingly Muslim; Punjab and Sindh remained quite pluralistic despite being Muslim majority areas. The evolution of Sikhism within central Punjab and the reemergence of Christianity as a result of the presence of missionaries during the colonial era further increased religious plurality in Punjab. Although most of the Sikhs and Hindus left for India, and likewise Indian Muslims especially from eastern Punjab sought home in Pakistan in 1947, the Christians in Punjab did not move en masse across the new borders. As a consequence, Christian communities in Punjab also underwent partition, which still remains a largely under-researched subject. Most of its Hindu citizens live in lower Pakistan, and even during the stormy days of 1947 amid the world's largest migration, the level of communal volatility here remained low. There is a small community of Sikhs, again mostly in Punjab, who are either engaged in business or are attached with the Sikh holy places.

Parsis, or Zoroastrians, make up one of the world's smallest religious communities and have traditionally lived in subcontinental cities such as Mumbai and Karachi. This enterprising community is quite successful in business sectors, and in Pakistan, except for a few well-known families in Lahore and Gujranwala, most of them live in Karachi, although successive migrations to the West have been diminishing their numbers.

Other than a smaller and almost invisible community of Bahais, there are several million Ahmadis, who, despite their own identification as a Muslim sect, were officially declared a minority as a result of their own specific views on the finality of prophethood. Pakistan's parliament had passed legislation declaring them a minority in 1974, and their leadership eventually sought shelter in London. Mostly concentrated in central Punjab, Ahmadi families are found in several other towns and cities and excel both educationally and professionally.

GOVERNANCE AND ECONOMY

Pakistan is a federation that consists of the four provinces of Punjab, Sindh, Balochistan, and the NWFP, along with FATA and FANA, and is run through a three-tier administration. Azad Kashmir is technically not a formal part of Pakistan and has its own government headed by a president and run by a prime minister. The latter is a small piece of land wedged between Pakistan and the Indian-controlled Kashmir, which was liberated by the locals around Partition and has often contested India's claims on Kashmir. Pakistan itself has had many constitutions in its early years, until 1973, when a final document was agreed on that allowed a parliamentary form of government administered through a bicameral legislature. The upper house, elected on the basis of parity among the federating units, consists of 100 senators; the lower house, known as the National Assembly, is elected for five years through an adult franchise. The party in the parliamentary majority forms the central government and is headed by a prime minister. As a result of successive amendments, especially in recent years, the Pakistani president has now assumed greater powers, including the dismissal of the cabinet and parliament, which has led to a presidential form of government. Pakistan's second tier is anchored on four provinces that retain their own separately elected provincial legislatures where chief ministers and their respective cabinets form governments on the basis of electoral majority, although here again vital powers have been delegated to provincial governors who sit as chief executives and are appointed by the central government in Islamabad. The third tier of administration involves local government in villages, towns, and counties where several powers have been devolved to the elected councils, yet the tradition of a strong bureaucracy remains largely sacrosanct. In the same vein, Pakistan's judicial system follows Western legal traditions inherited from the British, but since the 1980s, several Sharia benches have been added at the higher level to implement certain specific legal injunctions as interpreted in the Islamic writings.

Pakistan's civil service, consisting of various cadres, is selected through a complex system of merit and positive discrimination—called a quota system—to allow some representation to numerous underprivileged groups. Given the centralized nature of governance, bureaucracy at the higher levels remains quiet powerful, although the army is the strongest pressure group, and a small group of generals have traditionally made vital decisions on domestic and external matters. As shall be seen in subsequent chapters, Pakistan has periodically experienced military coups, but the blame has been routinely pushed on to politicians for poor administration and corruption. The army is so entrenched in the system that the possibility of a full-fledged civilian system operating on its own with full autonomy is often slim. Other than the education system, the army employs the largest number of Pakistanis, although many of the foot soldiers come from Punjab. Pakistan's free press, both in English and other national languages, is usually vocal on the issues of governance and corruption and has been a strong voice for civic causes. The country has several political parties varying from national to ethnic, and religious to sectarian, and in many cases their politics revolves around some resourceful dynasties. As a result of administrative authoritarianism, Pakistan's political parties have often fallen victim to bureaucratic high-handedness, and for a long time, three national political leaders remained in exile in London. Benazir Bhutto, the leader of Pakistan People's Parity (PPP); Mian Nawaz Sharif, the leader of a strong faction of the Muslim League (ML-N); and Altaf Hussain of the Karachi-based Muttahida Qaumi Movement (MQM)—an ethnic urban group—were based in London for longer periods, as the army disallowed their return. In addition, there were several cases pending against them in the higher courts, which they often decried as fictitious and venomous. Pakistani newspapers and television channels in the Diaspora ensured the political survival of these Pakistani leaders, who were away for unlimited time obviating the possibility of their return unless they could strike some arrangement with the generals.

Pakistan's economy, compared to the state of affairs at its formation and also seen within the context of a burgeoning population pressure, is quite impressive. In recent years, despite a severe post-9/11 downturn, the country's economic growth has been among the top three or four fastest growing economies. Most Pakistanis are agriculturalists, but urbanization has been allowing a steady development of industries and other economic sectors such as manufacturing and services, the latter being the fastest to grow. Textiles, sports goods, surgical instruments, leather commodities, food items, and dry fruit have been some of the notable Pakistani exports, along with about four to five million citizens working abroad. The export of oil, weaponry, chemicals and heavy industries continue to underwrite trade imbalances. The foreign exchange reserves have grown in recent times, and Pakistan has escaped any default on its loan servicing, although the volume of domestic and external borrowing remains quite high. The lack of land reforms, a smaller tax base, and a burdensome nondevelopment sector persist as serious economic challenges. For ordinary people it is not the lack of resources but the absence of will amid corrupt practices that prevents substantial economic improvement of the poor, who account for one-third of the total population. Founded on the basis of a mixed economy, despite the nationalization of several concerns during the 1970s, Pakistan has been pursuing privatization since the late 1990s. Remittances by Pakistani expatriates, further streamlined since 9/11, along with some foreign aid, have helped the economy rebound from an earlier slowdown, although long-term structural changes and more efficient planning within a balanced sectoral allocation might produce tangible dividends. In addition, peace within and without could ensure further economic uplift and optimism among the teeming millions. For the eradication of poverty, other than the numerous charity organizations and societal generosity, the government would have to make specific efforts in the larger interest. Given the untapped resources in Balochistan and FANA, an efficiently run Pakistan can certainly accelerate its economic growth and equitable wealth redistribution. Despite the usual hazards of consumerism and class-based divisions, the country's overall preference for frugality, recourse to traditional moral values especially in reference to alcohol, gambling and safe sex, and extensive support for the vulnerable in the family and locality are important informal assets within a largely unrecognized social capital.

NOTES

1. Chaudhary Rahmat Ali was one of those students who spearheaded the movement for the political reconfiguration of Indian Muslims and suggested *Bengalistan* for Muslims in eastern Bengal. Their counterparts in southern India, especially those living in the princely state of Hyderabad ruled by the Nizam, were advised to group themselves as *Osmanistan*. Such an opinion reflected the diversity of views about the political rearrangement of India on the eve of the expected British departure and also showed that religion was turning into a major identity marker for all the diverse communities of the most pluralistic region in the world. See, Choudhary Rahmat Ali, *Now or Never* (Cambridge: University of Open Press, 2005) (reissued); also, Mohammad Aslam Khan Khattak, *A Pathan Odyssey* (Karachi: Oxford University Press, 2004).

2. For further details see, Iftikhar H. Malik, *Religious Minorities in Pakistan* (London: Minority Rights Group, 2002).

3. Given the nature of claims and counterclaims on this scenic and strategic border region, there is a whole spectrum of books and reports on Kashmir that includes several regional and religious communities, although the valley remains the most populous, with Muslims accounting for a majority of the inhabitants. See, Alastair Lamb, *Kashmir: A Disputed Legacy, 1846–1990* (Hertingfordbury: Roxford Books, 1991); Victoria Schofield, *Kashmir in the Crossfire* (London: I.B. Tauris, 1996); Iftikhar H. Malik, *The Continuing Conflict in Kashmir: Détente in Jeopardy* (London: Research Institute for the Study of Conflict and Terrorism, 1993); and, Raju C. Thomas, ed., *Perspectives on Kashmir: The Roots of Conflict in South Asia* (Boulder, Westview, 1992).

4. An earthquake in 1974 in Pattan and Chilas areas, just by the Indus, cost thousands of lives besides injuring many more. In 1935, Quetta, a cantonment town farther south in Balochistan, suffered a serious earthquake that destroyed the entire population. Geologists are predicting more earthquakes in Pakistan's northern regions for the next several decades given the seismic changes and the younger nature of these immensely high mountains.

5. The figures claimed by a two-decade long armed defiance in the Indian-controlled Kashmir and the resultant fatalities in this earthquake are assumed to be almost equal, acutely debilitating one of the world's most scenic and equally controversial regions.

6. It is also pronounced as Tirichmir and is visible from the town of Chitral itself.

7. Nanga Parbat has killed more mountaineers than any other mountain in the world and its first successful assault was not possible until 1979. The first

successful attempt of Nanga Parbat occurred in 1953 by a combined German and Austrian expedition.

8. The epicenter of the 2005 earthquake was in the town of Balakot, toward the south of the mountain and lying in the proximity of Muzaffarabad, the capital of Azad Kashmir.

9. The Line of Control (LOC) dividing Indian and Pakistani parts of Kashmir passes to the south of most of these glaciers, although Siachin is contested by both neighbors. More soldiers have been killed on Siachin by frostbite than as a result of gun battles that have gone on since 1984. For details, see Robert G. Wirsing, *India, Pakistan and the Kashmir Dispute* (London: Macmillan, 1994).

10. The Karakoram Highway is virtually built on glaciers at places such as Passu and often requires rebuilding not just because of landslides but also because of the glacial movements.

11. For a useful discussion on languages and ethnic identification, see Tariq Rahman, *Language and Politics in Pakistan* (Karachi: Oxford University Press, 1996). Just making language as the only anchor for ethnic identity will be fallacious as economy, politics, geography, and class all play their respective roles in such a trajectory. See, Feroz Ahmed, *Ethnicity and Politics in Pakistan* (Karachi: Oxford University Press, 1998).

12. The founder of Sikhism was born in Nankana Sahib, 26 miles outside Lahore. Lahore has some temples dating from the Sikh period in the early nineteenth century, whereas Hassan Abdal houses the Punja Sahib, the third most sacred Sikh temple (Gurdawara). Lahore also boasts a few splendid churches and cathedrals besides some other known monuments representing traditional and modern architectural designs.

13. Plural of a *Muhajir* that literally means an immigrant.

14. For more on ethnic pluralism, especially in Sindh during the 1980s and 1990s, see Iftikhar H. Malik, *State and Civil Society in Pakistan: Politics of Authority, Ideology and Ethnicity* (Oxford: St. Antony's-Macmillan Series, 1997).

15. It is believed that there are more Baloch living in the Lyari area of Karachi than in the entire province.

16. According to Sunni tradition, an imam is the one who leads prayers but according to Shia views, an imam is a spiritual as well as an earthly leader whose words are to be followed on all religious and civic matters. The Aga Khanis are a smaller community of Shia Muslims, who are known for their higher educational and financial achievements. "The Aga Khan" was the British title for the leader of the Ismaili Shias, whose followers happen to be in several regions; the Imam himself lives in Paris.

17. Tariq Rahman, *Language, Education and Culture* (Karachi: Oxford University Press, 1999).

18. For many Western observers, these seminaries have become the home of a militant culture. See, Peter W. Singer, *Pakistan's Madrasahs: Ensuring a*

System of Education Not Jihad (Washington, Brooking Institute: Analysis Paper No. 4, 2001); and, Jessica Stern, "Pakistan's Jihad Culture," *Foreign Affairs*, November-December 2000. Such critics often ignore the historical background to this tradition in the Muslim world and owing to the Taliban factor rush to generalize.

19. Such problems converge with uninspiring texts and lower self-esteem for those already involved in teaching. For details, see, K. K. Aziz, *The Murder of History: A Critique of History Books Used in Pakistan* (Lahore: Vanguard, 1993); and Pervez Hoodbhoy, ed., *Education and the State: Fifty Years of Pakistan* (Karachi: Oxford University Press, 1998).

20. Among several publicized cases of gang rapes is that of Mukhtar Mai, who refused to be cowed by her relatives to keep quiet over an assault on her. Instead, she has made her story a national issue and has been offering help to other battered women. See, Mukhtar Mai with Marie-Therese Cuny, *In the Name of Honor: A Memoir*, translated by Linda Coverdale (London: Virago, 2007). On February 20, 2007, Zille Huma Usman, a woman minister in Punjab government and mother of two children, was gunned down in Gujranwala as she prepared to speak to a political rally. Her killer, Maulvi Sarwar, believed that women should be confined inside their homes and reportedly had already murdered six women, accusing them of prostitution, although he never faced any long-term imprisonment for those crimes. For further details, see "Demise of Gujranwala" (leader), *The Daily Times*, February 22, 2007.

21. Many people believe that since the late 1990s, Islam has assumed a center stage not only among most Muslims but also in their relationship with the Western countries. 9/11 and the Anglo-American invasions of Afghanistan and Iraq have occasionally affirmed the hypotheses about the clash of cultures. Some people may even exaggerate political tensions to suggest that Muslims and the rest have always been on a collision course. For more on this see, Iftikhar H. Malik, *Crescent between Cross and Star: Muslims and the West after 9/11* (Karachi: Oxford University Press, 2006).

22. The Prophet was survived by a daughter, Fatima, whose husband was Ali, a cousin and close companion of the Prophet Muhammad. Muhammad did not will for any successor to guide the new community in its political and spiritual affairs, and this led to a schism among Muslims at an early stage. Ali became a successor (caliph) but only after three other companions had preceded him. That is where the political divisions eventually led to two theological schools of Sunnis and Shias. For more on this, see Karen Armstrong, *Islam: A Short History* (London: Weidenfeld and Nicolson, 2000).

23. For a recent and interesting account of these stormy events and the fall of the last Muslim king of Delhi see, William Dalrymple, *The Last Mughal: The Fall of a Dynasty, Delhi, 1857* (London: Bloomsbury, 2006).

2

The Indus Valley Civilization: Dravidians to Aryans

The Indus River, like the Nile in Egypt, not only has been the lifeline for Pakistan since ancient time but also denotes the name of one of the oldest human cultures. The Indus Valley civilization evolved in the areas fed by the mighty river and its tributaries. In addition to signifying several prehistoric cultures, Indus, locally known as *Abasin, Sindh,* and *Sindhu,* is the root of the words *India, Indica, Hindu, Hinduism,* and *Hindustan.* It has symbolized the cultural history of the entire south Asian subcontinent. The ancient Indus Valley inhabitants, often known as Dravidians, established their settlements many millennia before the development of great Indian religions such as Brahmanism, Hinduism, Jainism, and Buddhism. As their ancient hymns suggest, these religions evolved in the Indus regions.

Because of our inability to decipher the language of pre-Aryan Indus Valley residents, and despite the availability of thousands of seals and such other artifacts displaying inscriptions, pictographs, and carvings, knowledge about the food-gathering and agrarian ancestors of today's Indians and Pakistanis remains limited.[1] The ancient Indus history is still a mystery and largely based on assumptions concerning the evolution of earliest human and animal life in South Asia. The most ancient collection of Sanskrit tales, the *Rigveda,* describes battles, victories, and an extravaganza of gods and goddesses largely

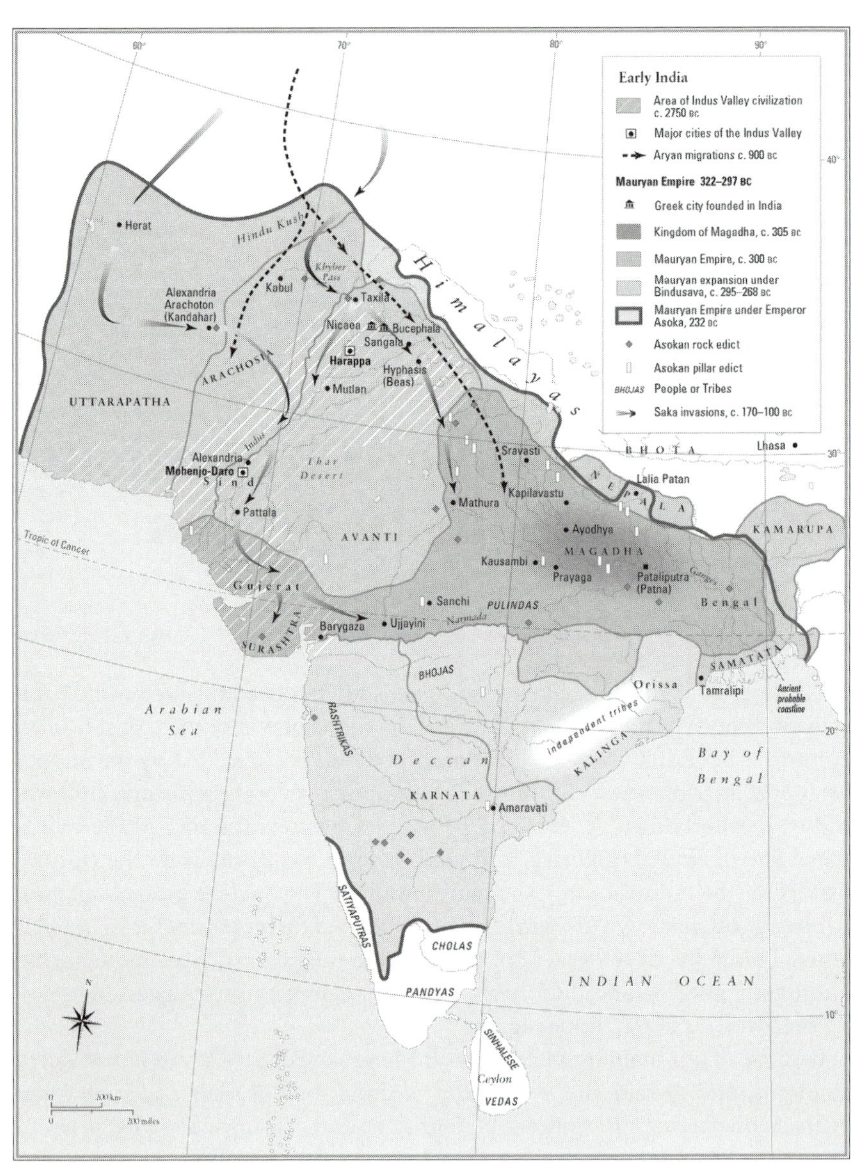

Civilization in Early India.

concentrated in areas that make up present-day Pakistan. The *Rigveda* itself dates from 1500–1000 B.C.E., however, and thus focuses on the Aryan exploits, whereas the pre-Aryan Indian past either remains obscure or is relegated to stereotypes shared by victors toward their vanquished.

The Aryans, or "noble men," ushered in a new era in the northern subcontinent and formulated Brahmanism in its all religious, social, and literary realms. Despite recent political- and ideology-driven theories that the Aryans were indigenous Indians, it seems that earlier inhabitants pioneered the Indus Valley civilization. With a possible ability to decipher their pre-Sanskrit language, major gaps in ancient history could be bridged, enabling a more complete reconstruction of the Indus past. The ruins of the two ancient cities of Harappa and Mohenjo Daro discovered in Pakistani territory during the 1920s also continue to offer archaeologists and historians a steady stream of information on pre-Aryan Indus regions. Questions about the origins and sudden disappearance of the ancient cultures in the Indus Valley challenge historians, who might otherwise routinely focus on the better-known evolution of Aryan domination and the subsequent evolution of Brahmanism.[2]

Another major question concerns the land of origin of the Aryans, whose Vedic age saw the documentation of early Hindu creed and practices in Sanskrit that evolved in the Indus regions. Now understood by only a few scholars, Sanskrit was a synthesis among the ancient Indians who had recently settled in the northern subcontinent. The Indus Valley and subsequently the Gangetic regions became home to the Aryans and their caste-based communities, but recent nationalist discourse has sought to define them not as invaders and immigrants but as inherently *Indian.*[3]

WHAT'S IN A NAME?

Etymological controversies about terms such as *India, Hindu, Indica, Bharat,* and *Indus* defy consensus on their origins, time span, and spatial frontiers. One could write a whole volume on the historical and ethnic connotations of the term *Indian.* In the early modern era, exploring Europeans often identified the regions all the way from southern Africa to China as India. Columbus and his successors stumbled on the Native Americans who were and are still largely identified as "Indians."[4] Like the ancient Greeks and Persians, however, British historians and administrators pioneered a monolithic definition of the subcontinent in reference to its geography, territory, religions, and history. Except for the Buddhist Emperor Ashoka (273–232 B.C.E.) and the Great Mughals (1526–1707 C.E.), who both made multiple efforts to unify India along with present-day Afghanistan, the subcontinent remained a vast region of varying natural, political, and ethnographic characteristics. Efforts to consolidate India certainly merit some attention, especially when its leaders such as Mahatma Gandhi (1869–1948) and Pundit Jawaharlal Nehru (1889–1964) continuously attempted to retain a unified India, despite its cultural, religious, and political pluralism. The Ultra Right Hindus, in recent decades, have gone several steps beyond these leaders with demands to reclaim a united India all the way from Afghanistan to Burma, but also to establish this Greater India as *Hindustan* or *Bharatvarsha*—the land of (only) Hindus. This notion of communalized utopianism not only spawned intercommunity tensions, but to a great extent led to Partition in 1947 and has kept the communal cauldron boiling with dissentions and anxieties.

Bharat is the name for ancient Hindu India that has often been used for the post-1947 Union in textbooks. The name can be controversial, however, as historically it lays claim on the areas making up contemporary Pakistan, Afghanistan, and Bangladesh. Bharat was an Aryan leader, mentioned in the Vedas, whose name is derived from *Bharati,* the goddess of goodness. In *Rigveda, Bharat* referred to the Aryan victory in the battle of 10 kings that took place 3,000 years ago in present-day Pakistan and resulted in triumph for the *Bharatas* clan. These victorious tribesmen called their land *Bharatversha* or *Bharatvarta* (the land of Bharat). In contemporary, post-Dravidian literature, this region is also known as *Aryavarta*—the land of Aryans. Both *Bharatvarta* and *Aryavarta* were loosely defined in a territorial sense, but in modern times they have been appropriated by some Indian nationalists as synonymous with Hinduism.[5] Consequently, these terms have become irredentist, romanticizing the entire Aryan past and their claims for the entire Indus Valley civilization.

In contrast, *Hindustan,* a Persian term also used in Turkish and Urdu, means the land of Indus or *Sindh,* as well as the home of *Hindis/Hindus,* making it a geographical term. Application of this term for sheer religious purposes would exclude several non-Hindu communities and ignore the vast and complex topography of the subcontinent. *Hind* was used by the Achaemenid Persians because of the centrality of the Indus until after the Greek invasion, when it began to be called *Indica. Indica* came into currency with the invasion of Alexander the Great, who crossed the Hindu-Kush in May 327 B.C.E. and fought with the tribes in northern Pakistan until he was able to cross the Indus in February 326 B.C.E. He was welcomed by the ruler of Taxila (Takshashila) who assisted the Greeks with troops, horses, and cattle in their march to the plains of Punjab. After defeating King Porus by the Jhelum, Alexander moved on beyond Lahore but decided to return home from the eastern fringes of the Beas. He returned to Susa, Persia, in 324 B.C.E. and died a year later in Babylon.

Indica, according to ancient Greek historians, referred to the entire subcontinent, and *Hind* began to reappear in Middle Eastern accounts only after the decline of the Greek military presence in southwestern Asia. The Achaemenids were Parthian-Aryans who referred to their own country as *Paras,* which later yielded the terms *Faras, Parthia,* or *Persia.*[6] These Persians and their Indus

Valley contemporaries were two rival branches of the same ethnic group. The Persians subscribed to the beliefs of Zoroastrianism; the Indo-Aryans developed Brahmanism, which eventually evolved into Hinduism.[7]

Borrowing from ancient Persians, the Arabs called this whole region *Al-Hind,* a term still in use but now primarily referring only to the northern and northwestern territories, many of which now form Pakistan. According to these west Asians, a *Hindi/Hindustani* would refer to anybody living in the subcontinent irrespective of religion or region; thus for a long time *Hind* remained a territorial rather than a religious identity.[8] Ultimately, the Greek term *Indica* was anglicized as *India* by modern Europeans; *Al-Hind* and *Hindustan* remain prevalent in Urdu, Persian, and Turkish even today.[9]

PERIODS IN THE SUBCONTINENT'S HISTORY

Like any other complex and immensely contested historical matter, south Asian history has precipitated several theoretical debates. Until recently, many historians had unhesitatingly accepted the division of south Asian history into ancient, medieval and modern periods, originally attributed to the early British chronicles of India. In the breakdown of these three overarching phases, the Indus Valley civilization and classical Hindu period would usually form the earliest phase combining early history with prehistoric times. Curiously, the Dravidian past received little attention in this category, but the Aryan and Hindu epochs, particularly in the northern regions, monopolized a major portion of scholarship. This long period was further subdivided into two separate phases: the Greco-Buddhist or Indo-Greek period and the Christian era. The Hindu empires of the early Christian period are, accordingly, followed by regional kingdoms owing to the periodic regionalization of the subcontinent and a series of invasions from the north.

The medieval period begins with the establishment of Muslim sultanates, as well as some Hindu regional empires in the south (Deccan). Some British historians group the Mughal era with the medieval dynasties; some view it as proto-modern. The full-fledged inauguration of the modern era, according to this classification of Indian history, however, ensued with the advent of British control and specific efforts for modernization after India's failed rebellion against the East India Company in 1857. According to this grand narrative of Indian history, the contemporary era began in the twentieth century with India's integration into the global scheme of empires, wars, expeditions, and economies.

The preceding categorization of Indian history is challenged by several recent historians who refuse to accept a Eurocentric classification of south Asia's totally distinct and complex heritage. To many of them, the emphasis on *modern* itself seems a self-celebratory commendation by the Raj, which proudly ascribed India's administrative unity and industrial progress to itself. The other parallel classification of Indian history divides the entire realm into interconnected periods respectively defined as prehistoric (Dravidian), Hindu (Aryan), Zoroastrian (Persian), Gandhara (Greco-Buddhist), Hindu Shahis, Muslim (Delhi Sultans, Bahimnis, and Mughals), Deccan kingdoms (Shatavahanas, Pandyas, Cholas, Chalukyas, Vijayanagar, and Bahmanis), British/European (British East India Company and the Crown), and Sikh and Nationalist (secularist and Hindu in India, Islamic in Pakistan and Bangladesh). The main objection to this classification is its focus on religion as the main anchor of collective identities, assuming India to be inherently communal if not communalist, with people owing allegiance only to their own religious group. Such a categorization may be acceptable to religiopolitical parties in south Asia, yet for secularists and liberal historians this is a dangerous oversimplification of an otherwise diverse heritage in which various communities and cultures had fluid, even co-optive, boundaries.[10] Certainly, the colonial period and communal tensions have been the underlying factors for this historiographical debate, which goes beyond the polarity between the imperial and nationalist schools of Indian history. The former credited the British with discovering and identifying a unified India, whereas nationalists believe that a united Indian identity had always existed in south Asian history and did not owe itself to a modernist engineering.[11] Emerging historical scholarship is diverse and explores areas such as gender, peasants, tribes, ethnicities, ideologies, resistance, ecology, arts, ideas, and subalterns. Such a wide range of historical perspectives accounts for an expansive debate.[12]

THE INDUS VALLEY CIVILIZATION: THE HARAPPAN PAST

Long before the Aryan and the Vedic eras culminated in the classical Hindu period, the Indus Valley had developed its own urban culture featuring township, trade, and statecraft, although agriculture remained the mainstay of these indigenous people, often called Dravidians. As suggested earlier, there is scant information concerning them or their ancestors who inhabited these valleys several millennia before the birth of Hinduism. The south Asian land mass had been formed around 50 million years ago, when the Indian plate, like Australia, broke away from Africa and began to thrust itself into the Eurasian plate. As a consequence of this collision, the Hindu-Kush, Karakorams, and Himalayas emerged, pushing the Indian plate farther underneath their weight and causing frequent tremors in the adjoining territories, which continue to occur even today. These monumental geological changes also formed two major water systems: the Indus system, which initially flows westward before heading south toward the Arabian Sea, and the Gangetic system, which moves eastward before shifting its course toward the Bay of Bengal in the south. The Indus, or Sindhu as it was later called in *Rigveda,* was joined by six other rivers in its southward journey: the Jhelum, Chenab, Ravi, Sutlej, Beas, and Saraswati. The Sarawati dried up long ago somewhere in Rajasthan, but not before establishing its historical sanctimony in the Hindu epics. Around 40,000 to 12,000 years ago, a period generally identified as the Middle Stone Age, the erstwhile food gatherers who traversed the river valleys in India began to settle down in smaller communities. By about 10,000 years ago, they had formed agricultural settlements.[13] Further graduation to sociopolitical institutions rapidly followed, as political authority evolved in the persons of priest-kings who looked after the religious and temporal needs of their respective communities. Thousands of seals excavated from the Indus Valley display the figures of these bearded leaders often accompanied by inscriptions still waiting to be deciphered. The period since the evolution of agriculture is known as the ancient Indus Valley civilization and is called the Harappa culture after one of the historic sites in Pakistani Punjab.

A distinct Indus Valley or ancient Indian civilization was unknown and unacknowledged in all the British historical accounts, and the subcontinent, beginning with the arrival of the Aryans around 1500 B.C.E., was believed to have inherited a culture that was a mutation of the Mesopotamian heritage. In the 1920s, a number of significant archaeological discoveries put a distinct Indus civilization on the map. These discoveries were largely owed to Sir John Marshall, the head of the archaeology department in India. His studies and those of his associates benefited significantly from information on the historical authenticity of these sites from earlier researchers. For instance, in 1829 Charles Mason, a British explorer in southwestern Asia, had noticed a huge mound near Harappa along with the old course of the Ravi River and left an account in his personal papers. Four years later, Alexander Burnes, a Scottish officer, drew maps of the Indus and its tributaries and, after visiting Harappa, left notes about the possible antiquity of the site. In 1858, Alexander Cunningham, the first head of the Archaeological Survey of India, expressed deep interest in the mounds at Harappa and Mohenjo Daro, but no systematic effort was undertaken to further preserve and study these two sites, which were 600 kilometers apart. Instead, when the railway tracks were being laid down between Lahore and Karachi, the uniquely slim bricks were taken away from the mound and other ruins of ancient Harappa to be used in the construction of the line. Like local inhabitants who had pilfered the site in the past, the British officials in Punjab irreverently ignored the significance of the place, which was denuded of all its bricks down to the ground level.

Lord Curzon, the viceroy in India, reinvigorated the archaeology department in 1901 and appointed John Marshall as its head a year later. Based on early British accounts and the maps left by Cunningham, Marshall employed a team of Indians in 1921 to supervise excavations at Harappa and Mohenjo Daro where efforts began to bear fruit. Soon the elaborate ruins of two well-planned cities that once housed the ancient Indus civilization came into public view. With their straight streets, well-patterned houses, granaries, and, most of all, underground sewage system, the Harappan heritage began to be recognized as the fountainhead of a hitherto unknown culture. Further excavations confirmed that the Indus Valley civilization in its heyday was twice the size of its Egyptian counterpart and four times bigger than the Sumerian civilization in Mesopotamia. Indus seals discovered in the Mesopotamian ruins and a swastika inscribed on the entrance to the main temple at Ephesus in Anatolia offer evidence that the Indus Valley inhabitants, especially during their peak between 2600–2300 B.C.E., held trade linkages with people hundreds of miles away.

Some historians prefer to call this ancient civilization the "Indus Age" instead of the Harappan civilization partly because the latter seems to exclude other important urban centers across the valley.[14] Historians of ancient civilizations enjoy comparing various known human epochs and, until recently, would identify the Egyptian and Mesopotamian cultures as pioneers, superior to their counterparts. However, given the area it covered and the finesse with which its craftsmen built its cities with all the civic amenities, a lateral pre-eminence has now been given to the ancient Indus Valley civilization.[15] Because stone was not to be found in the plains and deserts of Punjab and Sindh within the immediate proximity of the Indus, the ancient inhabitants baked slim bricks and used them to build all their dwellings and other communal structures. Harappa, Mohenjo Daro, Kot Diji, and Mehrgarh retain remains of buildings used for spiritual rites yet lack other monumental structures such as the pyramids so unique to Egypt.

The great communal bath in Mohenjo Daro was 39 by 23 feet, with a depth of 8 feet and was located in the center of the acropolis, the main worship center. This bath was connected to an extensive water supply and sewage system and was located near a magnificent building, which could have been the seat of government. In the same area, there was a huge granary 150 feet long by 75 feet wide with properly ventilated compartments. Although one cannot be sure when during the Indus civilization this urban engineering occurred, it is generally assumed that around 9,000 to 10,000 years ago agriculture had already set in as the major occupation, soon to be followed by the growth of regular cities and their social organization.

The ancient Indus people evolved from living in villages to living in urban communities and developed regular religiopolitical institutions. The system of government, which combined the sacred with the secular in the persons of priest-kings, was purported to supervise multiple aspects of governance and the ensuing civic professionalization. There are still questions about the class system, laws governing statehood, and the languages and religions of these ancient Indians, and the undeciphered seals in their enormity and sophistication hold the key to them. The pictographic inscriptions on these square seals offer a formidable philological challenge to archaeologists dealing with the Bronze Age, but they also affirm the high ratio of literacy among the Indus societies. The script is found on 4,000 to 5,000 seals carved in stone, terracotta, and faience amulets, as well as numerous ceramic pieces, stone implements, ornaments, and other household objects. These seals also carry motifs, animal depictions, and cultic scenes of deities and worshippers. The humped bull, zebra, unicorn, tiger, rhinoceros, and elephant are frequently sketched on these seals.[16]

An ancient Indus city such as Mohenjo Daro or Harappa would traditionally have a center with a public building set on a raised structure along with a communal bath used for worship. Most of the houses, street floors, and drainage paths were built of baked bricks; the religious and political buildings were made of special, rather costly bricks. The public stores housed commodities built by craftsmen along with granaries meant to store harvests. As is confirmed by diagrams on several seals, these people had been using the wheel for a long time and were familiar with wheeled vehicles.[17]

Because these agricultural and urban Dravidian communities were ultimately overcome by pastoral Aryans, various hypotheses about their origins abound. Some trace their evolution to Africa,[18] whereas others believe them to be the ancestors of Indians presently living in southern India.[19] The mass graves in Mohenjo Daro, the persistence of fertility rituals in southern India, the prejudices against darker complexion, and the use of terms such as *Varna* (color) and *Rakhshasas* (demons), often mentioned in *Rigveda,* affirm the Aryan-Dravidian conflict that led to the downfall of the Dravidians over an extended period.

The Aryans began to move into northwestern regions of the subcontinent from their native homes in Central Asia between 2000 and 1700 B.C.E., gradually overpowering the natives. As mentioned previously, one branch of the Aryans, the Parthian-Aryans, became the ruling elite in Iran, and the Indo-Aryans initiated the Vedic Age, characterized by Brahmanism until its transformation into Hinduism first in the Indus Valley and then more substantially in the Gangetic regions. The Gangetic regions were a safe distance from their Iranian cousins, who were always eager to capture the Indus Valley. The Aryans gradually overpowered the Dravidians and inflicted all the prevalent practices of ethnic cleansing and enslavement, although not without first accepting several of the agricultural, urban, and even religious traditions of their victims.

Some writers may believe that the dramatically sudden disappearance of the ancient Dravidian culture resulted from epidemics, geological changes, or massive floods, but a more persuasive argument exists for the gradual subjugation of a relatively peaceful urban society by the Aryans. It is true that some of the Indus cities were periodic victims of floods and were rebuilt about 20 times, but these epidemics could have equally affected the invaders if they are to be considered as a viable explanation of the sudden decline.[20] Like subsequent invasions, the ancient Indians fell victim to the better organized, more disciplined, ruthless assaults by their foes. Like oceanic currents, civilizations also merge and diffuse into one another. They do not disappear altogether but instead assume newer identities as did the Dravidians when the Aryans overtook them. In this way, the northern cultures and religions gradually overpowered those of the indigenous peoples in southern India through the processes of Hindiization, Aryanization, and Sanskritization.

THE ADVENT OF THE ARYANS AND THE VEDIC ERA

During the eighteenth and nineteenth centuries, it was usually believed that the Aryans were fair complexioned, tribal people who lived pastoral life styles in the mountainous valleys of central Asia; were pushed out of their natural homeland for some demographic, natural, and adventurous reasons; and moved into Europe and southwestern Asia. The hymns and mythical accounts of the *Rigveda* shed some light on the establishment of Aryan communities in the northwestern subcontinent during the second millennium of the pre-Christian era. The other literature found in the Vedas, which illustrates the early Vedic era in Hinduism, was recorded in Sanskrit, which over the centuries was replaced by several more popular regional languages. The religious hymns, traditions, and mantras of the *Rigveda,* however, were recited in their original text by Brahmans, who enjoyed higher social and racial status. Studies conducted by Sir William Jones, the British East India Company's official scholar during the late eighteenth century, convinced him that Sanskrit was actually the mainspring of several Indo-European languages.

During the nineteenth century, scholars such as Max Muller believed in the Caucasian appearance of the Aryans, which further solidified theories about the non-Indian origins of the Aryan tribes. Rivaled by their Iranian cousins, the Indo-Aryans developed their own sociopolitical organization, often borrowing from the Dravidians. Higher status was granted to Brahmans, who safeguarded and interpreted religious knowledge and administered sacrifices, which were quite common among these tribes

The Aryans moved into the Indus Valley from 2000–1750 B.C.E. when the Dravidians had begun to decline as a political force. As in the modernist reconstruction of India, *Hindu, India,* and *Aryan* became interchangeable in the late nineteenth century, although, as previously discussed, all these terms had different meaning at different times. *Arya* or *Airia* itself is an Iranian word found in the ancient Pehlavi language and was used in *Avesta*, the Zoroastrian holy book. It does not appear in the contemporary Vedic literature, although in Sanskrit it suggested a higher social status. In the revivalist and reformist terminology of nineteenth-century India, *Arya* became synonymous with *India* and the higher caste Hindus. Such racialization was partly derived from the quest for identity in a pluralistic and increasingly competitive India and partly a product of European categorization of Aryans as a superior race.[21] Adolf Hitler certainly took this prejudice to extremes in the twentieth century with his attempt to create a fair-haired Aryan master race, but he had surely been influenced by racialized views of Aryan supremacy.

Within ancient India this powerful sense of superiority, bolstered by the subjugation of Dravidians and assumption of control over the vast, fertile valleys of western and northern regions, underwrote a rigid caste system. The Indo-Aryans began formulating their religious and social ideas in the Indus Valley and did not shirk from accepting new ideas concerning town planning, agriculture, jewelry-making, and priesthood from their vanquished predecessors.[22] Even Lord Shiva—the Dravidian deity—was adopted as a destroyer and builder by the Aryans who, like the ancient Greeks, evolved their own unique pantheons of male and female deities, attributing them various special powers. The victory of the *Bharata* tribes recorded in *Rigveda* led to the early form of Brahmanical Hinduism known as Santana Dharma in the Indus regions, although a more concrete form would not emerge until the Gangetic valleys became the heartland of Hinduism during the millennium preceding the Christian era. The threat from the Iranian cousins and a longing for more land and fertile valleys originally led the Indo-Aryans into the Gangetic lands. The Persians, however, did not lose interest in expanding into Indus regions until the Greek conquests temporarily limited their prospects.

Rigveda, the most ancient Hindu book, was composed in the Indus Valley during 1500–1100 B.C.E. and supersedes the other four major texts from this era in terms of quantity and quality of historical information. It contains 1,028 hymns (*suktas*) with 100,000 verses that are divided into 10 books or cycles of songs (*mandalas*). In addition to depicting historical battles and victories over "barbarians," the text expounds on themes such as creation and natural manifestations. It elevates the practice of sacrifice, which held a central position in Aryan traditions. During sacrifices, priests or Brahmans (children of Brahma/God) would recite hymns, mostly learned by heart. Sacrifice was meant to please gods while soliciting their blessings in daily life. To appease and please fire (*Agni*), rain (*Indira*), and sun (*Surya*), elaborate rituals and hymns accompanied periodic acts of sacrifice, necessitating the retention of Brahmans as a powerful group of knowledgeable, high-status individuals.[23] Known as the Early Vedic period, this era was mostly concentrated in the territories comprising Pakistan today and led to the evolution of Hinduism, which was largely dominated by Brahmans and characterized by the rigid Aryan hierarchical caste system.

In the later Vedic period, the Hindu political and cultural centers became concentrated in the Gangetic Valley. The Indus Valley, after Alexander's departure, came under the control of the Indo-Aryans (Mauryans), who subsequently lost it to the Greeks, Bactrians, and Persians. The Aryans became the upper castes of society by assuming control of the religious, military, and commercial enterprises, and the subjugated Dravidians were grouped together as Shudras (Untouchables). Their women were relegated to a lower status of *Dasis* (slaves) and were often offered to Brahmans and temples in return for blessings and favor. The number of *Dasas* (male slaves) and *Dasis* also determined the wealth and status of the upper castes including priests, warriors, and merchants. The ruler, often called a *raja,* was assisted by priests (*Prohits*) who performed holy rituals including sacrifice on special occasions.

The later Vedic period in the Gangetic Valley lasted from 800 to 500 B.C.E. At this time the Indo-Persians started to encroach on the Indus Valley and eventually captured it, led by Cyrus the Great, the Achaemenid king. It was in the fertile regions around the Ganges, Saraswati, and Jumna that reformulation of Hinduism took place along with the composition of several more sacred books in Sanskrit.[24] Belief in transmigration of the soul through reincarnation, stoical conviction in life being constant pain until one attained emancipation (*Muksha*), and several related rituals and prayers were codified by Brahmans in scriptures known as *Brahmanas.* As the name denotes, these compositions were under the strict monopoly of the Brahmans, who had been enjoying special status since the early Vedic era. Another series of philosophical works, *Upanishads,* focused on tutor-student relationship and contained lessons to be imparted on a one-to-one basis. Unlike *Brahmanas,* these texts, about 108 altogether, were more accessible to the common laity and played an important role in providing the basis for a more mystical and even egalitarian view of the human soul. Also, a number of other hymnal works called *Sutras* (threads) were composed during this period, which is hallmarked by two great Hindu epics: *Mahabharata* and *Ramayana.* Both focus on developments occurring between 1000 and 700 B.C.E. *Mahabharata* consists of 100,000 verses and celebrates monarchical victory over chieftains located in the central Gangetic regions. *Ramayana,* composed slightly earlier than *Mahabharata,* is the story of the heroic victory of Ram over Rawan, who had kidnapped Ram's wife, Sita. Here Ram or Rama, born in the town of Ayodhya in the present-day state of Untied Province, or Uttar Pradesh (UP), is helped by the monkey god, Hanuman. Rawan symbolizes evil and barbarianism. Ram's triumphs and establishment of Brahmanical rule spawned the movement for Ram Raj or Hindu divine rule, which is espoused in the modern era by many Hindu nationalists.

Unlike *Rigveda,* the events and warfare in these two classical Sanskrit epics are concentrated in the central Gangetic Valley, also known as Doab (confluence of two rivers); and cities like Allahabad (Priyag), Muthra, and Banaras (Varanasi) are depicted as the Hindu heartland. Here religion and statecraft combined, as with the ancient Indus Valley priest-kings, although the caste system became even more rigid, resulting in the almost invincible dominance of the Brahmans.

Initially, the caste system signified social classes on the basis of a division of labor, but gradually a strict color bar and a serious Brahmanical preoccupation with pollution created an acute gulf between the upper castes and outcastes. Brahmans were followed by the rulers and warriors (*Kashatriays*) and the merchants and professionals (*Vaisas*), respectively; the Dravidians and tribals were designated as outcastes (*Shudras*), making these boundaries further unbridgeable. Commonly known as *Varna,* this caste[25] was also called *jat,* which remains a basic identification in India even today.

Like the Indus Valley Aryans, these Gangetic Aryans preferred sons over daughters and followed a strong tradition of sacrifice to celebrate special occasions or to beseech divine help. Horses and bulls were usually sacrificed, and the Brahmans administered special rituals and prayers. These Aryans developed a unique way of using sacrifice for land acquisition that is sometimes traced to ancient central Asia. A horse was allowed to roam around over unclaimed land and then would be sacrificed at the sunset, allowing the raja possession of the areas covered by the horse. It was from among these rajas that the earliest Hindu kingdoms, also called confederacies, emerged in various regions from 500 to 324 B.C.E., when King Chandragupta of the Maghda state unified most of India under his control and built the earliest Hindu empire.

JAINISM AND BUDDHISM IN THE GANGETIC VALLEY

The dualism of raja and prohit, led by Brahmans and fortified by a segregationist caste system, reorganized Gangetic societies by mixing politics with religion, yet did not allow sufficient space to the lower castes, who suffered from serious discrimination. The control of the upper castes up until present times was aided by the diverse nature of the lower castes, which suffered from a lack of autonomous political or religious organization. Their continued economic dependency on the upper castes kept them confined within the sharp caste boundaries. The rural nature of Indian communities also worked against the lower castes, and it is only in recent times that education, urbanization, and some politicization have begun to ameliorate this enduring state of deprivation. Changes have not occurred, however, without strong retaliation from India's upper castes.

To pacify social violence resulting from the caste system and to establish greater human camaraderie over and above priestly monopoly, two new spiritual movements appeared in the Gangetic regions and soon became known as Buddhism and Jainism. Gautma, later known as Buddha or Siddhartha, the enlightened one, was a prince who left his family and luxurious life in Kapal Vastu to find peace and self-knowledge. Buddha is believed to have lived from 563 to 483 B.C.E. Mahawira, Buddha's contemporary, was born during the middle of the first millennium of the common era in that part of the Gangetic Valley that forms the present-day Indian state of Bihar and died around 477 B.C.E. Both were deeply disturbed by the Brahamanical control of mundane and ecclesiastic affairs, as well as caste-based violence, and they revolted against contemporary norms through their own teaching and pacifism. Jainism, pioneered by Mahavira, eventually led to greater respect for life, which turned into a more individualistic form of worship and connection with deities. The preservation of life in Jainism gradually resulted in the rejection of all professions that might claim the lives of humans, animals, or other such beings. Thus in trying to escape sin (*karma*), Jains gradually began to practice trade and business only.

Buddha, on the other hand, after finding enlightenment (*Gyan*) at the age of 35, rejected the priestly control over human freedom and both sought and preached individual ways to achieve reunion with the soul. He urged recourse to three truths: that the individual life was a sad experience but transient (*anicca*) and lacking in spirituality (*anatta*); that human suffering (*dukhha*) owed to the cycle of transmigration, and the ignorance of this truth led to the desire to live (*avidya*); and that all this malaise can be broken by *nirvana,* sought through character, awareness, speech, struggle, livelihood, aspiration, and meditation. Disciples were tutored to adhere to group-based (*sangha*) efforts, and greed and temptation were to be shunned by living in monasteries and not seeking power. Unlike Brahmans, disciples would accept whatever the community offered them without striving for office. Like Buddha himself, a disciple carried a begging bowl to highlight humility and otherworldliness, not to promote a parasitic existence.

Jainism, despite challenging several Brahmanical practices, remained a minority creed and usually avoided missionary efforts. It maintained its own distinct identity without being reabsorbed by a revitalized Hinduism or Buddhism and even today is followed by a small community living across the West Indian regions. Buddhism, on the other hand, was viewed as a serious threat, especially when the Maurya emperor, Ashoka (273–232 B.C.E.), accepted Buddhism and tried to popularize it across the subcontinent, Sri Lanka, and central Asia. A reformed Hinduism, however, which strengthened during the reigns of the later Mauryan and Gupta kings, staged a strong comeback. Buddhism, despite the tolerance shown by King Harsha in the seventh century

C.E., almost vanished from India until the 1950s, when several Dalits, led by Bhimrao Ambedkar, converted to Buddhism.

PERSIANS, GREEKS, AND THE MAURYANS, 530–185 B.C.E.

In addition to the religious divisions across the subcontinent over the six centuries preceding the Christian era, political regionalization was another enduring feature, with different dynasties controlling various regions of India. The Indus territories, however, despite their early Vedic cultural influences, were largely ruled by the west Asian dynasties. Here, Zoroastrianism had begun to be established, especially in those areas ruled by the Achaemenids, until the invasion by Alexander when Greek traditions began to mingle with west Asian mores. The influence of the Greeks was then followed by a resurgence of Buddhist influences. As mentioned earlier, Cyrus the Great of Persia (558–530 B.C.E.) crossed the Hindu Kush after conquering Kabul and received tributes from the rulers of Gandhara, a region located in what is now northern Pakistan whose capital at Taxila stood quite close to Pakistan's new capital of Islamabad. This area was comfortably prosperous because of its location along major trade routes connecting with the Silk Road, but it was equally vulnerable to several intermittent invasions by the central and west Asian tribes. Persian control of the Indus territories was challenged by Alexander the Great who, after his defeat of Darius III in 330 B.C.E., attacked Afghanistan, Uzbekistan, and then Gandhara. Alexander next marched into northern Chitral and fought a high-altitude battle in Swat before reaching Taxila to initiate his journey across the Salt Range into the plains of Punjab.[26]

Alexander built cities and temples all across his empire and fought a memorable battle by the Jhelum River where Raja Porus, a tributary of Persepolis, put up a formidable resistance.[27] Porus used his vast collection of elephants to fight the Greeks and their allies, but was finally defeated near the present town of Dipalpur in Punjab when Alexander crossed the Jelum at night to mount a surprise attack. Porus's elephants panicked when attacked by Alexander's cavaliers and snipers and, according to Greek historians and oral traditions, stampeded their own troops. Porus, however, was rehabilitated as a tributary, and the Greek conqueror moved on to the Beas, the eastern fringes of the Punjab as well as of the Persian Empire. Here his troops refused to fight the Nanda confederacy belonging to Maghda, and Alexander decided to return home. He would die not long after in Babylon in present-day Iraq. Thus ethnic and religious pluralism remained the hallmark only of the conquered Indus regions, whereas Deccan and other eastern, central, and southern areas escaped foreign invasions and saw centuries of rule by the same dynasties. Even these areas, however, would be disrupted during the early modern era when Vijayanagar and Bahmani kingdoms prevailed and the Europeans appeared on the coasts (*Ghats*).

It was again from the central Gangetic region of Magdha that an adventurer raja took it upon himself to displace the regional power holders and, with the help of Kautilya, the author of *Arthashastra,* established a new empire with its capital in Patna. Chandragupta, the founder of the great Mauryan Empire, struck his fortune after Alexander's withdrawal, which left a power vacuum in the northern subcontinent. The Greek successors of Alexander, the Selucids, could not manage a huge empire, and with the capital in distant Mesopotamia, the Indus possessions tended toward autonomy.

It is generally held that the great Brahman luminary Kautilya, also known as Chanakya, had been grievously insulted by Maghda's Nanda king and, out of revenge, aligned himself with Chandragupta. The author of a political classic, like Machiavelli two thousands years later, Kautilya had devised a policy of control, conquest, and imperial management that would ensure the longevity of a king's rule. According to Kautilya, the imperial authority must employ spies and build alliances with his neighbor's neighbors, as one's neighbors could never be trusted. This realistic strategic planning, anchored in a policy of alliances and espionage, would guarantee greater territorial security and expansion. Kautilya's *Arthashastra* became a blueprint for the dauntless Chandragupta, whose conquests would establish a transregional Hindu Empire in 323 B.C.E., only two to three years after Alexander's departure from the Indus Valley.[28]

After deposing the Nanda king, Chandragupta based his capital in Patna and used military offensives and matrimonial alliances to expand his possessions across the subcontinent. By 305 B.C.E., he had more than a million men in arms and felt strong enough to challenge Selecucus I, one of Alexander's generals, who, after the emperor's death, had established his own autonomous kingdom called Parthia. Chandragupta's troops had reached the Beas and threatened Selecucus's Parthian possessions in the Indus Valley. After a limited war, the Greek king agreed to cede the Indus lands all the way to Afghanistan to the Maurya king and also gave his daughter in marriage to establish closer fraternity. In return, Chandragupta offered a gift of 500 Indian elephants to the defeated foe and restored many of his privileges to keep him pacified.

For the first time in known history, both the Indus and Gangetic regions came under the control of a single ruler. Selecucus retained Megasthenes, an ambassador at the Mauryan court whose notes filtered down to subsequent generations, offering a host of information on ancient India. The Greek ambassador was deeply impressed by his hosts and wrote a detailed commentary, *Indica.* The work was eventually lost, but many of its details found their way into works authored by early Greek historians. According to these narratives,

Kautilya had ensured implementation of many of his ideas in the Mauryan administration, which sought help from a Parisad, or council of ministers, along with a civil service that helped run the empire. The empire had two major parts, each overseen by a viceroy; villages were administered by rural chieftains called *gopas*.

Around 300 B.C.E., Chandragupta, the founder of a unified Indian Empire, retired to pursue an ascetic life and surrendered his authority to his son, Bindusara, who pioneered the conquest of Deccan. In addition to the Indus and Gangetic regions, the south now also formed part of the Indian Empire, which reached even greater heights in administration, architecture, and human excellence under Ashoka the Great (273–232 B.C.E.). In 261 B.C.E., Ashoka undertook a successful campaign to conquer Kalinga (eastern India). In capturing it, however, he witnessed hundreds of deaths on both sides and large-scale destruction of property and animal life. These horrors made him recant his imperial designs and also led to his conversion to Buddhism. The emperor's multiple contributions in the arts and the humane administration of his empire did not receive recognition, however, until 1837 when a number of his inscriptions and edicts were deciphered by James Prinsep, who was able to identify the language as Pali. Pali was one of several derivatives from Sanskrit and was Buddha's own mother tongue. Ashoka used it for his edicts in Magdha in a local script called Brahmi.

Ashoka built magnificent stupas and monasteries all across his empire, extending from the western reaches of Afghanistan to western Burma. His edicts espousing tolerance, kindness, and humility were inscribed on the walls, rocks, and other public places across this vast kingdom. The Ashokan philosophy, known as *Dhamma,* advocated tolerance, humility, and honesty and, to a great extent, offered uniform moral foundations to an extensive empire.[29] Two giant statues of Buddha were carved in Bamian in central Afghanistan, and all across the Karakorams Buddha's profiles and sermons, along with Ashokan edicts, were carved at open and visible places for all to see. Ashoka believed in peace (*ahimsa*) and vegetarianism and appointed moralist preachers (*Bhikshus*) to administer state affairs more humanely. Thus he earned the respect of his subjects. His wheel and the lions that adorned pillars of his buildings are now India's national symbols, and the monasteries and Greco-Indian statues of Buddha, especially a fasting and meditating Buddha, have become emblems of this classical age.

REGIONAL KINGDOMS AND GANDHARA

After Ashoka's death, the Mauryan Empire began to regionalize itself, as a weaker central authority was unable to keep distant provinces together. Punjab, Kashmir, Kalinga (Orissa), and Deccan all became autonomous and revenues fell short of imperial needs. The Indus Valley once again came under the control of Alexander's successors, and the Gangetic plains went to the Shunga Dynasty, which incited a Brahmanical resurgence by reversing the spread of Buddhism. Buddha was declared to have been an *avatar* of Vishnu and thus a reformer within the Hindu tradition, not the architect of a separate religion. Under the persuasion of the kings and priests, the Gangetic Valley overwhelmingly reverted to Brahmanism, which established itself as an assimilative tradition, eventually evolving into Hinduism.

Later rulers of the Indus lands, also known as Indo-Greeks, slowly absorbed themselves into local Buddhist traditions of the Indus Valley to usher in a unique era, generally known as the Gandhara culture.[30] This unique and splendid culture, although largely Buddhist in religious composition, adopted Greek, Persian, Bactrian, and Hindu traditions, which allowed an unprecedented blend of diversity and mutual accommodation in ancient Pakistan. The Pothowar region and valleys across the Indus, Hindu Kush, and Karakorams not only became the cradle of Gandhara civilization, but the people living there also exported these values and artifacts into China through Swat, Gilgit, Hunza, Baltistan, and Chitral—the regions adjacent to present-day China and located on the historic Silk Route. The rock carvings, inscriptions, stupas, monasteries, and even universities, such as those in Julian near Taxila, ensured expansion of Buddhism into central and eastern Asia. Soon the present-day northern regions were being coveted by newly converted Buddhist monarchs of Tibet and China, beginning an early form of the Great Game featuring imperial rivalries.[31]

Amid the political instability prevailing in the subcontinent after the death of Ashoka, the successors of Selecucus I, who had earlier lost to the Mauryans, began to regroup. Led by Demetrius, the Bactrian king, they mounted campaigns to capture Gandhara. Demetrius, who ruled between 190 and 167 B.C.E., was able to conquer Gandhara but in the process lost his own native Bactria to Eucratides, one of his own Greek-Bactrian generals. Thus Demetrius converted the Indus Valley into his main imperial bastion. The prevailing Buddhist influences assimilated the king and his followers, who had been largely out of contact with the Perso-Greek traditions for generations. It was under King Menander, also called King Milinda, who ruled Gandhara from 155–130 B.C.E., that Buddhism emerged as the state religion of the Indus Valley. The king, known as one of the ablest monarchs in the subcontinent, often held debates with Nagasena, a Buddhist monk, who was able to persuade him to accept Buddhism. Milinda then tried to capture the Gangetic Valley from the Hindu Shunga rulers who put up a strong resistance, and Milinda had to content himself with the annexation of Rajasthan and Gujarat.

After Milinda's death in 130 B.C.E., the Indus Valley once again lay open to foreign incursions until the Scythians, another central Asian dynasty, captured it. The new rulers, eventually known as Shakas, had been pushed westward from central Asia by the construction of the China Wall. The Shakas had been expelled by the Yueh-chih, another rival central Asian tribe, and so moved south, conquering Bactria and Parthia (Persia). In 88 B.C.E., the Shakas annexed the lower Indus Valley where they ruled for four centuries until their defeat by the rising Guptas. The upper Indus Valley was reclaimed by the Parthians for a while until a new group of adventurers from central Asia ended the short-lived Indo-Greek revival in Bactria and Gandhara.

The Kushanas, a branch of the Yueh-chih, successfully captured Bactria. Along with their Scythian and Shaka contemporaries, they shared the northwestern territories, the area of present-day Pakistan and Afghanistan. Thus during the early common era, the southern regions of the Indus Valley were ruled by Shakas, the middle regions and Punjab by the Parthians, and the northern and western Gandhara by the Kushanas. The steady streams of people and ideas from the north and west continually increased ethnic and cultural diversity across the Indus Valley and Afghanistan. Unlike Deccan, the Gangetic Valley, and Kalinga, these Pakistani regions were perpetually exposed to multiple influences and periodically experienced great historical crosscurrents.[32] Kushana's control of the Silk Route played a vital role in transmitting economic, political, and cultural influences into other Asian regions, although a steady stream of invaders, immigrants, traders, and fortune seekers kept pluralizing Indus societies, in addition to their role as a buffer for trans-Beas Hindustan.[33] The most famous Kushana king, Kanishka, uniquely consolidated the Indo-Buddhist culture, ensured its expansion into China, and ended the long and often interrupted series of Greek periods in the political history of the Indus regions. Kanishka's rule began in 78 C.E. and is heralded as the golden era of the Kushana dynasty in the ancient history of Pakistan and Afghanistan. Trade between China and the subcontinent increased manifold and, as is evident from the contemporary gold coins and other archaeological treasures, Indian merchants and missionaries often ventured deeper into China. This general level of prosperity allowed the spread of a positive image of the Indus Valley to the outside world as the center of Buddhism along with being a rich kingdom, which for the first time had struck gold coins in the subcontinent. The dynasty ruled these regions until the third century C.E. when its territories were annexed by the Guptas who were to decisively define the classical era in India and restore Hinduism as the primary religious tradition across the subcontinent including the Indus Valley.

Since the dissolution of the Mauryan Empire, the regional kingdoms across south Asia continued their rule until the advent of Islam in the western and northern subcontinent. Other than the Shungas in the Gangetic Valley, the Kalinga monarchy in Orissa and the Andhra kingdom in the southwestern territories (state of Andhra Pradesh) prevailed in the delta of the Krishna and

Godavri. Because the Deccan regions escaped all the invasions that befell the Indus Valley, at places such as Tamilakam, the Pandyas, Cholas, and the Cheras ruled undisturbed until the early modern era. In 1652, the Muslim sultans of Golkanda and Bijapur captured many of these territories only to eventually cede them to European powers or to independent princely rulers including the Nizam of Hyderabad.[34] But during the earlier tenure of these regional kingdoms, despite a recurrent political instability, their population had largely reverted to Hinduism, being looked after by Brahmans and structured through a rigid caste system. This cultural unity played a pivotal role in once again establishing political unity under the Guptas.

THE GUPTAS AND THE HINDU CLASSICAL PERIOD, 320–540 C.E.

Despite several academic debates about the disappearance of Jain and Buddhist influences and the level of prosperity under an essentially revitalized Hindu monarchy, the Gupta monarchs were able to reunite the subcontinent politically and simultaneously restore Hinduism. Begun during the latter Gupta period, the Hindu renaissance itself took place after the dynasty's decline in the sixth century, although a high level of tolerance on the part of the rulers made a major contribution in this landmark intellectual and artistic phenomenon.[35] Other than regular education from the Buddhist and Hindu monasteries, Brahmanical control of religious scriptures was reinstated by Guptas who were themselves devout Hindus. The most famous classical writer of this period was Kalidasa who produced several collections of poetry and drama that were mostly translated from Sanskrit by William Jones and read by generations of impressed intellectuals in Europe. Kalidasa's play, *Shakuntala,* remains one of the classics in world literature, although ironically our own knowledge about the author himself is scanty. Other than religious texts such as *Puranas* and *Kamasutra*, which deal with rituals and love, the Gupta period harnessed a developed system of numerals including their unique knowledge of zero. In the area of architecture, several splendid temples and the known frescos of Ajanta cave complex highlight imperial devotion to religion and the arts. It was under the Guptas that Vishnu and Shiva emerged as two prominent deities while gods were allowed to have wives, and, more like in ancient Greece, Hinduism developed its own pantheon.

The founder of the Gupta Empire was Chandra Gupta who ruled from 320 to 330 C.E. and, through conquests and matrimonial alliances, expanded his Gangetic possessions to other territories. His son, Samudra Gupta (330–380 C.E.), ruled India for a half century and acquired the Indus Valley along with extending his power deeper into Deccan. At the time of his death in 380, Gupta, like Ashoka, controlled a huge empire consisting of almost the entire northern subcontinent, as well as vast southern lands. His son, Chandra Gupta II (380–415), brought an end to Shakas and, in addition to annexing most of Deccan, captured Sri Lanka (Sinhala) as well, although many Sri Lankans remained faithful to Buddhism. The trans-Chenab regions including Kashmir and Gandhara were controlled by the Sassanids during this time but were captured by Chandra Gupta II. Nepal came under the indirect control of the Gupta dynasty, which claimed to be of Nepali origins. One of the earliest known Chinese visitors to India, Fa-hsien, traveled across the subcontinent as a scholar in search of original Buddhist scripts. He lost many companions while crossing the snowbound northern Pakistani mountains to reach the holy monasteries in Taxila and Patna and left copious notes about his impressions of India during the reign of Chandra Gupta II. He could not find many of the sought-after manuscripts to take back home in 415, but he learned Sanskrit to understand the contemporary scholarly debates.

Kumara Gupta I (425–455) and Sakanda Gupta (455–476) followed each other during this peak time of the Gupta reign until, as in the past, the central administration turned weak, allowing autonomous forces to reassert themselves. In addition, a new wave of central Asians, the Huns, had begun to attack Gandhara in 485 and, after having defeated the Sassanids of Persia, proved a formidable challenge to the authorities in India. By 500, the Huns controlled the Indus Valley and Rajasthan with their capital at Sakal (present-day Sialkot in Pakistan), and their empire also consisted of the vast regions of Sinkiang and Afghanistan. Nevertheless, they were fiercely challenged by the Hindu kings of Malwa and the remaining Gupta dynasts. Such intermittent warfare did not produce any single king and India persisted with its regionalization. During the seventh century, however, Harshavardhana (606–647) tried to revive the old Hindu Empire through steady conquests, but his efforts were too late. Still, he was able to capture the Indus Valley from the Sassanids who had annexed it during the dusk of the Gupta Empire. His victories and efficient administration, greatly celebrated in books on the classical Hindu period, were recorded by Hsuan Tsang, another contemporary Chinese traveler to India. Hsuan Tsang traveled through the subcontinent from 633–643, and his return was facilitated by the king himself. Harsha was a tolerant ruler and a great scholar himself. He composed poetry and wrote plays in Sanskrit and is credited with opening universities. Despite being a Hindu, he appointed Buddhist scholars to higher positions, which annoyed many Brahmans. He was both a poet and a general—a scholar-king—who tried to establish a unified empire as extensive as that of the early Guptas. His reign is also viewed as an extension of the Hindu classical era. The king died childless, however, and soon several governors announced their own independence. This situation remained until in the early eighth century a new era began in several parts of the Hind with the arrival of Muslims in coastal regions.

NOTES

1. Such a state of affairs may not be that unique, for writing is a comparatively recent human profession, and our knowledge of history based on the written word or inscriptions is miniscule when compared to the enormity of human experience in the Neolithic and Paleolithic periods.

2. The terms *Hinduism, Hindus,* and *Hindoos* are quite recent, coming into vogue during the early nineteenth century. In its early connotation, *Hindu* simply signified a resident of the Indus region and was thus a territorial identity as opposed to a religious category.

3. Ideological and political efforts to turn post-1947 India into a Hindu republic instead of a pluralistic and secular polity have led to profusion of such views where Aryans are shown as the natives of India since the earliest era. The proponents of Hindutva such as the Bharatiya Janata Party (BJP) and its ultra-right affiliates have always desired to project Hinduism and Aryanism as synonymous with both being native to India. These issues appeared during the 1990s when BJP emerged as the ruling party in India and began changing history texts, much to the discomfort of many scholars inside and outside the subcontinent.

4. During the nineteenth century, the Americans would differentiate their native communities from the Indian Indians by calling the latter East Indians or Indian Indians, which again confused the inhabitants of the subcontinent with the people from Southeast Asia, known as the Dutch East Indies.

5. That is why the use of *Bharat* becomes so emotional for its followers and their opponents. For the former, it signifies the Arya Land and is an essentially Hinduist place; to others, it ignores the pre-Aryan and subsequent plurality of creeds and peoples. Thus "the Aryan Problem" becomes more than a historical quest of the inhabitants of the classical era with its direct bearing on the ideological and political orientation of contemporary India.

6. Iran itself literally means "the land of Aryans." Afghanistan's national airline is also called Aryana.

7. It is not surprising to note that even today the followers of Zoroastrianism, both in India and Pakistan, prefer to be called Parsis, which certainly denotes the Persian origins of their ancestors and their religion. *Avesta,* the ancient Zoroastrian holy book, at places resembles *Rigveda.* Both have often referred to similar battles between the forces of good and evil and are written in two contemporary ancient languages that are extinct or are confined to some selected scholars. Both of these powerful expressions eventually led to the evolution of several more languages.

8. The main national language of India, now popularized by the Mumbai film industry (Bollywood) is also known as Hindi.

9. The prime ministers and many officials in the Indian Union have often preferred *Hind* over *Bharat.*

10. For an interesting perspective, see Sugata Bose and Ayesha Jalal, *Modern South Asia: History, Culture, Political Economy* (Delhi: Oxford University Press, 1999).

11. The nationalist histories were mostly written in the early half of the twentieth century and were a quest for identity. For example, see Jawaharlal Nehru, *The Unity of India* (London: L. Drummond, 1941); and, *The Discovery of India* (Oxford: Oxford University Press, 1989) (reprint).

12. These areas may be distinct from one another or could all be aggregated as "voices from below." See various volumes edited by Ranajit Guha and others in *Subaltern Studies* (Delhi: Oxford University Press, 1981–2005).

13. Bridget and F. Raymond Allchin, *Birth of Indian Civilization: India and Pakistan before 500 BC* (Harmondsworth: Penguin, 1968) and, *Origins of a Civilization: the Prehistory and Archaeology of South Asia* (New Delhi: Viking, 1997).

14. Gregory L. Possehl, *Indus Age: The Beginnings* (Philadelphia: University of Pennsylvania Press, 1999). The Harappan Age has been divided into various phases and archaeological sites and begins in 3300–2800 B.C.E. and ends in 1900–1700 B.C.E. when it finally encounters a sudden eclipse. For further details on the early, transitional and the final phases, see Richard H. Meadow (ed.), *Harappa Excavations: A Multidisciplinary Approach to Third Millennium Urbanism* (Madison: Prehistory Press, 1991).

15. Gordon Childe acknowledged its almost perfect adjustment to environment, whereas the Allchins highlight its exceedingly consistent and superb town planning. Gordon Childe, *New Light on the Most Ancient East* (New York: Praeger, 1953); and Bridget and Raymond Allchin, *Birth of Indian Civilization.*

16. The majority of these seals carry the depictions of a unicorn. One also finds several parallel lines drawn or crisscrossing one another as in a swastika. Some seals have figures of gods such as Shiva sitting in a lotus position.

17. For a comprehensive work, see Jonathan Mark Kenoyer, *Ancient Cities of the Indus Valley Civilization* (Karachi: Oxford University Press, 1998).

18. R.C. Majumdar, *The History and Culture of the Indian People,* pp. 215–217 quoted in Mohammed Yunus and Aradhana Parmar, *South Asia: A Historical Narrative* (Karachi: Oxford University Press, 2003), p. 8.

19. Robert Eric Mortimer Wheeler, *Civilisation of the Indus Valley and Beyond* (London: Thames and Hudson, 1966); also, *Five Thousand Years of Pakistan: An Archaeological Outline* (London: C. Johnson, 1950).

20. According to a British historian, the Indus changed its course drastically and the inhabitants had to leave their towns for other places, and hence many of these habitations became ghost towns. See, H.T. Lambrick, *Sindh: A General Introduction* (Hyderabad: Sindhi Adabi Board, 1964). Interestingly, Mohenjo Daro literally means "the mound of the dead." For further details, see Mortimer Wheeler, *The Indus Civilisation* (Cambridge: Cambridge University Press, 1960).

21. The copper plate celebrating the inauguration of the Indian Institute building at the University of Oxford in 1885 by Prince Albert specifies this facility "for the use of Aryas (Indian and Englishmen)."

22. For further details, see A. L. Basham, *The Wonder that was India* (New York: Grove Press, 1954).

23. Romila Thapar, *A History of India,* Vol. I (London: Penguin, 1966).

24. River Ganges is a holy river for Hindus, who believe that its source in the Himalayas, Gangotri Glacier, is, in fact, the place that a deity selected to land on earth. They call it *Ganga Ma* or Mother Ganges and use its waters for bath (*ashnaan*) besides spreading the ashes of their loved ones in the holy waters. Newlyweds also visit the river and throw in marigolds for good luck. It is reported that because of global warming, rivers like the Ganges and Indus are experiencing declining water levels. *The Daily Telegraph* (London), March 12, 2007. The Saraswati River flowing into the Indus system through Rajasthan is mentioned in the Hindu epics but is believed to have dried up long ago.

25. Etymologically, the word itself is derived from Portuguese.

26. The Kalasha people in the three valleys of Chitral, hemmed in within the Hindu Kush, are often referred to as the descendants of the Greeks who decided to settle in this part of the world. In the late nineteenth century, Rudyard Kipling, the British writer, further popularized their Greek origins through his *The Man who Would Be King.*

27. In Taxila there are pillars of a temple built by Alexander. The remains of the temple and specially designed wall patterns offer a unique resemblance between ancient Pakistan and ancient Greece. The temple is the only surviving structure of its type in south Asia. (Based on personal visits to the site and interviews with Professor A. H. Dani and Muhammad Saleem, the known archaeologists in Pakistan.)

28. For more on this ancient period, see John Keay, *India: A History* (London: HarperCollins, 2000).

29. John Keay, pp. 96–97.

30. Statues of fasting Buddha with Indo-Greek features, along with jewelry, figurines, and inscriptions across the valleys of Peshawar, Swat, Mardan, Takhtbhai, Mansehra, and Taxila testify to the existence of multiple cultural mainstreams.

31. The discovery of the Dunghuang Caves in Western China, which contain thousands of scrolls, scriptures, textiles, figurines, coins, and cave murals, and the excavation across this region over the past century have revealed a closer relationship between western China and southwestern Asia.

32. Such cultural crosscurrents continue today, as evidenced by the recent geopolitical developments that affect Pakistan.

33. Even today Pakistan often serves as a buffer for various geopolitical and demographic developments in west Asia, shielding the Indian Union from their impact.

34. The Nizam of Hyderabad used to be the Mughal viceroy until he became independent in 1722 and his family ruled Andhra until 1948, when the Indian government annexed this territory by force.

35. According to some historians, it was Hindu nationalism itself that led to the rise of the Gupta Empire and not vice-versa. See, D.D. Kosambi, *An Introduction to the Study of Indian History* (Mumbai: Popular Prakashan, 1975), p. 313.

3

Islam in South Asia: The Indus and Delhi Sultanates

The advent of Muslim political power in south Asia resulted from a number of factors including the absence of a strong, central authority in the subcontinent. Islam expanded because of its pronounced emphasis on human equality, which attracted underprivileged groups to its fold. Establishment of Muslim empires in the Middle East benefited from an enduring power vacuum resulting from wars among the Greeks, Persians, and Romans that had sapped their vitality. In the same vein, Judaism, Christianity, and Zoroastrian could not stop Islam's entry because of its persistent emphasis on simplicity, anticlericalism, and the humanness of the prophet Muhammad (570–632). Despite his modest and disadvantaged upbringing, his personal life, both as a messenger and a successful statesman, enthused Arab tribes seeking to carve out their preeminence on the world map. For generations, these tribes had been either looked down upon by other civilizations or periodically conquered by the Romans, Byzantines, and Persians. Taking pride in their Abrahamic genealogy and associations with the Kaaba in Makkah, one of the oldest worship houses in the world, underpinned the common Arab desire for a mainstream role, which had not come their way yet, unlike their other Semitic cousins. Thus the Prophet not only appeared at the opportune time with a befitting message in one of the oldest and widely cherished languages, but also symbolized a journey from humble origins to a sublime status. His role modeling toward a cherished universal profile kindled hopes and dynamism among the peninsular Arabs, whose urban and nomadic divisions appeared to have gradually declined to underwrite a new assertion that historians detect among communities at the threshold of major breakthroughs.

Islam's political and spiritual presence in the Indus Valley since the late seventh century gradually helped the emergence of an enduring Muslim factor that over the subsequent centuries, became quite pluralistic as its indigenous, Arab, African, Persian, and central Asian strands converged to form what came to be known as the epochal Indo-Islamic culture. With Persian as the native language and Persian imperial structures imbibed by dynasty after dynasty in India, including the British, there evolved a multidimensional political, literary, and artistic tradition. Known as Persianate, it decisively globalized the subcontinent by integrating it with other Muslim regions, collectively known as the Islamicate. In a powerful way, this interplay between Islam and Indian values continued with their cultures, as both avoided completely assimilating each other. South Asian Islam was part of a larger Muslim tradition, but it simultaneously reflected its own Indian embodiment in many areas, which made this interaction complex but mostly constructive. Islam did not Islamize India, nor did the latter overshadow Islam's own distinct character.[1] For a long time, similarities and competition characterized this multicultural exchange in south Asia, unlike some other places where one culture might come to dominate everyone else.[2]

The latter-day Hindu nationalists decry the Muslim Sultanate as an inherently anti-Hindu and non-Indian Turkic trajectory, while Pakistanis and Bangladeshi see in it the victory of Islam and the early formation of their own separate identities. But history demands a more responsible and comprehensive perspective of the three centuries of the Delhi sultans. First chosen by Qutb-ud-Din Aibak, a former Turkish slave of the deceased Muslim king of Afghanistan, Delhi remained the capital of various dynasties and kingdoms, collectively known as the Delhi Sultanate. Along with Aibak's own immediate successors, Delhi was the capital for 320 years of the future dynasties of Khaljis, Tughluqs, Sayyids, and Lodhis. Despite their fondness for Agra, the Mughal emperors preferred Delhi as their imperial capital from the inception of their power in 1526 until 1857, when the East India Company formally deposed the last Mughal monarch, Bahadur Shah Zafar. Thus Delhi and other regions across the subcontinent, including present-day northern India, Pakistan, and Bangladesh, have been the repositories of an endowed Indo-Muslim culture. Historically, Afghanistan has been part of a larger Indus Valley heritage, but its own pluralism and distinct cultural heritage also reflect the country's role as the crossroads between several cultural traditions. Surely, Afghanistan had been the vanguard region of the Delhi Sultanate, which owed itself to the rulers and conquerors venturing in from the former. In 1757, it became a sovereign monarchy under Ahmed Shah Abdali, whose Durrani Pushtun descendants have ruled this country until recently.

MUSLIM ARAB RULE IN THE INDUS VALLEY

Soon after the Prophet's death, the Muslim caliphs devoted attention to the consolidation and expansion of the newly formed Muslim state that was eager to make its existence and message felt across the neighboring lands. By 644, the Medina-based Muslim caliphate led by the second Caliph, Umar al-Farooq, had been able to conquer Palestine, Egypt, Syria, Iraq, Persia, and Yemen, along with some coastal regions across the Arabian Sea. After the victory over the Persian Sassanids, Caliph Umar had, in fact, sent some fact-finding missions to coastal regions of Balochistan and Sindh. These missions brought information that warned him of inclement weather, scarce resources, and the prevalence of highwaymen. But the total defeat in 651 of the remaining Sassanids by Caliph Usman, the third caliph, brought Muslim troops into Indian coastal regions in close proximity to India's Rajput kingdoms. It was under the Umayyads in 711–712, however, that Spain, central Asia, and the Indus Valley were formally annexed by the Damascus-based Muslim caliphate. The conquest of Sindh and lower Punjab was motivated by an act of piracy on a Sri Lankan ship bound for Basra with Muslim pilgrims and expensive goods. The perpetrators were reputed to owe their allegiance to Raja Dahir, the Hindu ruler of lower Sindh. Hajjaj bin Yusuf, the governor of Mesopotamia and a man of iron will, demanded of the Raja a punitive action against such frequent acts of piracy and not being happy with the latter's inaction dispatched Arab troops to Sindh in 711 C.E. These forces were led by Muhammad bin Qasim, the 17-year-old nephew and son-in-law of the governor, who landed at Deebul, near Karachi, and was able to defeat Dahir in 712.[3]

Ibn Qasim's victory did not end with a homeward journey; instead it turned into a south-north conquering campaign until the Arab general—more like his contemporary Tariq ibn Ziad in Spain—reached Multan in Punjab. The Muslims were tolerant of the inhabitants of the Indus Valley and, despite the former's aversion to idol worship, designated them as *dhimmis* (tax-paying citizens) at par with Christians, Jews, and Zoroastrians of west Asia who had been defined as "people of the Book." This was a worthy title guaranteeing respect for fellow believers but would absolve them of military service in lieu of paying a tax called *jizya.* Muslim kings applied this system to non-Muslim subjects in India and elsewhere and avoided clerical and other pressures for en masse conversions of non-Muslims under their control. The tax money, in a visible way, deterred Muslim rulers from forcibly converting their subjects to Islam along with pure logical reason of not alienating vast sections of the population within the kingdom. That is why at places like India, Spain, or Sicily religious identity was largely a private matter, although Muslim rule certainly added to the hopes and status of Muslim scholars (*ulama*) and mystics (Sufis). The *ulama* often exerted pressure on monarchs for conversion of non-Muslims, yet the stately considerations and even a greater element of tolerance deterred rulers from state-led proselytization. Islam's own emphasis on simplicity and equality carried significant attraction for possible conversions, which usually came from the underprivileged groups and lower castes seeking better status under a new dispensation. Muslim rulers of the subcontinent and their west Asian elite often married Indian women, and these matrimonial alliances led to greater tolerance on all sides.

The Arab conquests of the Indus Valley happened rather quickly but were stalled owing to Ibn Qasim's sudden recall by the new caliph in Damascus who was not enamored of an ambitious Hajjaj and his victorious nephew. Arab rule of these territories continued as a low-profile affair, and most of the local population remained peaceful because the Arab rulers, who were interested only in establishing homes and raising families in their adopted lands, avoided mass-based conversions and even slaughters. A stable peace, further helped by the arrival of religious publicists and Sufis through the western passes, led to considerable conversions within the Indus societies, which were now part of a diverse and expansive Muslim caliphate that included numerous areas across the three continents. This new role opened up fresh commercial and cultural opportunities for the Indus people and helped to integrate them into one of the most forward-looking and tolerant systems of the time.

Arab rule of the Indus Valley was followed by that of Ismailis, a branch of Shia Islam, who, like the Fatimids in Egypt and Tunisia, carried on the policies of their predecessors and avoided forcible conversion. The Ismailis had been a smaller Muslim sect who found these territories conveniently distant from Syria and Iraq, the heartland of the Muslim caliphate. In 750, Umayyads had been deposed by another Arab dynasty of the Abbasids who were helped by the Persians in gaining control of the Muslim Empire. The Abbasids built Baghdad as their capital instead of Damascus at a time when Spain had become autonomous with its own Umayyad caliphate. Muslim rulers in India and elsewhere would often accept the spiritual primacy of the Abbasid caliph in Baghdad, but they were otherwise autonomous, pursuing their own policies until the Crusades and the Mongol invasions from the tenth to thirteenth centuries destroyed the Arab-Persian caliphate. It was at this juncture that the central Asian Turks began to play a leading role in Baghdad and also pioneered efforts to establish regional kingdoms in Persia, Anatolia, Egypt, and Afghanistan. A new series of invasions of the northern subcontinent began in Afghanistan and led to the establishment of the Delhi Sultanate.

GHAZNAVIDS AND THE INDUS REGIONS

Islam's emphasis on human equality and the prophetic example of anti-racism allowed better status for slaves, and in several cases the latter were able to win over the confidence of their masters. Unprecedented loyalty aided with proper grooming led to several slaves becoming members of the royal households and eventually obtained senior royal positions. The Mamluks, Ottomans, and the Slave Dynasty among the early Delhi Sultans are the three case studies in Muslim history where erstwhile slaves, owing to their sagacity, reached the pinnacle of highest power.[4] Although the early prosperous Arabs owned African slaves, their expansion into Persian and Byzantine heartlands from the seventh century onward facilitated access to central Asian Turkish communities. After the Persians, the Turks proved to be dependable and equally daring bastions of Muslim caliphate until the latter were able to form their own empires. The Turkish slaves, soldiers, and ruling elite infused fresh blood and ideas into the Islamic world and, especially after the Mongol destruction of Baghdad in 1258, they resuscitated Muslim fortunes. As a consequence, these Turks were able to form three contemporary powerful empires of the Mughals, Safawids, and Ottomans until the Europeans were able to colonize the Muslim world and a serious phase in Muslim decline began.

Among these several fortune-seeking Turks, one comes across a central Asian adventurer, Alaptigin, who, in 962, was able to capture the city of Ghazni in eastern Afghanistan. His subsequent military campaigns enabled him to transform his possessions into a smaller kingdom extending to the western regions of present-day Turkmenistan. Toward the end of his life, he willed for his slave, Sabuktigin, to succeed him. Sabuktigin, again from humble Turkish origins but loyal to his late master-king, had proven his leadership in consolidating the Ghaznavid empire during the two decades of his rule (977–997). He was able to annex Peshawar by defeating Raja Jaipaul of eastern Punjab in 991 and aimed at conquering Hindustan. His son, Mahmud (998–1030), however, continued this series of expansion toward the east through his 17 invasions of the Indus regions. Mahmud, instead of calling himself Amir, selected the Persian title of sultan and came to be known as Sultan of Ghazna.[5] His invasions of India, attributed to greed for Indian riches by several Hindu historians and credited as Jihad by their Muslim counterparts, were in line with the age-old tradition of invasions of the subcontinent from the west. During one of his campaigns, Mahmud brought the famous scholar, Al-Beruni, with him to observe and record his views of Indians. Like his other well-known contemporary and courtier-poet, Firdausi, Al-Beruni studied Indian geography and society, displaying a dispassionate and rather deeper scholarship. His book in Arabic, *Kitab Al-Hind*, remains a unique treatise on India and Hinduism. After conquering Punjab and Sindh, Mahmud annexed the Gangetic Valley and coastal regions of western India but never stayed for long, always returning to his capital, Ghazni. After Ghazni, Lahore and Multan were the other two significant metropolitan centers where traders, Sufis, poets, and travelers from different parts of the world gathered, adding to the cosmopolitan atmosphere of these Indus cities. Here Persian literature, philosophy, and natural sciences flourished in a tolerant environment and Sufis and scholars chose these towns for their respective pursuits.

DELHI SULTANS: THE SLAVE DYNASTY

After Mahmud's death, his successors squandered his vast empire, which was, in its western regions, confronted by the Seljuks, another Turkoman tribe, who were soon to annex parts of Persia and Anatolia to found the Seljuk dynasty.[6] A century after Mahmud, however, another Turkish general from the region of Ghaur in central Afghanistan was able to capture Ghazni in 1151 to formally close the chapter of Ghaznavid rule. The Ghaurid Empire was divided between his two descendants in 1173, with the eastern regions falling into the hands of Muhammad, also known as Sultan Shahab-ud-Din Muhammad Ghauri, who selected Lahore as his capital and determined to capture trans-Sutlej regions of Hindustan. Two years later, Muhammad Ghauri's campaigns farther south enabled him to capture Balochistan and Sindh from the Ismailis, and in 1192, after defeating Prithvi Raj Chauhan, the Rajput Raja, he captured Rajasthan and Delhi. His smaller but swift central Asian cavalry of experienced archers was able to overwhelm a bigger Rajput force of men and elephants. Ghauri's decisive victory at Tarain was assured when Prithvi fell to a Turkish arrow and his troops retreated. Like Raja Porus facing Alexander, the elephants on the Rajput side were no match for Turkish horse riders who would race toward the Indian flanks to suddenly stop and turn around while aiming arrows at their enemies. After his victory, Ghauri allowed the late Raja's son to govern in his behalf in Delhi, and he appointed his slave-general Aibak to administer the empire from Lahore because the Sultan had to tend to his western regions due to a revolt there.

Qutb-ud-Din Aibak was a capable general who, in view of attacks on the Ghaurid Empire from the Khiva's kingdom (also known as Khwarzam), advised Sultan Muhammad to control Delhi so as to establish a safer monarchy in the Indus and Gangetic regions. Consequently, Aibak captured Delhi from the younger Rajput prince in 1202. In the meantime, the Sultan was able to annex the Turkoman and Khiva regions, extending his empire from the Caspian Sea to the Ganges and Gujarat-Kathiawar territories. Muhammad, however, was mysteriously assassinated in Lahore in 1206, and his viceroy, Aibak, already ensconced in Delhi, was chosen by the powerful Turkish generals to succeed his deceased master.[7] Aibak concentrated his attention on the subcontinent and through matrimonial alliances secured his position vis-à-vis the Turkish elite, including a powerful slave-general Iltutmish, who became the former's son-in-law. Aibak's selection of Delhi for his empire in 1206 marks the formal beginning of the Delhi Sultanate; Aibak became known as the founder of the Slave Dynasty. Aibak died in Lahore as he fell down from his horse during a polo match and was succeeded by his son, Aram Shah, whose lackluster performance soon disappointed the powerful Turkish and Afghan courtiers. They desired to see a strong sultan at the helm of affairs to ensure consolidation of the newly formed Delhi kingdom. During this period, all of central Asia shook before the Mongols led by Chengiz Khan, whose interest in the proverbial riches of India knew no bounds. As the Mongols came closer to the Hindu-Kush, the inhabitants of the Indus regions and Delhi feared for their lives and properties. At such a critical juncture, an indolent Aram Shah offered no comfort. Soon, Aibak's son-in-law, Shams-ud-Din Iltutmish, a former slave, was formally invited by the Turco-Afghan generals to assume the royal charge, because his formidable position as a close member of the late sultan's household, along with his governorship of Punjab, strengthened his candidacy.

Iltutmish (1211–1236) consolidated the kingdom by introducing several reforms and establishing peace across the regions. He was the first Muslim king to make India his permanent home and, while reaffirming his subordination to the Caliph in Baghdad, chose the title of sultan for himself. Iltutmish tried to control the Forty Courtiers, who operated as an elite club of powerbrokers within the court.[8] Iltutmish defended his empire from intermittent Mongol invasions and thus saved India from large-scale devastation. When advised by some *ulama* to forcibly convert non-Muslims to Islam, Iltutmish resisted their pressures and attempted to create a wider institutional basis for his rule.[9] Despite the advice of his advisors, Iltutmish nominated his daughter, Razia, as his successor. Known as Razia Sultana (1236–1240), the queen soon did away with her palatial lifestyles and veil and began to lead military campaigns in addition to running an otherwise male-dominated court. Razia was able to establish her credentials, but some of the conservative Turco-Afghan courtiers did not accept a woman leading the empire and conspired to have her deposed. Her dependence on Jalal-ud-Din Malik Yaqut, an Abyssinian slave, did not endear her in the eyes of her critics, and after a defeat by Malik Altunia, Razia was finally dethroned in 1240. She married Malik Altunia and tried to capture Delhi but, despite the supportive citizens of Delhi, the revolt was not successful and both were subsequently killed by jungle tribes while living as wanderers. Malik Yaqut had also been killed by the courtiers who, after some split decisions and prevarications, installed Nasir-ud-Din Muhammad, a son of Iltutmish, as the new monarch. The new king reigned from 1246 to 1266, although the de facto power was in the hands of a general from among the Forty Courtiers and who also happened to be his father-in-law. Ghiyas-ud-Din Balban was a capable and ambitious Turkish general who ensured smooth governance under his son-in-law and secured the courtiers' support sultan, who himself spent most of his time praying and copying Quran.

Sultan Nasir-ud-Din Muhammad had no male heir and nominated Balban for succession, although Balban was already 60 years old. Balban (1266–1286) continued the policy of reforms, consolidation, and expansion of the Slave Sultanate that had been pioneered by Iltutmish and that had been resuscitated under Sultan Muhammad after a brief interlude of civil war that broke out after the dethronement of Sultana Razia. Balban curtailed the power and autonomous tendencies of his courtiers and other provincial elite and maintained a fully paid standing army to fight his internal rivals and the Mongols. His salaried and well-trained soldiers defended India from chaos and foreign occupation in addition to ensuring domestic peace and prosperity. Balban believed that a secure populace would guarantee the longevity of the kingdom and thus tried to eradicate robbers and bandits operating in the countryside. He was deeply enamored of Persian courtly grandeur and after organizing such protocols and related paraphernalia, he followed the regalia to the letter. His tradition was pursued by other kings and rajas until the Mughals and the British took it to even greater heights and elaborate formalities. Sultan Balban never left Delhi, but his efficient administration and stern control over civil and military officials ensured the territorial and administrative integrity of his kingdom.

KHALJIS (KHILJIS), TUGHLUQS, SAYYIDS, AND LODHIS

Sultan Balban's death in 1286 left a vacuum, as his immediate successors could not rise to the occasion until Firuz Khalji, one of the powerful Turco-Afghan courtiers, gathered his troops to march on Delhi, which awaited a strong ruler to ensure peace and order. In 1290, Firuz Khalji enthroned himself as Sultan Jalal-ud-Din Khalji by formally introducing his own dynastic rule, followed by conquests and subordination of regional rulers. He had been a senior official in Balban's administration and thus continued the policies of the late king, although he soon turned to piety and meditation. His otherworldliness was not liked by many courtiers who wanted to see more territorial acquisitions and a stronger rebuff to the Mongols, but the sultan was already more than 70 years old and was averse to warfare. In 1296, Jalal-ud-Din fell victim to the intrigues hatched by his more ambitious and unscrupulous nephew, Ala-ud-Din Khalji, who soon came to be known for his ruthless administration and deeper penchant for conquests. Immediately after his control of Delhi, Ala-ud-Din, began to organize his revenue system, as he needed more funds for a regular army to defend India against foreign invasions.[10] He is criticized for introducing a tax that might have been too burdensome for farmers and merchants. In addition, since his military encounters in Deccan, he knew that the southern Indian traders and princes enjoyed a favorable balance of trade with the Romans and Arabs, and sought their resources to finance his official expenditures. Soon after his ascension to the throne in 1296, Ala-ud-Din attacked Deogiri and amassed greater wealth from campaigns deeper into the peninsula. Here, Ala-ud-Din's booty, along with jewels and gold, included Malik Kafur, a Hindu convert to Islam, who was destined to rise higher in royal esteem owing to his loyalty and closer knowledge of the Deccan. The Sultan eventually promoted him to his viceroyalty in the south while he had to rush back north to deter a Mongol invasion. In fact, Sultan Khalji repulsed seven Mongol attacks and thus defended India from major devastation that had befallen other Asian regions. Ala-ud-Din Khalji might have pursued a unilateral pricing policy that hurt the Hindu moneyed classes, yet he was the first Delhi sultan to marry a Hindu woman. He even arranged marriages between his sons and Hindu princesses and, like Iltutmish, rebuked *ulama* sternly whenever they demanded Islamization of his subjects. He believed in keeping religion away from statecraft and employed Hindu bankers to operate his finances. His long rule featured conquests in distant regions, resistance against the Mongols, and a firm economic policy, all enforced with an explicit use of force.[11]

Sultan Ala-ud-Din's awe and mighty administration deterred periodic rebellions intrinsic to India. After his death in 1316, however, a brief era of usual palatial tensions ensued. His trusted lieutenant, Malik Kafur, was also assassinated in the same year, and soon a vast Sultanate faced a recurrent issue of succession. The late Sultan's third son, Mubarak, was able to assume power by seeking help from Khusrau Khan, the governor of Deccan, who, instead, began to harbor ambitions for his own elevation to the monarchy. He engineered Mubarak's murder, but still he could not ascend the throne, as he was not liked by powerful courtiers in the Khalji kingdom. The latter invited Ghazi Malik, a capable and trusted governor of Punjab, to assume control of the sultanate, as all the three sons of the late Khalji Sultan had been murdered, one after the other. Ghazi Malik marched toward Delhi and after defeating Khusrau Khan, ascended to the throne in 1320 by assuming the title of Sultan Ghias-ud-Din Tughluq. This founder of the Tughluq dynasty soon engaged himself in the consolidation of a vast empire left behind by Ala-ud-Din that was now suffering from a series of revolts. The new sultan was himself the son of a Turkish slave and a Hindu mother and showed deeper affinity with the Indian peasants and landowners. He lowered the land revenue that had skyrocketed under the late Khalji king. His five-year rule ended tragically, as a victory pavilion built to welcome him back from a triumphant campaign in

Bengal fell on him instantly killing him and his eldest son. After his funeral, his second son, Muhammad ibn Tughluq, was crowned in 1325 and ruled until his death in 1351. The new sultan was a highly educated man, but he often displayed tendencies of a weaker character. Bedeviled by Mongol invasions and resultant exorbitant costs, the sultan sought southern finances and, like Sultan Ala-ud-Din Khalji, he set out on campaigns in Deccan.

Sultan Muhammad, unlike his predecessor, decided to build his new capital near Deogiri to stay closer to the prosperous regions in the south; he named the capital Daulatabad (city of wealth). He ordered his officials and families to move en masse to Daulatabad, 700 miles south of Delhi where the lack of proper infrastructure and distance from the northern recruiting heartlands made the capital unpopular for everyone. After spending eight years in the south, Sultan Muhammad ordered a return to Delhi and in the process incurred public anger and stupendous costs. The paucity of silver for coinage led to an abrupt royal order for minting copper coins, which turned out to be another disaster. Soon the Sultan planned on undertaking an invasion of Khurasan in Persia, but he was deterred by his advisors. Muhammad bin Tughluq founded many new cities and undertook the construction of a new city in Delhi, called Tughluqabad. The city had an impressive circumference wall buttressed by huge pillars and watchtowers; the wall was accessible through 13 gates.[12] Here he erected memorable buildings including a Hall of One Thousand Pillars, which now lies in ruins in the abandoned Tughluqabad.[13] With a new road cutting across the heritage site, the ruins of this impressive and elevated town sit facing the unique Tughluq mausoleum, where Ghias-ud-Din and his son, Muhammad Shah II, are buried. Built with red stones, these square structures of sloping walls are capped by while marble domes and reveal a combination of central Asian and Persian influences. The entrance to the mausoleum and the gardens around it is through a magnificent gate, and the entire structure is on a raised plateau. Sultan Muhammad bin Tughluq was a literary-minded person as is recorded by Ibn Battutah (1304–1377), the contemporary Moroccan traveler, who left written memories of his visit to the Middle East, Africa, India, Maldives, Sri Lanka, and China. According to Ibn Battutah, the Sultan was liable to varying moods and could be vindictive and generous concurrently.[14] The events of his reign were also recorded by a known early historian, Zia-ud-Din Barani (1284–1356),[15] whose contemporary accounts, although not unbiased, offer primary information on various Delhi sultans.[16]

Sultan Muhammad bin Tughluq died childless while campaigning in Sindh and had not even nominated an heir, so the influential courtiers put his nephew, Firuz Tughluq, on the throne. The new king tried to restore order and stability within the kingdom and displayed religiosity in personal life. Soon he came under the influence of *ulama* when he imposed *jizya* on non-Muslims, although he did lower taxes for the benefit of all. He rescinded most of the policies earlier pursued by his uncle and preferred a peaceful policy in dealing with his subjects and neighbors. During his reign, the strong kingdom of Vijaynagar emerged in the south, partly as a reaction against the invasions from the north and partly to establish independent commercial relations with the outside world. Bengal had also assumed autonomy and remained independent of Delhi for almost 200 years until it was annexed by the Mughals. Sultan Firuz Tughluq died in 1388 at the age of 90, and the Delhi throne once again waited for another powerful monarch to sustain the sultanate. After the reigns of four weaker princes, the last Tughluq king, Sultan Nasir-ud-Din Mahmud, ascended the throne in 1392 and ruled until 1412, when a new dynasty of the Sayyids took over the Delhi kingdom.[17] Two major developments during the reign of Nasir-ud-Din Mahmud were of great importance and left their imprints on south Asian history for a long time. First, Bengal and Gujarat continued their autonomous status, becoming even more prosperous through overseas trade and agriculture. Second and more dramatically, Amir Taimur (Tamerlane) invaded India in 1397, and in the process Delhi was subjected to large-scale misery and destruction. After killing about 80,000 inhabitants, Amir Taimur, the central Asian conqueror, moved swiftly to west Asia and defeated the Ottomans. Like many of his predecessors, however, he did not stay in India, Iran, Iraq, or Anatolia but instead hurried back to his native Samarkand, where he strove to make it into the most beautiful city in the world. After Tamerlane's death in 1406, it was more than a century later that his great-grandson, Babur, followed in his ancestor's footsteps to found the Mughal Empire in 1526.

India's attraction for west Asian fortune seekers never diminished even after a devastating invasion by Tamerlane who took India's riches and several of its artisans to Samarkand. The internecine warfare in their native lands and periodic population explosions, along with the material attraction of regions such as Persia and India, triggered frequent invasions by central Asian tribesmen and fortune seekers. Tamerlane's death and a steady decline of his vast empire soon led to the rise of regional politics, creating a significant power vacuum. Sultan Mahmud Tughluq ruled a desolate Delhi and its environ until his death in 1414, when a wily general, Khizr Khan, benefiting from the chaotic situation, captured Delhi and established the Sayyid Era in the Delhi Sultanate. Claiming their descent from the Prophet, the Sayyids tried to pacify their subjects through various measures, but in 1451 they lost power to an Afghan general, Bahlol Lodhi, whose son and grandson formed the last dynastic rule among the Delhi Sultans. Bahlol Lodhi proved a capable administrator whose tenure ensured the primacy of the Afghan elite over their Turkish counterparts, although the Lodhi kings, in general, avoided heavy taxes and unnecessary wars. Bahlol Lodhi's son and successor, Sikandar Lodhi (1489–1517), patronized learning and further stabilized his north Indian kingdom, although his son and heir lacked the military acumen of his ancestors and eventually lost to Babur in 1526.[18] Sultan Ibrahim Lodhi's own relatives such as Daulat Khan, largely driven by personal ambitions, had invited Zahir-ud-Din Babur to attack Delhi, assuming that the Uzbek king of Afghanistan, like Tamerlane, would hasten back to his own kingdom, leaving the northern subcontinent for the Lodhi claimants. Instead, Babur decided to stay and, after defeating the Rajputs and remaining Afghans, controlled an empire larger than its Gupta predecessor. By his early death in 1530, Babur, despite his own reservations about the Indian people and climates, had decided to make the subcontinent his home, although in his will he made provisions to be buried in his favorite garden in Kabul.

The series of Muslim-ruling dynasties since the Arab conquest of the Indus Valley in 712 added to south Asian socioreligious pluralism and established a long tradition of Muslim rule. The indigenization of the Muslim ruling elite and the conversion of many local inhabitants, owing to the efforts by Sufis and publicists, had established a visible Muslim presence in various parts of the subcontinent. A vast majority of Muslim rulers avoided forcible conversions and, in spite of their personal piety and religious inclinations, resisted attempts by *ulama* to Islamize India. That is why Muslims have always remained an overall minority in south Asia despite being a visible majority in the Indus and Gangetic regions. The growth of Indo-Islamic culture, anchored on Persian, Turkish, and Indian literary, political, and artistic traditions, allowed the flourishing of letters, arts, and other intellectual pursuits. Areas such as music, architecture, cuisine, weaponry, calligraphy, and urban planning reflected creative strands derived from a wide variety of sources. The evolution of common idioms and historical accounts raised India's literary profile, whereas Indian sciences and philosophy found new audience across west Asia and Europe. India attracted conquerors, fortune seekers, writers, and merchants of Muslim extraction who, in most cases, settled down here. In place of sheer brutal exploitation, most of the Delhi Sultans defended India against invasions and internal chaos.

The establishment of Sufi orders and contributions of people like Data Gunj Bakhsh, Baba Farid-ud-Din Ganj Shakar, Baha-ud-Din Zakaria, Nizam-ud-Din Aulia, Amir Khusrau, and numerous others have been fully recorded. Through their spiritual efforts, they sought communal harmony.[19] Like the rest of south Asian societies, Muslims here were also divided into several regional and ethnic communities, with Islam and Persian offering some common denominators at least to the prosperous elements among them. The ruling elite—*ashraf*—belonged to Turco-Afghan stock, whereas the local members of the community—*ajlaf*—engaged in agriculture, soldiery, trade, and some other urban professions. Over the centuries, Muslims and Hindus shared the soil and its resources, yet matrimonial relationships were not so common. Their religious and dietary practices also varied and despite even sharing neighborhoods and other personal associations, they lived as two parallel and distinct communities. This is not to suggest that there was a permanent strand of hostility underpinning their collective interactions, but cultural and religious preferences certainly played a crucial part in defining their respective identities. Since the Khalji era, the elite would often marry Hindu women from affluent and influential families, but they avoided marriages between Muslim women and Hindu men. In Deccan, the state of Vijaynagar had a dominant Hindu character, whereas Bahmani kingdoms reflected Muslim traditions of kingship, but their subjects avoided engaging in communal violence. Despite a dominant native section in the Muslim populace of India, more recent historical surveys often identified the former as *Turks*, juxtaposing their presumed foreignness with an element of attributed violence. In most cases, Indian Muslim rulers befriended non-Muslim priestly classes and avoided wreaking collective vendetta or any orchestrated onslaught on temples.[20] Muslims built *sarais* (rest houses), graveyards, mosques, and shrines in addition to secular buildings and did not shirk from borrowing Hindu and Jain architectural patterns. Despite a religious conviction against idol worship, kings and Sufis pursued tolerance and coexistence. A few cases of temple desecration occurring under some Mughal rulers had been driven mainly by political factors. In other words, it was not a clash of civilizations. Like Hindu rajas, Muslim kings sometimes fought internecine wars involving their siblings and even parents on opposite sides. Thus the course of Islam in India is a complex and multilayered phenomenon and must not be reduced to just two opposing paradigms of total assimilation or complete rejection.

NOTES

1. A rather critical perspective has been offered on Islam within the Indian environment by a leading historian of Muslim intellectual history who sees it as part of a larger tradition interacting within a regional context. See, Aziz Ahmad, *Islamic Modernism India and Pakistan, 1857–1964* (Oxford: Oxford University Press, 1967); *Studies in Islamic Culture in Indian Environment* (Oxford: Oxford University Press, 1964).

2. For an interesting view of Islam as an indigenous and reformative force within India, see Tara Chand, *Influence of Islam on Indian Culture* (Allahabad: Indian Press, 1964).

3. Ibn Qasim used *manjeeqs,* the stone- and rock-throwing mechanisms, which would cause havoc in the besieged towns and were the precursors of artillery guns. His favorite *manjeeq* was called *Aroosa,* the bride, and there are varying accounts of its capacity to throw massive rocks over considerable distances. The towns and cities in mainly agrarian Indus Valley would easily fall before the Arab artillery and cavalry.

4. A critical American historian finds this tradition to be unique in statecraft, displaying several problems of inequality. See, Daniel Pipes, *Slave Soldiers and Islam: The Genesis of a Military System* (New Haven: Yale University Press, 1981). Needless to say, Professor Pipes has been exceptionally critical of Muslim political and religious traditions as is evident from his recent studies such as *Militant Islam Reaches America* (London: W. W. Norton, 2002).

5. Mohammad Habib, *Sultan Mahmud of Ghaznin* (Delhi: S. Chand, 1951).

6. C. E. Bosworth, *The Ghaznavids* (Edinburgh: University Press, 1963).

7. For more details, see Peter Jackson, *The Delhi Sultanate* (Cambridge: Cambridge University Press, 1999).

8. They were called *Umrai Chahilgaan*, or 40 preeminent courtiers, comprising a well-knit group of senior generals and ministers. They all sought stability for the kingdom but were often split over the issue of succession.

9. Ishtiaq H. Qureshi, *The Administration of the Sultanate of Delhi* (Lahore: Shaikh Muhammad Ashraf, 1942).

10. For more details see *The Campaigns of Alaudin Khilji, being the Khazainul Futuh: Treasures of Victory of Amir Khusrau*, translated into English with notes and parallel passages from other Persian writers by Muhammad Habib and with an historical introduction by S. Krishnaswami Aiyangar, Bombay: Taraporewala, 1931.

11. The graves of these Sultans are found in several older and congested parts of Delhi and were once surrounded by gardens and seminaries but now suffer from urban encroachments and rubbish. Aibak is buried in Lahore and the Slave Sultan, Khaljis, and Tughluqs are mostly buried in Delhi. The Qutb Minar and the adjacent Masjid-i-Quwwattul Islam are the earliest Muslim buildings in Delhi, dating from the period of Sultan Aibak. Moth Ki Masjid, Hauz-i-Khas, Alai Madrassa, and the graves of Iltutmish and several other monarchs and their ministers, numerous older mosques and shrines, although preserved as national monuments, require major restoration work that is often reserved for Mughal buildings. Not too far from impressive Humayun's Tomb, lies the historic and predominantly Muslim area of Nizam-ud-Din, where the famous Sufis, Nizam-ud-Din and Amir Khusrau are buried and remain busy with visitors. In the same neighborhood lies the grave of Mirza Asadullah Khan Ghalib (d.1869) the most famous Urdu and Persian poet and a witness to the Rebellion of 1857. Purana Qila and the Old Delhi have mainly Mughal monuments, although some other buildings may predate the Mughal era. New Delhi itself dates from the British era and consists of Luttyen's official buildings designed for the Raj in the early twentieth century. This brief information is based on several personal visits to historic sites in Delhi.

Sir Syed Ahmed Kahn (1817–1898), a native Delhi Muslim intellectual, wrote a timely and detailed book on Delhi's historic buildings (*Asaar-us-Sanadeed*) just before the Rebellion of 1857 (Mutiny), which in many cases, were razed by a vengeful East India Company. Moreover, Thomas Metcalfe, a senior Company official during the 1840s, had commissioned a Muslim artist to sketch different sections of Delhi for a special volume, now preserved in London's British Library. Compared to present-day megalopolis, the pre-1857 counterpart looks artistically designed and more charming.

12. Located outside contemporary Delhi, it is all in ruins and inhabited by thousands of monkeys. Some of its ramparts and outer walls have been restored yet the traces of houses, palaces, and halls remain desolate and lost in dust.

13. Tim-Mackintosh Smith, *The Hall of a Thousand Columns: Hindustan to Malabar with Ibn Battutah* (London: John Murray, 2005).

14. Tim-Mackintosh Smith, *Travels with a Tangerine: A Journey in the Footnotes of Ibn Battutah* (London: Picador, 2002) (ed.), *The Travels of Ibn Battutah* (London: Picador, 2002).

15. Mohammad Habib (ed.), *The Political Theory of the Delhi Sultanate Including a Translation of Ziauddin Barani's Fatawa-i Jahandari, circa, 1358–9 A.D.* (Allahabad: Kitab Mahal, 1960).

16. The Indian Muslim historian denies Muhammad bin Tughluq's hand behind the construction of the victory pavilion that claimed the lives of his father and brother in 1325. Zia-ud-din Barani, *The Tarikh-i Feroz-shahí,* edited by Syed Ahmed Khan (Calcutta: Royal Asiatic Society, 1860–1862).

17. The Sayyids all over the Muslim world claim to have descended from the Prophet and enjoy special esteem among ordinary Muslims.

18. Surrounded by some modern-day posh buildings, the graves of the Lodhi Sultans lie within the mosque compounds in Delhi and are better preserved than their other predecessors. Known as the Lodhi Gardens, these historic Muslim monuments have green parks all around them, which have become popular picnic spots.

19. Richard M. Eaton, *Sufis of Bijapur, 1300–1700: Social Roles of Sufis in Medieval India* (Princeton: Princeton University Press, 1978); Mohammad Habib, *Hazrat Amir Khusrau of Delhi* (New Delhi: Cosmo, 2004) (reprint).

20. For some balanced analysis, see Richard M. Eaton, *Essays on Islamic and Indian History* (New Delhi: Oxford University Press, 2001); Yoginder Sikand, *Sacred Spaces: Exploring Traditions of Shared Faith in India* (New Delhi: Penguin, 2003); *Hindu-Muslim Syncretic Shrines in Karnataka* (Bangalore: Himayat, 2001); David Gilmartin and Bruce Lawrence (eds.), *Beyond Turk and Hindu: Rethinking Religious Identities in Islamicate South Asia* (Gainesville: University Press of Florida, 2000).

4

The Great Mughals and the Golden Era in Indo-Islamic Civilization, 1526–1707

After the dissolution of the Lodhi Empire, three centuries of Muslim political and cultural influences in south Asia entered a new and rather unique era under another Turkish dynasty that is credited for enhancing India's global prestige and profile. The Mughal administration, especially the revenue system and land settlement, was retained by the East India Company and the British Crown with some minor changes until 1947. In addition, the sovereign states of India, Pakistan, Bangladesh, and Afghanistan hold a rare regional consensus on the contributions of the early centuries of the Mughal Empire and its achievements in various cultural, intellectual, and artistic domains. As observed by an American historian, the "Timurid [Mughal] India far outstripped in sheer size and resources its two rival early modern Islamic empires—Safavids Persia and Ottoman Turkey. The Mughal emperor's lands and subjects were comparable only to those ruled by his contemporary, the Ming emperor in early modern China."[1] The Mughal Empire certainly had its own share of civil wars and feuds over succession owing to the absence of a consensual law of primogeniture, yet it avoided assuming any communal policies especially toward Hindus. Even the later problems with the Sikhs in Punjab or the Maratha confederacy were political by nature and not religious. The founder of the Mughal Empire, Zahir-ud-Din Muhammad Babur

(1483–1530), exhibited strong feelings toward some Jain sculpture, but it was mainly his own reservations against nudity and not narrow-mindedness. In the same vein, Emperor Aurengzeb (1618–1707) was unabashed about his own personal puritanical lifestyle and abhorred the luxurious courtly manners of his father and brothers, yet, unlike the Spanish Inquisition or the contemporary conquistadores in the Western Hemisphere, he did not impose Islam on his non-Muslim subjects. His 49-year rule, idealized by many Muslim historians, was interspersed with warfare directed against his Muslim, Hindu, Sikh, and European rivals but not geared toward turning south Asia into Islamdom. His battles with the Marathas and Sikhs, however, often assumed religious overtones on all sides but still within his domain Hindu-Muslim relations were not characterized by religious warfare. His military campaigns were financed by revenue that steadily increased, burdening Indian peasants of all persuasions with even more imperial demands and pressures. Finally, under a weak and indolent internal rule, the empire fell apart.

The fall of the Mughal Empire was a steady and slow process that developed from diverse domestic and external factors that began earnestly after the death of Aurengzeb, although some historians may place some responsibility for the decline on the frugal emperor as well. Taking a macroscopic perspective, however, based on the parallel decline of four major Asia-based empires—the Mughals, Ottomans, Safawids, and Qings—one can identify several global factors behind such major historical developments. The globalization of Western Europe, beginning with the "Age of Discoveries" and fortified by commercial and industrial revolutions, brought in its wake momentous processes such as colonization, enslavement of millions of Africans, and elimination of indigenous populations. Mobility, better military and technical organization, and most of all efficient naval power and the absence of any united opposition all helped new absolutist monarchies establish empires thousands of miles away. An energized Europe and expansionist czarist Russia rewrote the history of six continents as a long period of unevenness and imbalances, often defined as the East-West or North-South divide, or more ebulliently characterized as "the triumph of the West."[2]

ZAHIR-UD-DIN MUHAMMAD BABUR

The founder of the Mughal dynasty was a young Timurid prince, Zahir-ud-Din Babur (1483–1530), but the real architect and restorer of the rule itself was his grandson, Jalal-ud-Din Akbar (1542–1605), who, like Alexander and Ashoka, is known as Akbar the Great. The Mughals never liked being called "Mughals," as the term was derived from "Mongols" and echoed a violent and rather uncouth image of the central Asian invaders who had destroyed cultural and political center in China, and central, southern and western

Asia.[3] Instead, they preferred to be called Turks, or more specifically Chughtai Turks, or even Timurids—the descendants of Tamerlane—and sought common ethnic origins with the Safawids and Ottomans. Babur was, in fact, an Uzbek from the valley of Ferghana and on his father's side belonged to the 13th generation of Chengiz Khan; on his maternal side he belonged to the fifth generation of Tamerlane. Thus his aversion to being called a Mongol or Mughal is understandable, especially when his Indian and Afghan possessions had been the victims of Mongol onslaught for such a long time. Tamerlane had laid waste to Delhi and other places, but his pretension of fighting a holy war and then his devotion to the grandeur of Muslim cities such as Herat and Samarkand had endeared him to his future descendants. Babur was a man of letters and of superb aesthetic tastes for gardening, philosophy, poetry, metaphysics, and wildlife. Used to a regular consumption of opium and wine in the company of his friends, Babur was a generous and sociable man who wrote extensively about his victories, defeats, and virtues, as well as his vices. A Sufi dervish by temperament and choice, the emperor usually avoided excesses and composed excellent poetry that is extant.[4] Babur was a meticulous diarist and wrote excellent Turkish both in prose and poetry, proving to be one of the earliest classicists in that language. His knowledge of Persian imperial mores and literature in addition to an interaction with the Indian scholars allowed him to establish tolerant traditions of the Persianate, which was soon to witness its renaissance in India. Babur's daughter, Gulbadan Begum, and his son, Humayun, inherited their father's interest in books and intellectual debates and in a powerful way proved the antithesis of what was attributed to Mongols and Turks.

Babur's father, Omar Shaikh Mirza, was the grandson of Sultan Abu Said Mirza of Herat, the latter himself the grandson of Tamerlane; his mother, Qutlugh Nigar Khanum, had the Mongol lineage.[5] As is evident from his memoirs, he was overwhelmingly impressed by his grandmother, a dynamic woman who enthused the young prince with valorous stories of his ancestors. Babur was only 11 when his father died in an accident, and the young prince was enthroned as the ruler of Ferghana. Soon he was eyeing the great city of Samarkand and, during the next two decades, would conquer it three times after losing it to his cousins and other Uzbek rivals. There came a time when the Mongol-Turkic prince had lost everything, and, with enemies in pursuit, sought help from his cousins in Herat, who preferred an indolent life to forging a common alliance against Shaibani Khan, the Uzbek chieftain.[6] In 1504, Babur, with the help of a few loyal followers and benefiting from a raging political chaos in Kabul, captured the city and once again became a king at the age of 21. He soon began coveting lands beyond the Kyber Pass. During the next few years, he launched campaigns against the Pushtun tribals in the trans-Indus regions, followed by his advance into central Punjab, which was then under nominal Lodhi control. Officials in Punjab, such as Daulat Khan and his son, Dilawar Khan, had been appointed by Sultan Ibrahim Lodhi, yet aspired for their own monarchy and asked Babur to initiate an attack on Delhi. They had somehow assumed that Babur, like his ancestors, would lay waste to Hindustan and would then retire to the mountains of Afghanistan. They only sought his help to defeat their cousin, Sultan Ibrahim Lodhi; otherwise they shared no common interest with the Padshah of Kabul. Babur, always fascinated by India's riches and resourcefulness and encouraged by his five previous attacks (although not enamored of its people and places), undertook a well-planned invasion to wrest power from the weakened Delhi Sultan. In April 1526, Babur reached Panipat, the historic town north of Delhi and prepared his artillery and cavalry to confront a larger army of the Delhi Sultan, which lacked enthusiasm and capable leadership. Babur showed his military shrewdness, aided by Ottoman artillery, by tending to minute details on offensives mounted by his generals. Accordingly, the Mughal guns destroyed a larger section of the Lodhi army, also creating panic among its elephants. In the melee, Ibrahim Lodhi was killed and his troops fled the field. After the victory at Panipat, Babur visited Delhi and its historic sites and moved farther south toward Agra, which he made his new capital. The remaining Lodhi Afghan nobility began to ally themselves with the Rajputs, led by Rana Sanga of Mewar.

In a rather hostile Agra, Babur still found time to engage in his literary and artistic pursuits and, after distributing booty among his troops, decided to stay in Hindustan.[7] The news about the Afghan-Rajput alliance soon began to worry him, as the former began marching toward Agra. Babur's army was smaller by now, as many of his companions did not want to stay in a hot and distant Hindustan, and the king had already allowed them to return to Kabul. Reaching the outskirts of Kanauj with a rather tired army, Babur faced a larger and better prepared Rajput opposition. He did not lose heart, however, and in a fiery speech declared the battle a holy struggle (*Jihad*) against the "idol worshippers," thereby inspiring his soldiers. He gave them the option of dying as *shaheeds* (martyrs) or living as *ghazis* (holy warriors) and determined henceforth to stop using liquor by breaking goblets and caskets in the full public view. His oratory and the timely act of prohibition before his predominantly Muslim troops electrified everyone. By applying his best assets of artillery and archery, Babur began to harass the Rajput infantry and elephants. The decisive battle between the Rajputs and Babur finally took place on March 16, 1527 at Khanua, and after a day of fierce killing, a disheartened Rana Sanga fled, affording victory to Babur, who applied guerrilla tactics to create panic among the fleeing Rajputs.

Another battle with the Lodhi Afghan remnants took place near Patna in Bihar, which cemented Babur's crowning as the king of Hindustan. Despite his fondness for Kabul and Ferghana, the Timurid emperor would never return to those lands. He continued with his literary and aesthetic activities in Agra until the age of 48, when he fell seriously ill. His illness, as recorded by Gulbadan Begum, occurred when his favorite son, Humayun, had begun to recover after a bout with an acute ailment. Babur's death in 1530 happened after his nomination of Humayun as his successor with his other three sons—Kamran, Askari, and Hindal—sharing the governorships of various provinces in the newly formed Mughal Empire. Babur was initially buried in Agra in one of his personally designed gardens, Aram Bagh, but, subsequently, as willed, the remains were taken to Kabul for a final burial in 1543. Babur was entombed in Kabul in a garden designed by himself two decades earlier, located on a hilltop with the river and town down below on one side and the snow-clad Paghman peaks on the other.

NASIR-UD-DIN HUMAYUN

At his deathbed, Babur sought the allegiance of his advisors and courtiers for his son's succession to the throne; but, as had been the case with other kingdoms, Humayun (1508–1556) soon began to face challenges from his male siblings, cousins, and the powerful Afghans. The infant Mughal kingdom needed a determined monarch of strong resolution to reestablish his writ, but the young prince, despite his politeness, was not tailored to shoulder enormous responsibilities. Humayun, literally meaning "fortunate," was an unlucky king whose life was characterized by rebellions, defeats, and exile, all made worse by the betrayals of his brothers and cousins; and, despite being one of the most scholarly persons of his era, his own son and successor, Akbar, remained illiterate. Humayun was born in Kabul on March 6, 1508, and from his childhood he displayed the scholarly and intellectual aspects of his father's personality, although he remained rather deficient in military pursuits. As recorded by his contemporary historian, Abdul Qadir Badayuni, Humayun was a preeminent mathematician and astrologer, but was unfit for soldiery, although he was not lacking in personal valour.[8] He always carried his vast library with him and determined all his actions in accordance with the astrological signs and planetary movements. In fact, he had even decided to devise and operate his imperial administration in league with zodiac signs, but he never ruled for a sustained period of time. Even while he was the governor of Badakhshan, he neglected military and administrative affairs, much to the chagrin of his charismatic father. Despite several misunderstandings between the two, Humayun was the natural choice for Babur as his heir apparent in the fateful closing days of December 1530, when the first Great Mughal died. Humayun's ascension amid news about his otherworldliness emboldened his adversaries and rivals, but instead of tending to them, he led an invasion of

Gujarat. The treasures of the west Indian region besides the capricious ambitions of its ruler, Bahadur Shah, had triggered this campaign, yet common sense required Humayun to confront Sher Khan, an Afghan general, who had asserted his autonomy in the vital province of Bengal.

By the time Humayun undertook punitive action against Sher Khan, the rainy season had set in, and most of his troops were either drowned by floods or suffered from malarial diseases. Humayun's failure in reaching Gaur, Bengal's capital, amid reversals at Rohtas and Chunar, was further compounded when his brothers refused to help, and the Battle of Kanauj in 1540 resulted in his dramatic flight from the battlefield. Humayun, harassed by Sher Khan's astute tactics, left his troops and, after his bout with a near-death experience crossing the Ganges, reached Lahore, hoping to forge a united front with Kamran. With Sher Khan's troops on his heels, an isolated and demoralized Humayun departed for Sindh, eventually seeking exile in Iran. As recorded in detail by Gulbadan Begum, his ever-loyal sister, here in one of the parties Humayun met Hamida Banu Begum, a Persian Shia princess of dynamic qualities. After proposing to her, their marriage was solemnized in Sindh, and Humayun stayed in the area as his young bride began to show signs of pregnancy.[9] It was at Umarkot in present-day Sindh province of Pakistan that Hamida Banu Begum gave birth to Akbar. The royal family had to move on through Balochistan in its struggle to escapee pursuing Afghan troops sent in by Sher Khan. After traveling through the Bolan Pass, Humayun reached Kandahar but found no help from his brother, Askari, and decided to seek assistance from the reigning Persian monarch. Shah Tahmasp, the Safawid king, received Humayun with fanfare and offered 10,000 troops so that the Mughal prince could recover Hindustan, where Sher Khan had already declared his monarchy by assuming the title of Sher Shah Suri.[10] As we shall soon see, Sher Shah was a wiser and capable ruler who left his own legacy in India, but after his death in 1545, his throne was soon coveted by Humayun, who had returned to Kabul. In 1555, however, after the death of Sher Shah's successor, Islam Shah, Humayun returned to Delhi to reestablish his empire. Within a year, the scholarly king, addicted to opium, fell down the stairs of his observatory in Purana Qila, not far from Sher Shah's impressive mosque in this Delhi fort, and suffered a concussion. Humayun died instantly, but the news was suppressed for two weeks until his son, Akbar, had been informed. A hastily organized coronation took place in rural Punjab where the 14-year-old prince was heading a military campaign.

KING SHER SHAH SURI

Coming from a rather humble background, Farid Khan (subsequently to be known as Sher Shah, 1486–1545) was one of India's most capable rulers.

He was an Afghan from a trans-Indus Suri tribe whose grandfather dealt in horses and had moved to the Gangetic Valley during the Lodhi era. His father, Hasan Khan, administered a small estate of Sahsaram in Bihar and, given his multiple marriages, often ignored Farid Khan's mother. Farid Khan spent his early years learning war games and attending religious seminaries. A self-made man, Farid Khan joined Babur in his military campaigns. The Mughals, whom he found rather luxury loving and not too adept at military life, did not impress him. As a shrewd man, he knew that Babur had failed to provide a sustainable system to his Indian possessions and largely depended on his nobles and a rather uncertain revenue collection from the Indian farmers. Sher Khan bided his time until Humayun assumed the throne. Then he began gathering his forces in Bengal, although he stopped short of harboring ambition for his own kingdom. At the most, he desired to carve out a bigger role for himself, but his knowledge of Humayun's weaknesses emboldened the Afghan genius, who soon began to annex more territories and eventually became a de facto ruler in Bengal and Bihar. His intermittent defeats of Humayun came about owing to disarray in the Mughal camp compounded by Humayun's lackluster performance, along with Sher Shah's own acumen as an accomplished general. After the Battle of Kanauj with Humayun on the way to exile, Sher Khan designated himself as the king of India and pioneered his Suri dynasty.

Other than his achievements as a successful planner and strategist in the battlefield, Sher Shah's most significant contribution lies in introducing an efficient judicial and fiscal administration, which was followed by the Mughals and later by the British. Some of the terminology and structure introduced by Sher Shah are still apparent in the revenue administrations of India, Pakistan, and Bangladesh, and historians have often recognized his talents as an exceptional administrator. His untimely death during a siege, which was to be his last victory, closed an important chapter in Indian history; otherwise his own longevity and a more capable progeny could have certainly foreclosed restoration of the Mughal empire once and for all. Sher Shah worked industriously in several areas. He took a personal interest in the running of his bureaucracy and ensured greater peace and stability of his empire. He would sleep just a few hours and after early prayers would hold meetings with scholars and *ulama*, followed by court sessions, inspections, and other work until late in the evening and would take only short prayer breaks. He divided his empire into 37 divisions called *sarkars*, each headed by two well-paid officials, with one looking after the dispensation of justice and the other maintaining law and order, as well as being responsible for revenue collection. Each *sarkar* was further divided into subdivisions called *parganas* administered by paid officers. Each village was headed by a headman or *kotwal*, who was responsible for maintaining peace and justice in his locality. There were 113,000 *parganas* across the Suri kingdom, and a vigilant administration ensured speedy justice, official accountability, and dependable orderliness. For revenue collection and to avoid unnecessary disputes, Sher Shah ordered a proper documentation of land by dividing it into units called *khasras*, and revenue was fixed on averaging the produce every 10 years.

Sher Shah's civil administration, properly paid and supervised, remained efficient and transparent in addition to ensuring the proper appraisal and steady collection of yearly revenue. He would not tolerate any bribery, laxity, or corruption and was known to issue verdicts against transgressions by his own close relatives. Sher Shah ordered the facilitation of all-weather roads connecting Afghanistan with Bengal, and the Gangetic Valley with Gujarat and Sindh. His roads eventually were used by the British and post-1947 nation states as the main arteries of communications and were upgraded as motorways and railway lines. Every sixth mile on these routes, the government built a rest house for travelers called *caravanserai*, which were monitored by the police and ensured smooth trade and postal service. Approximately 1,700 posts were spread all over the Suri Empire and proved quite efficient in transmitting prompt intelligence on security matters, thus operating as eyes and ears for the regime. Sher Shah built some massive forts in Bihar and Punjab and was planning several more to shelter the civilian population during emergencies, but he did not live long enough to realize this objective. He was killed when a mortar ricocheted during the siege of Mewar.[11] His son, Saleem Suri, also known as Islam Shah, continued his policies, sometimes too harshly, but after his death in 1554, civil war between the Suri heir apparent and his uncle allowed Humayun to recapture Hindustan. On his return to Delhi, Humayun moved into Purana Qila to occupy the Suri premises in the metropolitan city. He died here a year later while walking down the stairs at dusk.

JALAL-UD-DIN MUHAMMAD AKBAR

Soon after receiving the news of Humayun's death from Delhi, Bairam Khan and other senior Mughal courtiers ensured the prompt enthronement of Akbar, who was away in Punjab leading a military offensive. As usual, there were several old and new contenders to test the young king's mettle, and other than Suri Pushtuns, several Rajput claimants tried to test their military prowess. Born in 1542, young Akbar had been left in the care of his uncles, Askari and Kamran, during his father's escapade to Persia, and he was often used as ransom by the scheming uncles. Akbar, like Sher Shah, was streetwise and tough. He survived against the odds and, despite having seasoned tutors such as Monem Khan and Bairam Khan, remained uneducated although not short on intelligence and worldly wisdom. While Bairam Khan and Akbar wrestled with the Suri claimants, Delhi had fallen to Hemu Baqal, a shrewd

Hindu general who had served the Suris; but during this chaotic phase, he decided to fend for himself. Hemu was also a stubborn commander who, amid a severe famine in Hindustan, worried only about feeding his huge army of elephants. While ordinary Indians starved, each elephant was daily fed 250 kilograms of grain, alienating people from this new claimant to the Delhi throne. Akbar, despite the advice of some of his advisors, decided to fight Hemu's army of 100,000 troops and 1,500 elephants and used his artillery to its most devastating effect. The Mughal guerrilla raids under Quli Khan Shaibani unnerved Hemu's troops, and the army launched a pitched assault on November 5, 1556 at the historic battleground of Panipat, where Babur had defeated Ibrahim Lodhi 30 years earlier. Bairam Khan's inspired archers were able to target Hemu riding the lead elephant and successfully struck his eye, which left the general unconscious. His elephant ran in panic until it was escorted to the Mughal command post where Bairam Khan himself killed the dying Hemu. The leaderless army became an unruly crowd, and the Mughals were able to reassert their authority, sending a powerful message to other rebellious princes and errant rajas.

Among Emperor Akbar's numerous achievements, three stand out. First, he transformed the Mughal empire into a subcontinental force by forging closer alliances with his non-Muslim subjects. Second, he built a strong institutional framework in civil administration, which sustained the dynastic regime for a longer time. Third, he introduced a policy of tolerance and cultural synthesis, which augured a golden era in the Indo-Islamic culture. In attaining these achievements, Akbar was helped by a select team of advisors—often called *Naurattan* (Nine Jewels)—including the Muslim Abul Fazal and Hindu Todar Mal, who advised the emperor on vital issues.[12] Likewise on religious matters, Akbar was receptive to various views and opinions, but he always made up his own mind to stay resolute in his decisions. Undoubtedly, Akbar, at the prime of his power during the last quarter of the sixteenth century, was the most powerful and widely respected monarch of his age. With the Afghan and Turkish dissidence contained, Akbar turned his attention to the Rajput princes who posed a serious threat to the newly restored Mughal Empire. Here, instead of fighting endlessly, he chose to negotiate by co-opting the Rajput chieftains, offering them senior court positions and even extending his hand in marriage to the Rajput princesses. Akbar's matrimonial alliances ensured loyalty of a number of powerful Rajput chieftains and built fraternal relationships with the Hindu warrior elite who sought status at the Mughal court and in return offered support and loyalty. Akbar approached Raja Bihari Mal of Amber in 1563, seeking the hands of his daughter in marriage and in the process obtained the support of her two powerful brothers, Man Singh and Bhagwan Das. In another similar marital arrangement with Jodha Bai of Jodhpur, Akbar again abstained from insisting on her conversion to Islam and instead built a Hindu temple in his palace for Hindu queens. Jodha Bai was the mother of Salim, the crown prince and the future emperor. Subsequently, Salim himself married a Rajput princess who bore him Khurram, the future Emperor Shah Jahan. Akbar appointed Todar Mal to the senior cabinet position of finance minister, and Man Singh held senior military and civil positions at a time when Akbar abolished *jizya* earmarked for non-Muslim subjects. Akbar could not win over Rana Udai Singh, the ruler of Mewar and a descendant of Rana Sanga. In 1567, he personally led an attack on the princely capital of Chitor. His Rajput relatives and allies fought on Akbar's side against their own co-religionists and the Mughal Empire attained further strength, territory, and prestige. After consolidating his power in northern India and Gujarat, Akbar initiated military missions to capture Vijaynagar and other princely states in Deccan.

Benefiting from the capable talent all around him, Akbar adopted administrative and fiscal policies originally pioneered by Sher Shah Suri and ensured further land settlement and revenue reassessment. Akbar sought a break from the past practice of appointing hereditary officials in the provinces and territories on a permanent basis and instead loyalty and merit became the sole criteria for such postings, often featuring transfers to different places. These officials were categorized in reference to the number of horses and troops that they would maintain in addition to ensuring revenues to the central government. They were given *mansabs* (ranks) according to their varying capabilities and services to the state with future prospects for promotion. Known as *mansabdars*, these officials owed their positions to the services of the empire along with a capability of providing the required number of troops and horses during emergencies. This hierarchical system was not totally feudal, but appeared more like the European nobility without offering permanent roots. The sons and descendants of these *mansabdars* had to start afresh, as the erstwhile hereditary privileges were replaced by personal valor and merit. The revenue was often flexible given the vagaries of the weather because Akbar did not want to alienate peasants and even ordered constructions of warehouses to store grains for emergencies.[13] Akbar's elaborate administrative setup was derived from long-term imperial considerations and was to credit for a comparative peace and stability that his empire enjoyed. Along with benefiting from Sher Shah's legacy of an efficient and just administration, Akbar continued with his military campaigns so as to ensure its territorial expansion and security. In 1585, he shifted his capital to Lahore and built a huge fort, which now faces the grand mosque built by his great-grandson, Aurengzeb, and symbolizes Mughal glory in Pakistan.

The province of Punjab was prosperous, given its water resources for agriculture and the contemporary industrial potentials, which Akbar skillfully put to his own advantage. From Lahore, Akbar sent expedition to capture Swat,

Mardan, and Kashmir. He had been troubled by the Yusafzai Pushtuns and in the process captured their trans-Indus possessions after building a massive fort at Attock to ensure military supplies into Pushtun regions. It was from Lahore that Akbar expanded into the lower Indus valley and captured Sindh and neighboring Balochistan in addition to displaying vigilance against any possible Uzbek attack from farther north. In 1595, the Persian governor of Kandahar fell out with Shah Abbas and shifted his loyalties to the Mughal court, although the Mughal-Safawid relations had remained cordial. After spending a decade in Lahore, Akbar returned to Agra and prioritized the conquest of princely states in Deccan. By that time, he had lost interest in visits to Sufi shrines and reinvigorated his quest for some ultimate truth and a consensual creed.

Other than showing greater tolerance towards Hindus, Akbar tried to induct some reforms for the betterment of Hindu women and banned child marriages and *Sati* (the rite of burning widows on the pyre of their dead husbands) and sought to encourage widow remarriage. He also tried to put some curbs on financial assistance to many seminaries, shrines, and *ulama* so as to assert his own mundane policies, along with neutralizing the pressures from the clergy for conversion. Muslim clerics did not like Akbar's secularist policies, marriages with non-Muslim women, and construction of temples; but Akbar, both by temperament and geared by imperial demands, wanted to transform his state into an inclusive entity. His own autonomous and even critical thinking on religious matters was displayed by holding interfaith dialogues with the Portuguese Jesuit, Hindu, Jain, and Zoroastrian priests where he even involved some Muslim scholars. Akbar did not renounce his Islamic identity altogether and followed a more syncretic and Sufi version of Islamic traditions, which annoyed some orthodox *ulama.*

After several years of trying to have a male heir, Akbar began to visit Sufi shrines in Ajmer and Fatehpur Sikri and even acknowledged the birth of Salim to the blessings of Sufi Shaikh Salim Chishti, a Sufi in Fatehpur Sikri. In his devotion to the saint, Akbar named his crown prince after him and went to the extent of building a whole new capital at Fatahpur Sikri, 26 miles outside Agra near the Chishti shrine.[14] This elaborate town built of red stones with ample courts, palaces, and plazas had to be eventually abandoned owing to a scarcity of water, yet a curious Akbar persisted with his quest for some overarching religious truths and metaphysical subjects.[15] His debates took place at a specially constructed chamber called Ibadatkhana and led Akbar to devise his own belief system—away from Islam and other established religions—called Din-i-Ilahi or Divine Faith. Pursuing his policy of *Sulah-i-Kul* (peace for all), Akbar did not pressure his advisors and subjects to subscribe to his creed, although a halo around his head began to appear in all the Mughal paintings, giving him some divine status. Akbar's 49-year rule ensured stability of the state and its expansion into Deccan, but toward the closing years, he had to confront a rebellion from Salim, who had been catapulted into defiance by some palatial intrigues.

As recorded by Abul Fazl and visiting Jesuit missionaries, Akbar was an intelligent and tolerant person and unlike some other Mughals, avoided extremes in drinking or consuming opium.[16] In addition, tobacco had been introduced in Mughal India during the closing years of his rule, but he did not use it.[17] Akbar's encounter with the Christians began in 1572 during his military campaign in Gujarat. He asked Julian Pereira, a Jesuit in Bengal, to teach him about Christian theology but the latter had his own limitations as a missionary. In 1578, the Portuguese governor of Goa, Dom Diego de Menezes, sent Antonio Cabral to the imperial court to inform the emperor on Christian theology. Akbar's conversations with Cabral familiarized him both with Christianity and Europe, and he requested that the governor send him two more competent missionaries for the Mughal court. Accompanied by the Mughal ambassador and brimming with hope to convert the most powerful monarch of his time, three Jesuits arrived in Fatehpur Sikri from Goa. Rodolfo Acquaviva, an Italian Jesuit, led the delegation, which included the Catalan Spaniard, Antonio Monserrate, and Francesco Enriquez, a Muslim convert. Monserrate was the most vocal of all and recorded his observations of the emperor, Mughal court, and debates that occurred during this sojourn on the mainland. Not only did Akbar build a chapel in his palace, he even allowed missionaries to propagate their religion freely to Indians. Averse to the raised expectations by the Jesuits, Akbar did not go beyond showing utmost respect to Catholicism and never converted. His alertness and ease in relating with people of high caliber and often of diverse dispositions stemmed from a persuasive level of self-confidence and openness.

Salim, a prince devoted more to hunting, arts and drinking, began to develop doubts about his succession, as he feared to be superseded by his son, Khusrau. Sensing rebellion from his son, Akbar sent his close aide and advisor, Abul Fazl, to dissuade the prince, but the emissary was mysteriously killed on his way to Agra by a Hindu chieftain loyal to Salim. Akbar suspected Salim of ordering Abul Fazl's assassination but strove for reconciliation. Akbar was deeply worried about Salim's fondness for alcohol and disinterest in administrative responsibilities. Daniyal and Murad, Akbar's other two sons, had tragically died of alcoholism and with Salim on a similar path, Akbar's closing years in life were rather gloomy. Akbar's courageous and equally favorite wife, Salima Begum, took it upon herself to bring father and son together, in addition to persuading her son to reform for his own welfare. Salima Begum, like Hamida Banu Begum—Akbar's mother—was a dynamic Mughal queen. She escorted the errant prince back and left him with his grandmother before his audience with the emperor. Akbar himself visited Hamida Banu Begum's residence and, after embracing his recalcitrant son, put his own turban on his head to reassure the prince of his succession. The turbulent relationship between the two flared up again in 1604, and the emperor decided to assume personal charge to save his son from an impending disaster. But the emperor could not undertake the journey, as on September 10, 1604, his own mother, Hamida Banu Begum, died. He made one more effort to forcibly dissuade Salim from wine and opium and put him in a solitary confinement in addition to employing physicians, but without any significant benefit. Thus Akbar, otherwise the illustrious architect of the Mughal glory and now tormented by a sad family life, began to show signs of disenchantment and insomnia until he developed a serious illness. Confined to his bed during the last few days of his life, Akbar was visited by Salim. He reassured his son that he would inherit the throne. On October 25, 1605, the Great Mughal died at the age of 63. Following Muslim funeral rituals for Akbar in Agra in October 1605 and his burial at Fatehpur Sikri in a specially designed mausoleum, Salim succeeded his father as the fourth Mughal monarch.[18]

NUR-UD-DIN MUHAMMAD JAHANGIR

A man of exceptional literary and artistic taste, Salim (1569–1627) was a romantic by disposition who preferred sedentary life over military adventures and administering a vast empire. Titling himself as Jahangir, his reign (1605–1627) is known for the rise of Queen Nur Jahan as the de facto Indian ruler at a time when her spouse spent most of his time painting, drinking, or hunting wild animals. Despite his drinking habits, Jahangir was not an incapable monarch. A stable and peaceful empire left by his father had also contributed to his lack of interest in military expeditions, except for his victory over the Rana of Mewar in his early years. Jahangir's autobiography, like that of Babur, offers a frank and balanced account of his life and pursuits and is written in an elegant Persian.[19] Jahangir also developed political problems with the Sikh Gurus, although Rajputs usually remained faithful to him even when his own son, Khurram, rebelled against his father. Toward the end of his regime, Jahangir became totally dependent on wine and left the imperial administration to Nur Jahan, the daughter of a Persian nobleman who had migrated to India in the early years of the Mughal rule. Jahangir married Mehrunnissa—born in Kandahar in 1577—and titled her as Nur Jahan ("the light of the world"), although they did not have any children from their life together. As observed by the visiting European emissaries and missionaries such as William Hawkins, Thomas Roe, Jean-Bapiste Tavernier, and Jerome Xavier,[20] Jahangir and Nur Jahan "were good companions, who shared many interests. She was as enthusiastic about hunting as he was, and was an excellent shot, who once felled four tigers in six shots."[21] She had been married earlier to Sher Afgan, a Mughal general, and had borne him a daughter, Ladli Begum.

Nur Jahan's brother, Asif Jah, was elevated to prime minister and his daughter, Mumtaz Mahal, became Prince Khurram's wife in 1612. Nur Jahan's influence increased manifold and she was able to run the civil and military administration quite effectively until, to the chagrin of her brother and Khurram, she began to maneuver for the nomination of Shahryar as Jahangir's successor. Shahryar had been married to Ladli Begum, and Nur Jahan, with the help of some generals such as Mahabat Khan, conspired for the former's succession over Khurram—Jahangir's eldest son and heir apparent. Resultant skirmishes and battles led to victories for Khurram, and Nur Jahan had to assume a rather docile rule, as the reigning monarch had fallen ill and eventually died in 1627. Nur Jahan outlived Jahangir by another 19 years, which she mostly spent in Lahore in solitude until her natural death in 1646. During these last two decades, she supervised the construction of a beautiful tomb for her late husband in Lahore, but for herself, she preferred an ordinary grave—a few hundred yards away from Jahangir's grand mausoleum by the River Ravi.[22]

Sikhism was a creed that had evolved in central Punjab during the Lodhi era when a Hindu mystic, Guru Nanak, tried to bridge Hindu-Muslim differences by offering some shared values that reflected agrarian norms. He was deeply anguished over the rigid caste system and yearned for human equality. Nanak was born in 1469 in a village outside Lahore in a Hindu family but had grown up with some Muslims, and after wider travels he settled in Punjab preaching peace and coexistence. He had been influenced by the Bhagti movement that emerged in the late medieval era and highlighted commonalities in human experiences. He was grounded in Hindu teachings, as well as Sufi egalitarianism. Believing in one God but avoiding several other rituals and rites of both Hinduism and Islam such as daily prayers and priesthood, Sikhism was practiced in a worship house called Gurdawara, where prayers would be followed by shared food (*langar*). Over the successive centuries after Guru Nanak, however, Sikhism developed its own holy book (*Guru Granth Sahib*) and a martial character that often conflicted with the Mughal authorities.[23] Arjun Singh, the fifth guru, had sided with Prince Khusrau in his rebellion against Jahangir, which Jahangir never forgot. When Khusrau fled from prison and was given shelter by the guru in Punjab, Jahangir was infuriated. He ordered punitive action against the Sikh spiritual leader and after his arrest, Guru Arjun was executed under imperial orders, as was Khusrau, the eldest son of the emperor. Thus a political event like the war of succession led to a future Muslim-Sikh schism, which reverberated in future developments including the Partition in 1947. Jahangir, however, was not a bigoted person and is often praised by his admirers for his strict adherence to justice. In addition, Jahangir, like his father, was quite eclectic in his beliefs and pursued dialogues with Jesuit priests such as Jerome Xavier and Pinheiro, although the emperor showed more interest in obtaining European paintings from his Portuguese guests. Jahangir, as will be seen in the next chapter, would receive the emissaries from British East India Company, whose presence in Agra had infuriated his Portuguese visitors.

SHAHAB-UD-DIN MUHAMMAD SHAH JAHAN

After the death of Jahangir, Prince Khurram ascended the Mughal throne in 1628, assuming the title Shah Jahan ("ruler of the world"), which, in fact, his father conferred on him during his victories in Deccan. He was born in Lahore on January 15, 1592 to Jodha Bai, the Rajput princess of Marwar, and was named Khurram ("happiness") by Emperor Akbar, his grandfather. Although quite generous to his former rivals and enemies, Emperor Shah Jahan ensured expansion, as well consolidation of his empire, which, in size, prosperity, and development of the arts and architecture, was destined to become unrivaled in its time. He himself led the costly military campaign into the south, although by that time the coastal regions had long been penetrated by the Portuguese who, despite their dislike of Islam, engaged in shipping and human mobility between the Middle East and India for Mughals. Shah Jahan, like his ancestors, ignored building a strong navy and spent his resources mostly extending the frontiers of his land-based kingdom into southern, eastern, and western regions. His empire included newly captured Assam; to the west, he annexed Kandahar and aimed at capturing Samarkand and Bokhara, the land of his ancestors. He often succeeded in capturing these cities, especially, when his third son, Aurengzeb, commanded the campaigns, but Mughal soldiers did not want to stay in Tamerlane's imperial cities—too distant from their native India—and thus central Asian regions reverted to local contenders. Kandahar, however, changed hands between the Mughals and Safawids several times and remained a bone of contention until the 1730s, when it was forcibly annexed by Nadir Shah Afshar before the latter's sack of Delhi in 1739.

On his return from Deccan in 1636, Shah Jahan built a new capital city in Delhi that consisted of open boulevards, spacious houses, and, most of all, the Red Fort meant to house the imperial family, the bureaucracy, and troops. Facing the fort, the impressive Jamia Mosque stood on a hill, making it India's largest center for Muslim worship. Cities such as Agra, Lahore, Srinagar, Thatta, and Burhanpur were chosen to house immensely beautiful Mughal buildings.[24] Shah Jahan's favorite queen, Mumtaz Mahal, had died during childbirth in Deccan in 1631, and the emperor was determined to build the most beautiful mausoleum on her grave in Agra. Known as the Taj Mahal and built over 20 years by thousands of artisans with exquisite marble and red stone and surrounded by specially designed gardens, the Taj is certainly a unique monument of love and beauty. It stands by the River Yamuna and a few miles from the Agra Fort, where Shah Jahan was destined to spend the last eight years of his life. Here in the Agra Fort, he was imprisoned by his son, Aurengzeb, and from the palace the deposed emperor spent his time looking at the changing horizons over the white domes and minarets of the Taj. Shah Jahan employed Iranian and Indian engineers to design mosques, canals, forts, palaces, and gardens, as he was quite fond of architecture, which by now blended Persian, Turkish, and south Asian traditions. Usually built with red stone and topped by white marble, these buildings were decorated by specially designed multicolor tiles embodying Quranic calligraphy. By this time, the Mughal art, as observed by travelers such as Francois Bernier, had already assumed a unique and synthesized personality in various realms of architecture, calligraphy, miniatures, textiles, ceramics, jewelry, and other metallic works. The patronization of arts and certainly of architecture created fabulous images of India in the outside world, especially among Europeans, who were imbued with renewed energy and dynamism to seek out new routes and markets in the world. Despite this glittering wealth, however, India had its own share of problems, including periodic famines, and Shah Jahan is often accused of being unresponsive to the basic needs of ordinary people. To finance his buildings all over India, Shah Jahan raised land revenue to half of agricultural produce and thus shifted the financial burden to farmers and landowners.[25] He was a religious man, but not an extremist, and he pursued tolerant policies of his ancestors. As recorded by Niccalao Mannuci, he enjoyed music and parties.[26] According to a contemporary Muslim historian, Abdul Hamid Lahori, Shah Jahan ruled a wealthy empire, and his annual revenue stood at 220 million rupees, of which his personal income was 30 million, although his personal jewelry and diamonds accounted for 50 million rupees. A monarch of sentimental disposition, Shah Jahan, in the early two decades of his rule, dispersed gifts worth 95 million rupees.[27]

Shah Jahan had divided the administration of his vast empire among his four sons—Dara Shikoh, Shah Shuja, Aurengzeb, and Murad Bakhsh—although he desired Prince Dara to be his successor. Dara was the eldest and most scholarly of all, but he was not liked by Muslim *ulama*, who felt uncomfortable with his libertine ideas and shared views with Akbar. Dara had translated various Hindu classics into Persian, mingled with Sufis such as Miyan Mir of Lahore, and followed eclectic philosophy. On the other hand, Aurengzeb, the most capable son of Shah Jahan, excelled in military areas and was quite religious by disposition. He avoided drinking and mixing with nonreligious crowds and instead preferred reading Quran and conferring with religious circles. Shuja and Murad were akin to Dara, yet held their own ambitions to succeed Shah Jahan, especially when the Mughals never devised a proper mechanism for succession nor did they fully practice primogeniture. Dara Shikoh was duly helped in his ideas and scholarly pursuits by Jahan Ara Begum, Shah Jahan's daughter and confidant, making the other three princes apprehensive of their hold on their father when rumors about his deteriorating health began to circulate in the empire. Shuja served in Bengal, Murad was the governor of Gujarat, and Aurengzeb controlled the vast regions of Deccan as a viceroy. Shah Jahan fell ill in September 1657. Shuja was the first one to head toward Delhi, commanding troops to defeat Dara, although he suffered reversals at Bahadurgarh in February 1658 and retreated to Bengal. Despite this victory, Dara Shikoh was unable to defeat Murad and Aurengzeb at Dharmat in April. Their next encounter at Samurgarh in May 1658 was a total defeat for Dara Shikoh, who had hastily assembled an army that lacked proper training and was exhausted as a result of two earlier battles.

Despite official support from his father, a beleaguered Dara Shikoh was unable to repel Aurengzeb in the fourth major battle in this war of succession and was eventually captured in Punjab by Aurengzeb's troops. Both princes despised each other and their antithetical personalities were further pushed apart, with Shah Jahan and Jahan Ara backing Dara Shikoh.[28] After arresting Dara Shikoh, Aurengzeb held his trial on the allegations of apostasy, resulting in his execution in 1659; Shuja was defeated near Allahabad in the same year, leaving Murad and a crestfallen Shah Jahan to face the approaching forces of Aurengzeb. Shuja, in the meantime, fled to the hills of Assam and was murdered by local tribesmen. Murad was arrested on Aurengzeb's orders and executed in 1661 for allegedly killing a noble. Aurengzeb put his father into forced seclusion at the Agra Fort and took control of the Mughal domains, beginning his long 49-year rule. Shah Jahan lived his remaining eight years officially confined to his palace in Agra Fort, nursed by Jahan Ara and never visited by Aurengzeb, although both often exchanged accusatory letters. In January 1666, an ailing Shah Jahan pardoned Aurengzeb and expressed his wish to be buried next to his wife in the Taj Mahal. On February 1, 1666, Shah Jahan died and after a simple funeral for an otherwise opulent emperor, he was buried in the crypt at the Taj Mahal.

MOHIY-UD-DIN AURENGZEB ALAMGIR

The third son of Shah Jahan from Mumtaz Mahal and a capable military commander, Aurengzeb, is accepted as the last Great Mughal, although for some historians he has been no less controversial as a result of his puritanical lifestyles. A staunch Muslim, he devoted his free time to prayers and recitations, avoiding the usual regalia and pomp and show of his ancestors. Born in Deccan in 1618 during Jahangir's reign, he lived an austere but active life and died fighting protracted battles in the south. His warfare against siblings and imprisonment of his father for eight years certainly did not endear him to a long line of critics, although, the Mughal emperor may have believed he was undertaking precautionary measures to ensure the longevity of a vast empire, prone to laxity and luxury instead of strenuous efforts that were needed to sustain it. His constant military campaigns ensured the territorial expansion of the Mughal Empire, but they also proved costly in part because such a large empire had too many enemies that defied its authority. The widening gap between the rising demand and volume of salaries of the *mansabdars* and the actual produce itself, known as "jagir crisis," created serious fiscal imbalances in its treasury. The greater need for more resources for official administration and military campaigns eventually drained the surplus produced by the peasantry,[29] although to some historians, the Mughal decline resulted from a lack of political cohesion and consensus. According to the latter view, even the political loyalty had gradually come to depend on sectarian loyalty.[30]

Associating himself closely with the *ulama*, Aurengzeb lent a religious flavor to his rule, which alienated Sikhs and Marathas who were already agitated because of an ever-increasing revenue. In addition, in 1679, he reintroduced *jizya*, the controversial tax that further angered his non-Muslim subjects. It is too rash to suggest that the Mughal Empire was confronted by some rising tide of Sikh and Hindu nationalisms, as Aurengzeb also fought wars with fellow Muslims such as the Pushtuns, and most of the strife had political roots accentuated by personal preferences. The fifth Sikh Guru, Arjun, had been executed by Jahangir in 1606 for abetting Prince Khusrau's revolt, and the sixth Guru, Hargobind, tried to develop some military orientation among his Sikh followers. After admonishment from Shah Jahan, he had sought refuge in Rajput territories. Following a quiet interlude under the seventh Guru, Tegh Bahadur, the son of Hargobind, assumed leadership of the Sikh community in 1664 as the eighth Guru and soon developed differences with Aurengzeb, who had been formally installed as emperor in 1668. Under official orders, Guru Tegh Bahadur was arrested in 1675 and executed, infuriating his followers. Guru Gobind Singh, on assuming Sikh leadership, instilled a military spirit among his followers by inducting a strong martial orientation. In 1699, under his orders, Sikhs were ordained to observe their five Ks including a dagger, comb, a pair of shorts, bangle, and unshorn hair—all denoting a Khalsa (pure) creed and identity. The tenth guru survived Aurengzeb by a year, but by then Sikh-Mughal relations had become quite volatile. Abdus Samad Khan, the Mughal governor of Lahore, had been ordered to curb Sikh activism. His use of greater force not only deepened the Sikh-Muslim gulf, but it also pushed many Sikhs into the hills to mount guerrilla attacks on Mughals.

Eventually in 1799, a Sikh raja, Ranjeet Singh, captured Lahore and declared his own kingdom, holding sway in the upper Indus regions and Kashmir until 1839, when his death resulted into a war of succession. In 1849, the Sikh kingdom was captured by the East India Company after fighting in Punjab, and the Company sold off Kashmir to a Hindu prince for a paltry sum.

Other than the Sikh unrest in Punjab, Aurengzeb's major challenge came from Deccan in the south where a reorganized Maratha confederacy revived the idea of a Hindu kingdom based in Delhi. Since Akbar's conquest of Vijaynagar and Mughal expansion deeper into south through the annexation of kingdoms such as Ahmadnagar, Golconda, and Bijapur, the Maratha reaction had been multiplying and awaited some charismatic leader. Of course, religion and history were the two main factors underwriting this revulsion against the Mughal Empire, yet it is too hasty to suggest that the Maratha rebellion symbolized Hindu nationalism, reflecting some clash of cultures. Shivaji Bhonsle is credited by many of his admirers for flagging dissent against Mughals, although his early confrontation had been with the Sultan of Bijapur, whose kingdom his followers would often attack. In 1659, the sultan had sent a punitive force commanded by Afzal Khan, who was able to crush Shivaji's opposition and went to his camp after Maratha entreaties for peace. During their meeting, Afzal Khan was treacherously killed by Shivaji, who overnight became a hero with Bijapur, seeking assistance from Aurengzeb. The Mughal troops defeated Marathas and arrested Shivaji, who was sent to Agra as a prisoner. He later fled from the jail by hiding in a fruit basket and returned to his native territory. In the meantime, Aurengzeb had been busy quelling a rebellion in the trans-Indus region, which allowed Shivaji to regroup and resume his guerrilla attacks on Mughal territory. Shivaji's closing years were characterized by internal strife until 1680. After his death, his son Shambhuji succeeded to the throne at Rajgarh in present-day Maharashtra. In 1682, Aurengzeb decided to personally lead his troops to contain unrest in Deccan and selected Aurangabad as his capital for the next 25 years. In 1689, after a decisive battle, the emperor defeated Shambhuji and executed the Maratha commander, which ushered in a period of instability until 1708, when Shivaji's grandson, Shahuji, emerged as the titular head. Shahuji, however, soon decided to lead the life of a *sadhu* (ascetic) and left his political affairs in the hands of a minister, called *Peshwa.* This ministerial system itself became hereditary and persisted until 1818, when the British East India Company finally marginalized it but not before the Maratha Peshwas were able to overshadow the Mughal emperors in Delhi. Even the crushing Maratha defeat at the hands of Ahmed Shah Abdali at Panipat in 1760 did not totally eliminate the Maratha factor, although it certainly smoothed the way for the Company's primacy in Hindustan.

Aurengzeb wanted his successors to act more responsibly, as is evident from his letters to his sons and governors, and tried to curb various rebellions that were challenging his empire. He was able to contain the Company's growing power by securing Surat in 1680. By assuming a more assertive role in Bengal, but without a proper navy, he could not reverse the ever-growing power of the Company, which had already defeated the Portuguese in addition to pushing the Dutch out of coastal India. The Company enjoyed access to a rich Coromandel Coast, which was never annexed by the Mughals. Given the destruction of the Spanish Armada in 1588 and the Portuguese defeat by Captain Best in 1612 in front of the inhabitants of Surat, the writing on the wall was already clear to any keen observer of Asian affairs. Here, land-based empires such as the Qings, Ottomans, Safawids, and Mughals were destined to lose out before the smaller, stronger, and better-equipped forces of post-Westphalia nations of Western Europe. Aurengzeb was undoubtedly the hardest working emperor that the Mughal dynasty ever had, but his efforts were of no use, as extended military campaigns only further drained resources and infuriated non-Muslim subjects. He was heartbroken even before he died in 1707, still carrying on his mission of subjugating the dissenters and rebels.[31]

History repeated itself for the umpteenth time, as the war of succession ensued until Prince Muazzam, known as Bahadur Shah, emerged. He tried to repair relations with the Marathas and Sikhs by winding down military expeditions. He also abolished *jizya*, but by that time his court was being torn apart by the capricious elite, whereas several distant provinces planned to declare autonomy. In 1712, he died and another war of succession further weakened the empire. Within less than a decade (1712–1720), 12 monarchs ruled in quick succession, and all met brutal ends until Muhammad Shah assumed power and chose to lead a life of debauchery. His hold was further weakened by the invasion of Nadir Shah Afshar in 1739, which not only resulted in the wanton killings of thousands of inhabitants in Delhi, but also depleted the city of its wealth. Another subsequent invasion from Afghanistan in 1760 led by the Afghan king, Ahmad Shah Abdali, could have saved the empire, for it brought defeat to Marathas at Panipat, but Abdali hastened back to Afghanistan and the Delhi Empire soon reverted to palatial conspiracies and regional warlordism. By that time, provinces such as Bengal, Oudh, Deccan, and Gujarat had become independent and the Mughal emperors—a long series of incompetent men—became totally dependent on the largesse either from some regional elite or from the Company itself. Long before 1857, when the curtain was drawn once for all on Mughal India, the empire had been suffering from serious reversals; thus 1707 marked the end of the Great Mughals, for it sealed the fate of a glorious period in Indo-Muslim culture. As in the past, external forces once again redrew the south Asian map, although this time the invaders had come from the sea and not from the steppes of central Asia or the mountains of Afghanistan.

NOTES

1. John F. Richards, *The Mughal Empire* (Cambridge: Cambridge University Press, 1996), p. 1.

2. J.M. Roberts, *The Triumph of the West* (London: Guild Publishing, 1985).

3. "Mughals" was also used as "Mughuuls," which literally meant uncivilized and thus was a stigma for the central Asians of Turkic origins.

4. Zahir-ud-Din Babur, *Tuzk-i-Baburi*, translated by A. S. Beveridge (London: Luzac, 1921).

5. Mohibhul Hasan, *Babur: Founder of the Mughal Empire in India* (Delhi: Manohar, 1985).

6. In this beautiful city of grand buildings and known seminaries, literary and artistic activities were preferred over defending the kingdom from the Persians or Uzbeks. The Heratis were so immersed in literary pursuits that even the wrestlers would compose poetry. Abraham Early, *The Mughal Throne: The Saga of India's Great Emperors* (London: Penguin, 2001), p. 10.

7. Stephen Dale, "Steppe Humanism: The autobiographical Writings of Zahir al-Din Muhammad Babur, 1483–1530," In *International Journal of Middle East Studies*, XXII, 1990, 37–58.

8. *Muntakhabu-t-Tawarikh*, by Abdul Qadir bin-Muluk Shah, known as al-Badayuni, translated from the original Persian and edited by George S. A. Ranking (Karachi: Karimsons, 1976–1978).

9. Gulbadan Begum, *Humayun Nama*, translated by A.S. Beveridge as *The Life and Times of Humayun* (Lahore: Sang-i-Meel Publications, 1974) (reprint).

10. It is said that King Tahmasp needed such a high-profile visitor to build up his own status as a regional power. In addition, the 25-year-old Persian emperor wanted to impress his Turkic cousin with his own royalty and power. Tahmasp offered assistance to Humayun only if the latter would convert to Shiaism and promise to hand over Kandahar to the former after its reconquest.

11. Usually a critic of these rulers, Badayuni has special praise for Sher Shah and his deeds. To him, Sher Shah would keenly protect the lives of his soldiers and subjects and was able to implement an unprecedented level of peace in the countryside where even an elderly woman with a pot full of gold coins could undertake a journey free of being waylaid. For more on Sher Shah, see I.H. Siddiqi, *History of Sher Shah Sur* (Aligarh: P.C. Dwadas Shreni, 1971).

12. For an official contemporary account, see Abul Fazl, *Akbar Nama*, or, *The Institutes of the Emperor Akber*, translated by Francis Gladwin, London: Routledge, 2000 (reprint).

13. Irfan Habib, *The Agrarian System of Mughal India* (London: Asia Publishing House, 1963); Ishtiaq H. Qureshi, *The Administration of the Mughal Empire* (Patna: N. V. Publications, 1973).

14. S.A.A. Rizvi, *Religious and Intellectual History of the Muslims in Akbar's Reign* (New Delhi: Munshiram Manoharlal, 1975).

15. Fatehpur Sikri's *Buland Darwaza*, the grand entrance, has an inscription saying: "The world is a bridge: pass over it, but do not build a house upon it."

16. Three Jesuit missionaries visited Akbar's court in succession and held debates with the emperor and other religious priests. In 1580, Akbar had been influenced by Zoroastrianism and followed Parsi rituals of fire worship.

17. Abraham Early, p. 169.

18. In 1619, some Jats attacked Akbar's impressive mausoleum in Fatehpur Sikri and destroyed all the graves. This brutal desecration did not spare even Akbar's remains, which were set afire and thrown into the river.

19. Nur-ud-Din Muhammad Jahangir, *Tuzk-i-Jahangiri*, translated by A. Rogers and H. Beveridge (London: Royal Asiatic Society, 1909–1914).

20. Hawkins and Roe represented the East India Company at the Mughal court, Xavier was a Jesuit priest with easy access to the emperor, and Tavernier was a contemporary French jeweler-merchant in India.

21. "They were a perfect pair, her strength firming up Jahangir and reassuring him of his self-worth." Abraham Early, p. 275. Even the English emissary, Thomas Roe, could not remain unimpressed by their mutual dependence and faithfulness.

22. Located between these two Mughal tombs in Shahdara stands the mausoleum of Asif Khan, Shah Jahan's father-in-law and Nur Jahan's brother.

23. For more on the history and religion of Sikhs, see Khushwant Singh, *A History of Sikhs, 1469–1839*, Volume I (Delhi: Oxford University Press, 1977) (reprint).

24. The Shalimar Gardens in Lahore, Shish Mahal inside the Lahore Fort, Chauburji in Lahore, the Wah Gardens near Hasan Abdal, and the beautiful Mughal Mosque in Thatta—in the vicinity of historic Makli—are some of the known Mughal buildings in Pakistan symbolizing the glorious past in the arts. For more on this subject, see Catherine B. Asher, *Architecture of Mughal India* (Cambridge: Cambridge University Press, 1992).

25. For various aspects of economy in Mughal India, see Tapan Raychaudhuri and Irfan Habib (eds.), *Cambridge Economic History of India*, Volume I (Delhi: Orient Longman, 1992).

26. Some of the observations by Mannuci and Bernier have been challenged by other historians, so their travel accounts have to be read with great care as they may be prone to exaggeration and some personal bias. Both of them visited India toward the end of Shah Jahan's tenure and, without any direct

access to the court, depended on rumors and gossip in the bazaars. However, they still offer some important information on the contemporary Mughal life styles.

27. Abraham Early, p. 313.

28. Roshan Ara, the other sister, favored Aurengzeb.

29. See Irfan Habib.

30. John F. Richards, pp. 290–297.

31. For more details, see M. Athar Ali, *The Mughal Nobility under Aurengzeb* (New Delhi: Oxford University Press, 2006).

5

The British Rule and the Independence Movements

The evolution of British control over south Asia has been a gradual process, embodying a complex interplay of forces of change and continuity, and of modernity and tradition. Acquisition of "the jewel in the crown"[1] was not a master stroke of superhuman dimensions, nor did Britain and India sleep-walk into it. It was certainly a historical development in which a powerful European force, appearing at an opportune hour and equipped with appropriate strategy and technology, was able to benefit from a prevailing drift and divisions in an otherwise vast subcontinent of diverse cultures. Similar fate was to fall on several other continents and communities where colonization was destined to begin a new era of unevenness in world history.[2] Within the subcontinent, the British influences, especially during the nineteenth century and more so after the Revolt of 1857, unleashed various imprints and registered complex responses to colonization. South Asia's reaction initially reflected curiosity and interest, whereas anger and sorrow characterized the collective attitudes during the nineteenth century. Hurt, humiliation, and a sense of loss, however, gradually led to introspection. In general, South Asians cooperated with the British government in several areas, but were also opposed to cultural and political hegemony. They rejected modernizations such as missionaries, the English language, modern education, natural sciences, and industrialization that the British and other Western influences introduced. This phase became more obvious around the mid-nineteenth century, but registered increase in polarity after 1858, when India found itself at a crossroads of old and new. Reform, rejection, and revivalism were some of the strategies that Indian Muslims adopted in their quest for self-definition. These cultural and ideological perspectives later assumed political shapes during the twentieth century. One of those responses, as articulated by political parties such as the All-India-Muslim League (AIML), sought a territorial solution to the Muslim predicament by demanding a separate Muslim state. Many others from religious or regional backgrounds thought a united and free India, after all, might still ensure their cultural and political well-being.[3] This ideological parting of ways—either seeking a separate homeland or staying with the rest in one homeland—divided Muslim opinions until the British departure in 1947.

At another level, the growing cultural awareness among Indians of various ethnic, regional, and ideological persuasions became a suprareligious nationalist creed, which was advocated by the Indian National Congress (INC). This mainstream political party sought India's independence within the framework of one country and single nationhood, over and above religiocultural diversities.[4] Most INC members and leaders were from India's majority community of upper caste Hindus. There were also parties such as Mahasabha and Akali Dal, who, like many Muslims, felt that India's religious and demographic realities had to be considered while deciding its political future. In other words, the demands for a Hindu-dominated India or a Muslim-dominated Pakistan confronted the INC's unitary form of nationalism. Thus it is important to keep in mind the plurality of movements and ideas at work before the dissolution of the Raj while also focusing on the question of whether the Partition was inevitable. In the same vein, grand narratives on India's unity, or the lack of it; stipulation about Britain solely creating and arranging the community politics in some mischievous ways to fit in with the idea of "divide and rule"; or the colonial state engineering the very concept of Indian nationalism(s) do not aptly explain a complex situation. In this chapter, we discuss the consolidation of the British conquest of the subcontinent and the subsequent processes, movements, and personalities that led to independence in 1947. Within the various realms of an ever-growing history of South Asia,[5] however, issues of the establishment of the Raj, formulation of community politics, and the coming of independence account for significant themes. In that sense, the making of Pakistan is a complex and even more vital development than what is sometimes acknowledged.[6]

When Vasco de Gama, the Portuguese sailor, reached Calicut on the west Indian coast in 1498, Babur had become the king of Kabul and, like his great grandfather, Tamerlane, planned on conquering the Indus regions and Hindustan. The rise of Portuguese power across the Indian Ocean coincided with the prominence of the Mughal dynasty, although the latter was strictly land-based and mainly depended on land revenue, whereas the former flourished on trade. Given the deficit of silver in India, however, Mughals were the indirect beneficiaries of the Portuguese presence, although Akbar was wary of their encroachments and had even corresponded with the Safawid Shah Abbas to unite in expelling the Portuguese from the Indian Ocean. In fact, it was the coastal princely states such as Bijapur and Gujarat, and not just the Arabs, who put up a serious resistance to the Portuguese. The Portuguese and the Spaniards enjoyed their unchallenged monopoly over international trade until 1588, when, after the defeat of Armada, England began to rival other European nations such as Holland and France. Spices, herbs, tea, opium, slaves, silk, ceramics, and other commodities found their way into Europe and the Western Hemisphere, whereas tobacco, silver, beans, coffee, and other exotic products from the New World were introduced to people elsewhere. The union of seven Dutch provinces in 1579 and the formation of the East India Company in 1600 opened a new chapter in European commerce with the East by using sea routes, newly mapped after the Ottoman conquest of Constantinople in 1453. The exploratory visits to India by William Hawkins and Thomas Roe during the reign of Emperor Jahangir resulted in the opening of British factories on the coast at a time when the English began to assert their naval supremacy both on the Atlantic and Indian Oceans. The East India Company's private enterprise had royal support and protection and gradually led to the construction of its offices, stores, and dwellings in towns like Calcutta, Madras, and Bombay.[7] Initial English attitudes toward the Indians were based on curiosity and respect, and, unlike the Portuguese, the English avoided forcibly converting locals to Christianity. They were certainly wary of the ambitious French East India Company, which had been an official venture of the rival French monarchy, and more than the Spanish and Dutch, was intent on making its overseas presence felt.

FORMATION OF THE BRITISH RAJ IN A FRAGMENTED INDIA

The steady decline of central authority in Delhi; independence of Deccan, Awadh, Bengal, and Gujarat from the Mughal Empire during the 1720s; and the growth of further disputes all over India promoted French and English territorial expansion.[8] A large section of central and eastern Deccan separated itself from the Mughal Empire under a Muslim general. He took charge of a predominantly Hindu region known today as Madhya Pradesh. Based at the southern city of Hyderabad, the ruler never designated himself as a king but only a Nizam or Nawab (viceroy); and the princely state, quite shrewdly, maneuvered its autonomous identity well until 1948. Successive Nizams sided with the British against the French and other regional antagonists, but through alliances and similar diplomatic strategies, they kept Marathas and the Sultans of Karnataka and Mysore at bay.[9] Saadat Khan, another Mughal courtier, sought independence of a vast region in the Gangetic Valley, and, with its headquarters in Lucknow, he named his princely possession Awadh. The Nawab of Awadh retained a powerful influence on the Mughal king in Delhi. The princely state of Awadh was officially a Shia principality and aided the spread of Urdu poetry and a unique urban culture, although given its chronic internal weaknesses, it remained dependent on the East India Company until it was annexed in 1856.[10]

The third region to secede from Mughal Delhi was Bengal, a prosperous territory whose revenues kept Aurengzeb's military campaigns afloat until, like Hyderabad and Awadh, its provincial governor designated himself as the Nawab of Bengal, Assam, and Orissa. Calcutta, the headquarters of the British East India Company, happened to be in Bengal, and the successive Nawabs often had thorny relations with the Company officials. The Company's first major territorial expansion took place in Bengal; it was a cold-blooded acquisition that was marked by the exploitative squeeze of the court, as well as of ordinary peasantry. Farther south, Madras, adjoining the Nizam's state of Hyderabad, housed a safe and secure Fort George that facilitated Company's access to factionalist political forces across Deccan. A similar arrangement in the enclave of Bombay, surrounded by Maratha and other maritime princely states, ensured the Company's secure commerce and naval movements across the Indian Ocean. A strong navy accustomed to "gunboat diplomacy" (especially after humbling other European rivals) ensured secure trade and the accompanying political clout. Bombay and Surat, in fact, facilitated British vigilance of Gujarat and the Maratha confederacy in addition to linking up with Madras and Calcutta to ensure sufficient military muscle against Mysore or Bengal. Thus by the mid-eighteenth century, India had once again become a patchwork of principalities that persisted by the weakening of the central Mughal authority, and they mostly pursued their own local interests while staying vulnerable to European predominance. By developing a dependency relationship with the British, however, these numerous states, in several cases, escaped forced integration, although their own internal administration was wrought with corruption and autocracy.

After the Persian invasion in 1739 and the Third Battle of Panipat in 1760, India reverted to its usual schismatic politics, allowing the French and English an open arena for pitting Indian principalities against one another. On the eve of the Seven Years War (1756–1763), as the French and the British wrestled over their influence and possession in the Atlantic and Indian regions, the East India

Company reinforced Fort Williams in Calcutta with fresher supplies and more troops. Apprehensive of the growing power of the mercantile interests, the new Nawab of Bengal, Sirajud Daula (1737–1757) sent a punitive expedition against the East India Company in Calcutta in 1756. His troops rounded up a number of Europeans and detained about 100 of them. About 50 of these interned Europeans did not survive the heat and confinement in what is known as "the black hole of Calcutta," arousing serious retaliation by the Company. Led by an ambitious clerk, Robert Clive (1725–1774), the East India Company's well-armed forces headed toward the Nawab's capital, Murshidabad. Before the start of the hostilities, Clive and his associates secretly built up alliances with some of Nawab's close relatives and ministers by promising money and other benefits and thus were able to cause divisions in his ranks. By gaining the support of Nawab's influential advisors such as Mir Jaafar, the Company defeated Sirajud Daula at Plassey in 1757 and gained vast territories and rights to levy revenues in various regions of Bengal and Orissa. The Company's hold on Calcutta was assured and Mir Jaafar became the new Nawab, but only after draining his own treasury by offering gifts and prizes to Clive and other Company officials. Corruption became so endemic that the unscrupulous Nawab's exchequer could not meet the newer demands, and Jaafar was soon replaced by Mir Qasim, another claimant to the throne. When Mir Qasim tried to assert his authority by imposing a small tax on the Company (9% for the Company in contrast to 40% for its Indian counterparts), he was stringently rebuffed and sought refuge with the Nawab of Awadh. An aging Mir Jaafar was once again appointed to head Bengal, although the Company had already become a de facto power in eastern India. The crestfallen Nawab of Bengal, Mir Qasim, sought a common front with the Nawab of Oudh and the Mughal Emperor, Shah Alam II, who also had been camping in Awadh because of the Abdali's invasion of Hindustan.

Shujaud Daula, the Nawab of Awadh, felt humiliated by the Company's unilateral dominance, and the Mughal monarch had his own reasons to forge an alliance with the Nawabs to take on the Company's forces, which had been emboldened after their early victory. The Battle of Buxar in 1764 in Bihar sealed the fate of these Indian allies once and for all, as Clive defeated them and squeezed further radical concessions from his crestfallen opponents. This battle transformed the Company into the most significant military and political force in India at a time when the English had been finally winning over France in the Seven Years War, which was being concurrently fought in Europe, North America, and India. The East India Company, now named as the Company *Bahadur* (brave) by the defeated and dependent Mughal crown, had come of age, although corruption among its officials knew no bounds. They were eager to build up their own personal riches and fiefdoms. The moral and economic plight of the East India Company led to parliamentary legislation in 1773, as well as the trials of Robert Clive, who saw himself as the architect of an emerging British Empire in India. The new governor, Warren Hastings (1773–1785) tried to reform the Company's revenues and established a judicial system patterned on the British style. Fond of Indian learning and languages and also aiming to facilitate a growing need for Indian clerks and translators, he established Fort Williams College in Calcutta, where leading British scholars such as Sir William Jones interacted with their south Asian counterparts. In his pursuit of centralization and westernization, however, Hastings lost many friends. Because of his treatment of many Indian ruling families, he had to face a well-publicized parliamentary trial led by Edmund Burke. To help a faltering East India Company and to subsidize wars in the south, Hastings had demanded huge financial contributions from the Nawab of Awadh, Nizam, and others. Hastings looked the other way when Shujaud Daula used force in Rohilkhand, and, averse to a pledge to help Awadh financially in case of any Maratha attack, did not comply. A merciless massacre of thousands of innocent inhabitants of Rohilkhand by a vengeful Nawab went unchecked by the Company forces.

In a similar and rather disreputable move, Hastings, prompted by the Company's financial needs and in view of the revolt by the American colonies, saw Benares as a prosperous town and incited its Hindu elite to revolt against the Nawab of Awadh, although Benares also had a sizable Muslim population. The Hindu-Muslim divide and a nod from Hastings led to a declaration by Chait Singh as the independent Raja of Benares. He also agreed to pay 2,500,000 pounds in annual tribute to the Company for ensuring the territorial security of his principality. In 1778, the tribute was unilaterally doubled. When the Raja failed to make the payments, he was overthrown and Benares was annexed by Hastings. In the same vein, Hastings, in pursuit of money, used heavy-handedness against the Awadh Begums, the widow and mother of Shujaud Daula, who had died in 1775. Under the existing arrangements, the Company controlled the finances of this princely state and, when prodded by the new Nawab, Asifud Daula, Hastings pressured the Begums to surrender their personal wealth.

During the closing decades of the eighteenth century, the Company faced opposition from the Sultans of Mysore—Hyder Ali and Tipu Sultan—who, more than any other Hindu or Muslim rulers, put up a strong resistance to the expansion of British power in India. Hyder Ali (1722–1782) was a Moplah Muslim from Mysore, who rose to a senior command position and eventually became the ruler of this southern state. His adoption of European military tactics and weaponry helped him subdue his southern neighbor. The princely state of Karnataka was ruled by a Muslim sultan who had been dependent on the Company for trade and naval protection. Hyder Ali soon developed problems with Company officials garrisoned in Madras and, in a battle in

1769, defeated them. His third victory was over the Marathas. He considered Marathas to be a threat to his state and thus entered into peace treaties with the Company and the rulers of Karnataka and Hyderabad. He restored the territory and privileges of the defeated Company on assurance that it would help him in case of Maratha invasion of Mysore. In 1771, when the Marathas attacked Mysore, the Company backtracked from its agreement, but Hyder Ali was still able to withstand the Maratha assault. When Hastings assumed power in 1772, Hyder Ali forged an alliance with the French, who were then based on the island of Mauritius. In 1779, Hyder Ali defeated the British contingent in Karnataka and expected a full-blown British retaliation. Before allowing a large-scale invasion of Mysore, Warren Hastings applied his secretive diplomatic skills and struck deals with the Nizam and Marathas to isolate Hyder Ali. Consequently, Hyder Ali was defeated in 1781 and died a year later but advised Tipu Sultan, his son and successor, to seek out a peace treaty with the British.

Tipu Sultan was aware of growing British power in India, as well as of Britain's invincible naval power. He sought help from other Indian princes and even sent emissaries abroad to France and Turkey. Despite some early victories and a heroic defiance, an isolated Tipu Sultan finally confronted the Company's forces at Seringapattam in 1799 and was killed fighting along with many of his loyal comrades.[11] This was the last major battle of the late-eighteenth century that added a major feather in the crown of Governor-General Richard Wellesley (1798–1805). Earlier, the Peshwas and the princely state of Hyderabad ruled by the Nizam had been turned into subordinate vassals by Hastings and his successor, Lord Charles Cornwallis (1786–1793). Despite his surrender to American revolutionaries, Lord Cornwallis was an aristocrat with a military background who was determined to turn the Company's army into a professional fighting force based on European style. In addition, he prohibited private gifts and businesses conducted by Company officials and ensured the separation of commerce, administration, and military, basically further Europeanizing all the major services. Cornwallis's policies of permanent land settlement were meant to ascertain a steady supply of revenue from Bengal, but they severely impoverished the local inhabitants.

Supported by Westminster during the Napoleonic era, the East India Company was seen as the right arm of British power overseas and had been benefiting from its trade with China, Africa, Europe, and North America. Imbued with greater self-pride and a global profile, British officials segregated themselves from the Indians and even looked down on some of their colleagues donning Indian clothes and marrying Indian women (*Bibis*).[12] Imperial, racial, and cultural pride was further refurbished by military and political victories. Napoleon's defeat and the rise of a messianic fervor underwrote contemporary self-righteousness, although some British utilitarians sought to pressure the Company into investing its profits in educating Indians. An unbridled moralization and self-commendation underwrote the attitudes of British officials across the empire and, despite the abolition of the slave trade in 1807, contemporary enthusiasm for colonization never slackened. Instead, as seen in the expansionist policies of governors such as Wellesley[13] and Minto,[14] or in Macaulay's well-known *Minutes* on education in 1835, Britain was perceived to be performing a historic and divinely ordained job in India. The arrival of missionaries and input from utilitarianism was reflected in official polices and works by historians such as John Stuart Mills. India symbolized the entire East—decadent, backward, and divisive—that needed Western political, cultural, and moral energies for its regeneration. The enslavement and shipment of millions of slaves, the opium trade subjecting millions to addiction, and the elimination of indigenous peoples did not deter any such self-congratulatory attitudes, which were further bolstered during the long Victorian Era, when Britain was not merely a sea giant but also an intercontinental power.

REFORMS AND EXPANSION IN THE INDUS LANDS

By the second decade of the 1800s, the East India Company was largely encumbered by periodic parliamentary laws and gradually overshadowed by several other competitive interests. It controlled vast regions in the subcontinent but still shied away from investing heavily in education, health, and social welfare, although a growing number of Indians espoused a proactive reformism. To the credit of Lord William Bentinck (1828–35), however, a whole raft of socioeducational reforms and institution building was introduced in India, receiving support from reformers such as Raja Ram Mohan Roy (1774–1833). Roy, a Bengali thinker and founder of the Hindu reformist Brahmo Samaj, was a well-traveled advocate of the modernization of India. William Bentinck had been to India as a young man. In 1803, at age 29, he was appointed governor of Madras. His tenure had been rocky, as he faced a revolt by Indian sepoys as a result of his ban on turbans and beards; and after the suppression of defiant soldiers, he rescinded the orders. Before his return to India as the governor-general in 1828, he had been transformed by Jeremy Bentham's utilitarianism and followed it to its letters during his term. He banned *satti* (the burning of Hindu widows), outlawed child sacrifice prevalent in some areas of Rajputana, and appointed Colonel Sleeman to control the menace of *thugee* (banditry), which was quite widespread in some regions. His emphasis on education and reforms and not on expansion and profit helped ameliorate social life in India. His work was carried on by many other senior administrators such as Sir Thomas Munro in Madras,

Mountstuart Elphinston in western India, and Sir Charles Metcalfe in Delhi and adjacent regions.

The zeal for changing India through modern education received a major impetus from the advice of Lord Thomas Babington Macaulay. Brimming with enthusiasm, the famous English historian found nothing useful in the entire Eastern scholarship and instead urged for modern Western education to produce well-educated westernized Indians (often derisively called *Babus*), who would help operate offices while staying loyal to the empire. He had served on the Supreme Council of India during 1834–1838, and his notes merited serious attention, for despite their Orientalist, derogatory, attitude, they radically changed the course of education and elite formation in south Asia. He advocated equality among Indians and Europeans before the law but derided Eastern languages and learning, because his idealism was derived from the prospect of turning Indians into Englishmen. Politics, education, administrative reforms, missionary work, and gradual industrialization were the hallmark of this pre-1857 era of reforms, but they produced mixed responses from a variety of Indians.

An important phase in the British expansion in Hindustan, Indus regions, and across the Passes happened under Lords Auckland, Ellenborough, and Dalhousie, who had no qualms in using both force and diplomacy to add more territories to the empire. Factors such as the heightened emphasis on colonial expansion, a perceived threat from an expansionist Russia leading to "the Great Game," and blind overconfidence in gaining more prestige and extensive territories underwrote this colonial sentiment.[15] Such an expansion had its own costs and benefits, but despite some local resistance at places like Punjab, Afghanistan, and Sindh, the Company was able to implement its unilateralism on regions that currently make up Pakistan and Afghanistan. Afghanistan, however, refused to be subdued, whereas a vanquished Punjab was soon won over by the Company and proved quite beneficial during the stormy days of 1857. After Sindh was annexed in 1843, it was joined with the province of Bombay, and Kashmir was sold to a Hindu raja in 1847. Except for areas around Quetta and the road connecting it with Sindh, the rest of Balochistan was reaffirmed as a loyal tribal territory. Such diverse yet crucial political and administrative engineering further catapulted the Company into a leading role as an imperial power, also bringing Britain closer to vital central Asia.

Under Lord George Eden Auckland (1836–1842) and Lord Edward Law Ellenborough (1842–1844), the British East India Company had been able to benefit from its formidable position in imposing its writ on Persia and even Afghanistan, albeit with costly effects. After the signing of a friendship treaty with Ranjeet Singh (1780–1839) in Punjab and the deposing of an Afghan king,

Shah Shuja now living in exile in India, the Company's forces attacked Kabul in 1839 and captured vast territories. The British had been apprehensive of a possible Russian expansion toward India and the Indian Ocean and suspected that the Shah of Persia had secretly collaborated with the czars. It is not a surprise that for the next century, Moscow proved a major preoccupation for strategists in London and India. Despite defeating Dost Muhammad Khan and the installation of a pliant Shah Shuja in Kabul, Afghanistan continued to elude pacification. Soon the Afghans rose in rebellion and, by mounting guerrilla attacks, caused multiple causalities among British troops. In a major assault in 1841, the Afghans wiped out the entire British force of 14,000 troops, and the British retreated toward India though the passes. Auckland's forward policy had proven costly, resulting in his recall. His successor, Lord Ellenborough, used flimsy pretexts and displayed opportunism to send troops into Sindh, which was ruled by the local chieftains—amirs—whose defeat was ensured after several battles. In 1843, Sindh became part of British India and the British slowly began to penetrate farther into the interiors of Balochistan.

Under Ranjeet Singh, Punjab had proved to be a stable buffer state and the Sutlej River had been agreed on as a common boundary between the Company's territories and those of the Maharaja of Punjab. The Maharaja, a practicing Sikh, expanded his kingdom north and west by conquering Kashmir and the trans-Indus regions, and by using Muslim elite and Persian as a lingua franca he had ensured some legitimacy, although he had to confront armed defiance during 1828–1830 when some Muslim revivalists declared Jihad (holy war) in the Frontier region. Ranjeet Singh built a strong army by employing European generals and trainers, but after his death the Lahore state was riddled with conflicting loyalties. Lord Hardinge (1844–1848), the governor-general, accused the Sikh troops of invading the Company's territories across the river and ordered troop deployment. After several battles in Punjab in 1845, most of the Sikh forces surrendered to the Company. Under the Treaty of Amritsar of 1846, Kashmir and eastern regions were ceded to the Company, and the Lahore court also agreed to pay 500,000 pounds in indemnity. The Company, desirous of seeking more monetary benefits and not ready to take on the responsibility of a vast region like Kashmir, sold off Kashmir for 100,000 pounds to a Hindu chieftain, Gulab Singh. This official in the Sikh administration had been secretly collaborating with the British during the hostilities, which enraged many Sikh generals who rose in revolt. The Second Anglo-Sikh War of 1849 occurred when Lord James Ramsay Dalhousie (1848–1856) headed British India, and it resulted in the defeat of the Sikh forces followed by the integration of Punjab and the Frontier into British India.[16] Soon the Sikhs were offered jobs in the army along with the restoration of their agricultural lands, which helped the Company win them over. Sir John Lawrence, the commissioner of Lahore, administered Punjab by forging contacts with the landlords and local influential persons, whose loyalty would benefit the British during the Uprising of 1857.[17] The annexation of the Indus Valley in 1849 was followed by the amalgamation of the princely states of Awadh and Jhansi, much to the chagrin of their respective ruling families, as an expansionist Dalhousie was determined to terminate the patchwork of principalities dotting the entire subcontinent.

REBELLION OF 1857 AND THE "HIGH NOON" OF EMPIRE

The Revolt of 1857 has often been called "Mutiny" or "Sepoy Revolt" by the British administrators and analysts; for the nationalist south Asians it was the first "War of Independence" when cross sections of people in the northern subcontinent rose to vent their frustration against an overpowering, alien, and often indifferent Raj. It is true that Karl Marx had supported British colonialism in India. He believed that this would transform a largely agrarian and feudal society into a pseudo-capitalist one so as to inadvertently prepare it for an ultimate proletariat revolution. Marx might have been thinking of the enormity of villages where local and caste-based loyalties disallowed any common ideological or class-based front that could be attributed to an urban, industrial environment.[18] The leftist historians in India and elsewhere, however, would see in the Uprising of 1857 symptoms of anti-imperial resistance articulated in the form of a peasant rebellion.

In any case, the revolt was certainly a historical event with several factors including a controversy over new gun cartridges, and proved a watershed in British Indian history. It made London more sensitive to the tenable nature of the Indian empire that could not be left to the discretion of a trading company; India soon came under the direct control of the British crown. Queen Victoria was officially named as the Empress of India and studied Urdu from her specially imported Indian assistant. Parliament now took complete responsibility for legislation in India, and a cabinet minister called the secretary of state shared colonial administration with a viceroy based in Calcutta. India's educational and industrial development gathered momentum after 1858, and some administrative and military reforms were inducted to overhaul the system. A growing number of Indians had been acquiring higher education in modern academic institutions and accounted for a newly formed middle class of westernized professionals seeking better opportunities and status for themselves. After 1857, some British also pushed for greater Indian co-option even if only in an advisory role so that the Raj could change its image as an alien conqueror. Areas like Punjab and Sindh underwent extensive irrigational development, and farming parents sought social status by sending their sons to join the rank and file of an ever-expanding British army.

Traditional resentment against the British had been pervasive at various levels and not merely confined to religious elements among Muslims and Hindus. The landowners or *talukadars* and the rulers of the erstwhile princely states that were already conquered or were apprehensive of impending annexation carried a deeper grudge against forcible integration, and many traditional moneyed sections felt dislocated with new classes forming as a result of modernization. The Indian peasants felt the burden of heavy revenue owing to the Company's warfare, and a stagnant agricultural sector was brimming with resentment. In a powerful way, the print industry had been feeding into awareness among the concerned sections on India's subordination by a smaller group of Europeans whose lifestyle, complexion, religion, language, and statecraft were new and foreign. The English language and Christianity were two powerful expressions of this new hegemonic culture that pushed many people toward defiance or introversion. The rulers and the court elite of Awadh, whose state had been recently annexed in 1856, were as upset with the Company's irreverent attitude as were the Rani of Jhansi, Rohillas of Bundel Khand, and the Maratha Peshwas of western India.[19] In Punjab, Sikhs had certainly been pacified but not the Muslim elite in Bengal, Awadh, and Delhi, who found themselves caught between several hostile forces. The Mughal Emperor, Bahadur Shah Zafar (1775–1862) was aware of his serious dependency on the Raj and, at an advanced age, could foresee the end of a proud Mughal dynasty, although his family desired to carry on the legacy even if it was just a token. Zafar's regime was not merely confined to Delhi but also to the Red Fort where he led an ordinary life, busying himself in artistic and scholarly pursuits while hundreds of members of the royal family known as Salateen lived like beggars in the inner quarters.[20] They were not allowed to venture outside their confined premises and the fort was a pathetic case in helplessness and poverty. Queen Zinat Mahal (1821–1882), the youngest among royal wives and the mother of Mirza Jawan Bakht (1841–1884), the youngest among the emperor's sons, desired her son's succession to the throne over and above elder heirs while the domineering Company officials stationed in Delhi pursued their own preferences.[21]

The initial contingents of rebels coming into Delhi from Bihar, Awadh, and other places pleaded to Emperor Zafar to lead them against the Company. Amidst a charged atmosphere, one noticed camaraderie between the Hindus and Muslims during the summer of 1857. The British troops and dependents at Kanpur, Lucknow, and Benares had been mostly killed by the rebels, whereas Delhi came under their active control for a while with the British forces retreating to the Ridge, outside the Mughal capital. They waited for fresh troops and supplies from Punjab to relieve them from their predicament. The eldest sons of the emperor and some Muslim generals such as Bakht Khan tried to instill discipline among the rebels, but problems in logistics, weaponry, and resources soon began to lower resistance. Several efforts to take the Ridge failed, and although in the long, hot summer of 1857 the besieged British suffered from illnesses, food shortage, and falling morale, they never surrendered. The arrival of fresh Punjabi troops and reinforcement from Calcutta eventually tilted the balance decisively in the Company's favor, enabling it to capture Delhi, Lucknow, and several other places from rebels. As recorded by contemporary prominent Muslim intellectuals, including Syed Ahmed Khan (1817–1898)[22] and Mirza Asadullah Khan Ghalib (1797–1869),[23] the fighting exacted a major toll from the Indian Muslims. The emperor was put on a bullock cart to be exiled to Rangoon with his immediate family, and all his grown sons had been executed in cold blood, as were most of the Muslim residents of Delhi and such other places where rebels had retained a visible presence. At times, it appeared that the Rebellion of 1857 had been openly and solely attributed to Muslims who bore the brunt of retaliation, as well as enduring hostilities for decades to come.[24] A greater sense of loss, economic underdevelopment, and ethnic divisions characterized Muslim attitudes across India, but for many other Indian communities, readjustment to the new political and cultural realities was not so hard.[25]

After 1857, a new aristocratic class of British administrators ran India at a higher level, and a district marked the basic unit of this large empire where, other than revenue collection, younger members of the Indian Civil Service (ICS) gained their initial knowledge of Indian cultures, peoples, and climates. British India featured a highly centralized administration that benefited from a newly furbished class of local intermediaries—tribal and rural landholders—while at the lower level local clerks ran the complex imperial machine.[26] Other than revenue collection and maintenance of law and order by the ICS, the Indian army also evolved into a strong arm of imperial policies dealing with western and eastern Asia. Its regiments would be housed in specially built suburban cantonments, away from the traditional population centers. The military officers all came from Britain, whereas most of the soldiers were "volunteers" who would never rise beyond junior noncommissioned ranks. Learning lessons from the Uprising of 1857, a more rigorous and vigilant organization of the regiments was undertaken in which a set of symbols and insignia mingled with the regimental and caste-based pride to solidify Indian loyalty to British defense and colonial imperatives.[27] During the Victorian Era when wars were quite frequent all over the empire, Indian troops played a crucial role in obtaining the required results for Britain.[28] The Indian forces captured Burma in the 1870s and later undertook another invasion of Afghanistan, as the expansionist British Prime Minister Disraeli feared Russian expansion toward Afghanistan and India. In 1874, Disraeli urged the viceroy, Lord Northbrook (1872–1876), to undertake a forward policy on Afghanistan, although the latter tried unsuccessfully to dissuade the British prime minister and eventually resigned.

The new viceroy, Lord Lytton (1876–1880), dispatched an army contingent across the passes to capture Kabul, as the Amir of Kabul, Sher Ali—the son of late Dost Muhammad Khan—was accused of maintaining secret liaisons with the Russians. Faced with a frontal attack in 1878 amid the Second Anglo-Afghan war, Sher Ali fled to central Asia and died within a few months. The British imposed a humiliating treaty on Afghans in addition to stationing a watchful resident in Kabul. Yaqub Khan, Sher Ali's son, was accepted as the new Amir, but he could not meet all the harsh conditions of the new treaty, and in the process, the Afghans rose in rebellion and assassinated the British resident. A punitive campaign was sent from India, but history was to repeat itself in Afghanistan where a quick conquest, followed by short-lived peace, would succumb to resolute guerrilla attacks by an immensely independent Afghan population. The British remained suspicious and wary of the Afghans until Amir Abdur Rahman, Sher Ali's nephew, became the new king and, through some sagacious moves, retained the sovereignty of his country, also keeping both the British and Russians at bay. The exaggerated fears of a Russian threat and the Pushtun revolt pushed both the British government and Kabul toward negotiations over border delineation. Sir Mortimer Durand, the foreign secretary of the Indian government, was assigned the task of border demarcation. In 1893, the Indo-Afghan borders, also known as the Durand Line, were established, adding Bajaur, Khyber, Kurram, and Wazir and Mahsud regions to British India. Here in these border tracts four semiautonomous tribal agencies were formed and administered by British political agents who, through special favors and courts, won over local chieftains. In addition, the tribal khans were allowed to run local administration on their own through customary laws, also protecting roads and British convoys heading toward the military posts guarding the borders. In addition, Britain obtained control of Chitral and Gilgit, which brought the former in the neighborhood of Sinkiang, controlled by China. From time to time, Pushtun Muslim clerics and disgruntled khans would rise in rebellion against the Raj. The most serious of these occurred in Tirah in 1896–1897, resulting in the largest military campaign ever undertaken by Britain between the Crimean War and World War I. These newly acquired areas were ceded to the province of Punjab until, in 1901, Lord Curzon designated the trans-Indus territory as a separate frontier region. In 1947, Pakistan inherited the settled land as well as the tribal regions that had been named as the North-West Frontier Province (NWFP).

THE INDIAN NATIONAL CONGRESS AND THE ALL-INDIA MUSLIM LEAGUE

Education, economic uplift (especially in urban areas owing to trade and professionalization), and modern means of communication such as English, railways, postal and telegraph systems, newspapers, and books strengthened the ideas of "Indianness" among a growing middle class. Many of these businessmen, reformers, educationists, and lawyers had studied in modern schools and desired equality before law while sharing bonds beyond the traditional boundaries of class, creed, and caste. The British state, in the meantime, through its hierarchical categorization of Indians in census surveys and other official gazetteers, had also helped regiment the parallel concept of community formation.[29] Although the Indian modernists and reformers felt no qualms in accepting modern education and several Western norms, many traditional elements among Hindus, Muslims, Sikhs, and others preferred a back-to-roots approach. Nevertheless, Lord Ripon's induction of a limited concept of local government such as municipal boards operated by locally elected Indians and headed by British officials in 1882 augured electoral practices that encouraged educated reformers to seek jobs and better opportunities for "natives." Highlighting this sentiment, some retired English servants such as Alan Octavian Hume and his Indian contacts from all over India met in Bombay in December 1885 to form an association of like-minded individuals. Known as the Indian National Congress (INC), its rationale was rooted in forming an effective channel between the British and Indians. Its annual conventions attracted Indians who, while reaffirming their loyalty to the Raj, would moderately seek better prospects for India. Known lawyers and activists such as Dadabhai Naoroji (1825–1917),[30] Surendranath Banerjea (1848–1925),[31] and Gopal Krishna Gokhale (1866–1915)[32] guided the INC for its first two decades until a younger and more vocal generation of nationalists joined its ranks in the early twentieth century. The establishment of the INC does not mean that contemporary India was undergoing some belated golden age; the colonial administration was anchored on a strong sense of moral righteousness, racial superiority, and self-imposed segregation by the Europeans from the rest of the population. Such realities ironically coalesced with widespread poverty and frequent spread of epidemics, as India, under an imperious Lord Curzon, entered the twentieth century.[33] The Japanese victory over Russia in 1905 and the partition of Bengal into two smaller provinces largely resented by Hindu moneyed classes had introduced more dissention and fresh blood in the INC, which gained further intensity during World War I.

In the meantime, a modest package of constitutional reforms known as the Minto-Morley Act of 1909 was being considered for India. This act would establish some modicum of electoral traditions while allocating separate electorates to Muslims. Muslims had been happy over Lord Curzon's division of Bengal in 1905, as they expected landless Muslim peasants to benefit in eastern regions with the decrease in the influence of rich Hindu landlords (*Bhadraloks*). Muslims who had graduated from modern colleges, such as Syed Ahmed Khan's Mohammadan Anglo-Oriental College at Aligarh, desired better prospects for their community and feared Hindu domination of the INC. Expecting the reforms package, several Muslim leaders formed a delegation to visit Lord Minto in Simla in October 1906, apprising him of existing Muslim disadvantages, and lobbied for separate elections and constituencies for Muslims. Two months later, many of these Muslim leaders met again in Dhaka and established the AIML to operate as a Muslim organization for safeguarding the community's economic and political rights. The Minto-Morley Reforms of 1909 allocated separate seats and franchise to Muslims for local bodies and also increased the latter's competence; yet it fell seriously short of Indian expectation.

The INC-led agitation against the partition of Bengal called the Swadeshi movement led to the boycott of European goods and continued until 1911, when the British government, to the dismay of Muslims, annulled the partition of Bengal. In the meantime, educated Indian Muslims began to worry about the political situation in the volatile Balkans, which threatened Muslim minorities, as well as the very existence of a weakened Ottoman Caliphate.[34] In 1913, the AIML was joined by one of the most preeminent Bombay-based lawyers, who not only energized the organization but also attempted to bring it closer to the INC. Muhammad Ali Jinnah (1876–1948), a young and dynamic legal mind pursued successful practice in Bombay and was soon to be known as the ambassador of Hindu-Muslim unity. His entry into the AIML enthused its cadres, although his policies, unlike that of Mahatma Gandhi, avoided agitation and instead depended on negotiations.

Despite the Allied victory in World War I, political activism in India assumed a mass-based dimension as a result of worries about the Ottoman Caliphate, which was defeated during the war. Concurrent with fighting the Turks and imposing further restrictions on political activities in India, Britain had been involved in the Third Anglo-Afghan War, further agitating Muslims on this side of the Khyber Pass.[35] At this juncture, Mahatma Gandhi (1869–1948), known for pacifist politics called *satayagraha*, returned from South Africa and soon began a new phase in mass politics.[36] His campaigns played a decisive role in politicizing Indians from all walks of life. In April 1919, on the eve of the campaign for the restoration of the Caliphate by Muslim leaders, Amritsar witnessed a massacre resulting from the indiscriminate shooting by British troops on a peaceful rally. Gandhi's charisma and nonviolent movement christened itself into noncooperation with the authorities and continued for some time, despite official clampdowns and numerous arrests. By 1922, however, the movement had slackened, and Hindu-Muslim unity over the Caliphate also turned weaker. Earlier, in 1919, another package of reforms known as Montague-Chelmsford Act allocated more powers to the elected assemblies in the provinces, also broadening the Indian franchise without making it universal. As a consequence, provinces now became the arena of competitive politics, and in addition to the INC and the AIML, several regional parties evolved, advocating local solutions and diverting energies from India-wide issues to provincial affairs.

During the 1920s, India presented a plethora of India-wide, provincial, and ideological parties who agreed on the subject of attaining independence but deeply differed over the mechanics and aftermath of independence. In 1927–1928, during the visit by the Simon Commission, a parliamentary fact-finding mission, India again witnessed strikes and a wave of noncooperation, which not only politicized many more Indians, but also added to interparty competition. Gandhi began his own march to the sea in 1930, aiming to abolish the salt tax along with rallying Indians around his demand for *swaraj* (independence) at a time when the British government invited Indian leaders to London to hold talks. These Round Table Conferences were attended by many regional and national leaders including Gandhi, Jinnah, and Muhammad Iqbal (1875–1938). A former Cambridge and Heidelberg student, Iqbal was a distinguished Muslim poet and philosopher who tried to reawaken Indian Muslims toward higher goals, including some form of political sovereignty. In the meantime, one of his contemporaries, Pandit Jawaharlal Nehru (1889–1964), had returned from Cambridge. While following in Gandhi's footsteps, he aimed at reactivating the INC.[37] The Act of 1935 finally came to India while its leaders offered different solutions to a stalemated politics and uncertain future. In pursuance of the act, elections in 11 British Indian provinces gave the INC a clear majority in nine provinces. The AIML's gains remained modest, although it was able to assert itself as the single-most effective voice of south Asian Muslims.[38] The Congress ministers in these provinces failed to win over the confidence of the Muslim political elite, especially those who sought better representation for their community. At this juncture, Jinnah, now the president of the AIML, began holding countrywide rallies to bring more Muslims to his side and strove to improve relations with provincial Muslim leaders.[39]

WORLD WAR II AND PARTITION

The outbreak of hostilities in Europe in September 1939 led to India's entry into World War II, although the viceroy, Lord Linlithgow (1887–1952), did not take the INC leadership into his confidence, especially when it had several ministers in the provinces. During the war years, Mahatma Gandhi advocated agitation against the British government, while another INC faction led by Subhas Chandra Bose (1897–1945) sought independence through an armed struggle and joined hands with the Axis Powers.[40] The INC revolt gained further intensity in 1942 after the Quit-India Movement, as negotiations broke down between Indian leaders and the British delegation led by Sir Stafford Cripps. The British administration in India filled prisons with the striking INC members, and Gandhi, along with Nehru and several other leaders, was jailed. This development allowed Jinnah to reorganize the AIML as the only countrywide Muslim political party. Earlier, in March 1940, the AIML had held its annual convention in Lahore and demanded the territorial rearrangement of the subcontinent, essentially creating the future state of Pakistan. The term *Pakistan* had not been used in this resolution itself, but the media and people identified the Lahore Resolution with the demand for a separate Muslim state in areas where Muslims were in the majority.

Jinnah spoke from an ever-growing sense of strength, as he was being supported by Muslim students, women, and many regional elite such as in Punjab, Bengal, Sindh, the United Provinces, or Uttar Pradesh (UP), and Bombay. In 1944, Jinnah and Gandhi held talks to improve the widening Hindu-Muslim divide and to seek out some common ground regarding independence for India. These talks proved futile, as Gandhi did not accept the idea of a separate Muslim state carved out of India. Gandhi had already resigned from the INC, but he still had widespread support worldwide. His austere lifestyle, espousal of nonviolence, and fasts unto death for political purposes had introduced a new political philosophy, much to the chagrin of Europe's colonial governments. In 1945, political negotiations involving the Viceroy Lord Wavell (1883–1950) and the leaders of the INC and AIML failed to produce a consensus regarding a timeframe for British departure and a subsequent political map of India.[41] The next series of elections in 1946 confirmed the representative character of the AIML as the preeminent Muslim political platform, with the INC still espousing the case for a unified India. With an accentuated polarization between the INC and AIML itself becoming a Hindu-Muslim divide, Britain tried to persuade them to agree to some mutually acceptable framework. A parliamentary delegation led by Lord Pethick-Lawrence, the secretary of state for India, tried to unite Indian leaders on a federal arrangement for an independent India with provinces enjoying full autonomy to the extent of allowing them to decide their ultimate political future. Known as the Cabinet Plan of 1946, it stipulated a weak central government but assertive provinces to form several zones in reference to the religious composition of their population. Despite early receptivity to these proposals, both parties rejected them. Sensitive to an increase in lawlessness and communal violence in India, Clement Attlee (1883–1967), the Labour British prime minister, declared Britain's commitment to leave India by 1948. To facilitate British withdrawal from India, Attlee, in March 1947, named Lord Louis Mountbatten (1900–1979), a member of the British royal family, to head the colonial government. Mountbatten soon found himself in a political dead-end despite his efforts for some consensus among Indian political leaders. He finally decided to partition the British colony into two separate states.[42] Accordingly, a partition plan proposing the division of Punjab and Bengal followed by new boundary demarcation was agreed upon, and all the leaders signed their agreement in June 1947. Eventually, amid the world's largest migration and accompanying mayhem, Pakistan and India emerged as two independent states in their own rights on August 14–15, 1947, respectively.[43] Mountbatten remained the governor-general of India, and Jinnah headed the newly established state of Pakistan.

NOTES

1. For some recent celebratory works, see Lawrence James, *Raj: The Making and Unmaking of British India* (London: Little, Brown, 1997); Niall Ferguson, *Empire: How Britain Made the World* (London: Allen Lane, 2003).

2. Simon Schama, *Rough Crossings: Britain, the Slaves and the American Revolution* (London: BBC, 2003).

3. K. K. Aziz, *The Making of Pakistan: A Study in Nationalism* (London: Chatto and Windus, 1967).

4. Bipin Chandra, *India's Struggle for Independence 1857–1947*(Harmondsworth: Penguin, 1989).

5. Among various interpretations including imperial, nationalist, Muslim, Hinduist and regionalist, the gender and subaltern perspectives have gained greater currency. See Ranjit Guha and Gayatri Chakravorty Spivak (eds.), *Selected Subaltern Studies* (New York: Oxford University Press, 1988).

6. Farzana Shaikh, *Community and Consensus in Islam: Muslim Representation in India, 1860–1947* (Cambridge: Cambridge University Press, 1989); Iftikhar H. Malik, *Islam, Nationalism and the West: Issues of Identity in Pakistan* (Oxford: St. Antony's Series, 1999).

7. Peter J. Marshall, *Problems of Empire: Britain and India 1757–1813* (London: Routledge, 1998).

8. The rulers of these important provinces never titled themselves as sultans or kings but instead preferred to be called nawabs or maharajas. The Maratha confederacy was also headed by a senior minister, known as Peshwa, thus allowing some nominal primacy to the Mughal emperor, who in most cases lacked authority and resources.

9. Omar Khalidi (ed.), *Hyderabad after the Fall* (Wichita: Hyderabad Historical Society, 1988); *Muslims in Deccan: A Historical Survey* (New Delhi: Global Media Publications, 2006).

10. For more on Lucknow culture, see Rosie Llewellyn-Jones, *A Fatal Friendship: the Nawabs, the British, and the City of Lucknow* (Delhi: Oxford University Press, 1992).

11. Both in Indian and Pakistani historiography, Tipu Sultan is seen as a heroic figure who resisted the British and died fighting in 1799. He wrote letters to France, Afghanistan and Ottoman Turkey seeking help against the British

East India Company. His favorite musical instrument—"Tipoo's Tiger"—now with the Royal Victoria and Albert Museum in London, was a wooden implement in the shape of a British Redcoat who is being mauled by a tiger. For many south Asian nationalists, the instrument showed Tipu Sultan's contempt and defiance of foreign rulers. For more on him, see B. Shaik Ali (ed.), *Tipu Sultan: A Great Martyr* (Bangalore: University Press, 1993); *Tipu Sultan: A Study in Diplomacy and Confrontation* (Mysore: Geetha Book House, 1982.

12. For an interesting study on the early phase of British-Indian relationships, see William Dalrymple, *White Mughals: Love and Betrayal in Eighteenth-Century India* (London: HarperCollins, 2002).

13. Wellesley (1798–1805) was a brother of the Duke of Wellington who ensured the acquisition of more territories from Awadh, as well as defeating the Maratha power in 1801. Earlier, in 1799, Tipu Sultan had been defeated and Wellesley ensured that Napoleon would have no friends on east of Egypt.

14. Lord Gilbert Elliot Minto (1807–1813) carried on with the policy of containing the Maratha power besides forging closer alliance with Maharaja Ranjeet Singh in Punjab. The boundaries between Nepal and British India were demarcated after a long phase of hostilities in 1814–1816, when Lord Francis Hastings held the governorship. His acceptance of Gurkha claims on Nepal in 1818 helped forge closer relations with these people, which persist even today to the larger benefit of the United Kingdom.

15. Peter Hopkirk, *The Great Game: On Secret Service in High Asia* (Oxford: Oxford University Press, 1991).

16. Andrew J. Major, *Return to Empire: Punjab under the Sikhs and British in the Mid-Nineteenth Century* (New Delhi, Sterling Publishers, 1996).

17. For further details on the work by the Lawrence Brothers in building the empire, see Harold Lee, *Brothers in the Raj: The Lives of John and Henry Lawrence* (Oxford: Oxford University Press, 2002).

18. Karl Marx was equally critical of the British exploitation of India and thus held two concurrent opinions on the British control of the subcontinent.

19. Tara Chand, a well-known historian, has observed: "It has to be admitted that the war against the British was not inspired by any sentiment of nationalism, for in 1857 India was not yet politically a nation. It is a fact that the Hindus and Muslims co-operated, but the leaders and the followers of the two communities were moved by personal loyalties rather than loyalty to a common motherland." Tara Chand, *The History of Freedom Movement*, Vol. II (Delhi: Ministry of Education, 1972), p. 42; also Percival Spear, *India: A Modern History* (Ann Arbor: University of Michigan Press, 1961).

20. William Dalrymple, *The Last Mughal: The Fall of a Dynasty, Delhi, 1857* (London: Bloomsbury, 2006).

21. For a recent work on 1857, see Saul David, *The Indian Mutiny 1857* (London: Viking, 2006).

22. Syed Ahmed was a prominent Muslim leader whose own family suffered from famine and bloodshed while he escaped as he had been serving as a civil official in Bijnour. He studied the causes of the Indian Revolt and subsequently founded the Muslim college at Aligarh. Many people consider him the most important reformer in Muslim India and even the first architect of Pakistan.

23. The most prominent Urdu poet and known for his Persian writings, Ghalib's letters and verses depict contemporary destruction of Delhi. He escaped because of his personal connections and spent the remaining years of his life lamenting the death of "Old Delhi."

24. Even some contemporary official accounts highlighted serious Muslim grievances that were exacerbated by official revenge. See W.W. Hunter, *The Indian Musalmans: Are They Bound in Conscience to Rebel Against the Queen?* (London: Trubner, 1871).

25. For a comprehensive work in this field, see Thomas Metcalfe, *The Aftermath of Revolt: India, 1857–1870* (Princeton: Princeton University Press, 1965).

26. For various regional administrations in British India, see Hermann Kulke and Dietmar Rothermund, *A History of India* (London: Routledge, 1995).

27. For instance, Punjabi peasants of Sikh and Muslim persuasions were characterized as martial classes whose pride would never let them run from the battleground. For details see David Omissi, *The Sepoy and the Raj: The Indian Army, 1860–1940* (Basingstoke: Macmillan, 1994). For their services, the Punjabi soldiers and junior commanders were allotted lands in newly irrigated canal colonies, which further added to incentives for joining the army. Thus a class of loyal peasants from "the sword arm of India" ensured an unending supply of recruits until 1947 and even after that to the new states. For more on this "hydraulic society" see Imran Ali, *Punjab Under Imperialism* (London: I. B. Tauris, 1988).

28. For an interesting and well-informed monograph on the subject, see Byron Farwell, *Queen Victoria's Little Wars* (London: Allen Lane, 1973).

29. For a detailed account of India's educational and economic transformation, see Judith Brown, *Modern India: The Origins of an Asian Democracy* (Oxford: Oxford University Press, 1994).

30. A Parsi by faith, Naoroji had been politically active in England. Aided by Indian students such as Muhammad Ali Jinnah, he won the parliamentary seat in Finchley, North London, and became the first-ever nonwhite member of the House of Commons.

31. A bright Indian who had been selected to the coveted Indian Civil Service, but was eventually forced to leave because of some contested charges. Banerjea spent his life teaching and publicizing the case for Indian equality with the British.

32. A lawyer from Bombay, Gokhale was a constitutionalist who sought Indian political rights through negotiations and influenced people like Jinnah. For more on Gopal Krishna Gokhale and Bal Gangadhar Tilak (1866–1920), see Stanley Wolpert, *Tilak and Gokhale: Revolution and Reform in the Making of India* (Berkeley: University of California Press, 1962).

33. "If at the turn of the nineteenth century the Wellesley generation had brought to bear a new British national pride on their attitudes towards Indian society, the Curzon generation at the turn of twentieth century exhibited a fully developed form of racial superiority and arrogance which had gathered momentum in the middle and late Victorian era." Sugata Bose and Ayesha Jalal, *Modern South Asia: History, Culture, Political Economy* (New York: Routledge, 1998), p. 105.

34. For the political and cultural undercurrents among North Indian Muslims, see Francis Robinson, *Separatism Among Indian Muslims: The Politics of the United Provinces Muslims, 1860–1925* (Delhi: Oxford University Press, 1996) (reprint).

35. This war finally ended with the Treaty of Rawalpindi with Britain recognizing the sovereignty of Afghanistan and both pledging noninterference in each other's affairs, although within a few years Afghanistan was to experience another crisis when King Amanullah Khan was overthrown by some of his own Afghan subjects who accused him of westernizing their country. Some people suspected British hands behind this tribal resentment.

36. Other than his autobiographical writings and correspondence, see Judith Brown, *Gandhi's Rise to Power. Indian Politics, 1915–1922* (Cambridge: Cambridge University Press, 1972).

37. For more on Nehru, see Stanley Wolpert, *Nehru: A Tryst with History* (Oxford: Oxford University Press, 1996).

38. Ishtiaq H. Qureshi, *The Struggle for Pakistan* (Karachi: University of Karacbi, 1969).

39. On the complex political negotiations between the British and Indian leaders, especially Jinnah, see Ayesha Jalal, *The Sole Spokesman: Jinnah, the Muslim League and Demand for Pakistan* (Cambridge: Cambridge University Press, 1994); Stanley Wolpert, *Jinnah of Pakistan* (Berkeley: University of California Press, 1984).

40. For more on this Indian revolutionary, see Leonard Gordon, *Brothers Against the Raj: A Biography of Sarat and Subhas Chandra Bose* (New Delhi: Viking, 1990).

41. For a biography of Wavell, see Victoria Schofield, *Wavell: Soldier and Statesman* (London: John Murray, 2006).

42. Larry Collins and Dominique Lapierre, *Freedom at Midnight* (London: HarperCollins, 1997).

43. For a contemporary Pakistani perspective, see Chaudhri Muhammad Ali, *The Emergence of Pakistan* (Lahore: Research Society of Pakistan, 1973).

6

Muslims in South Asia and the Making of Pakistan

Division of the Indian subcontinent in 1947 remains one of the most significant events in recent world history and has certainly proved a turning point in the course of Islam in south Asia, where the world's largest numbers of Muslims reside. Divided into the three states of Pakistan, India, and Bangladesh, this region witnessed the ascension of British power during the closing decades of a weakened Mughal Empire. Political decline only exacerbated anguish among the concerned Indian Muslims who felt that, educationally and financially, they had been an underprivileged community requiring some reorientation. At different times in subsequent centuries, Muslim intellectuals and activists proffered diverse solutions until, during the 1940s, it was the demand for Pakistan—a Muslim state—that caught their imagination. The emergence of Pakistan, divided into two parts in 1947, was thus the culmination point of a long Muslim heritage, which appeared to have been overshadowed by divided and unfavorable forces after 1720 when the looming political crisis assumed multiple dimensions. Traditionally, the ruling Muslim groups in India had been of Arab, Turkish, Persian, and Afghan extractions, although subsequently Indian elements also joined various imperial hierarchies. Yet ordinary Muslims fared like anybody else and remained scattered all over the subcontinent. Their ratio in the Indus Valley and eastern Bengal was proportionately higher but also overwhelmingly rural. The evolution of Indo-Islamic culture had built many cross-communal bridges, but religions kept all Indian communities apart as well. Muslim rulers often helped leading *ulama* and Sufi shrines through land endowments (*Aukaf*) but avoided sponsoring holistic conversions. Even Muslim metropolitan centers such as Delhi, Lucknow, Faizabad, and Lahore would not demand an absolute Muslim majority; nor did the rulers try to enforce demographic changes. In this chapter, we look closely at the issues of Muslim positions on their own collective identity over the past three centuries and how India and Islam both underwrote this discourse along with an increased politicization, which finally led to the evolution of Pakistan. In addition, we will seek the origins of the demand for Pakistan in those developments that characterized Muslim majority and minority regions within British India, soon to be aggregated within the fold of the All-India Muslim League (AIML) led by Muhammad Ali Jinnah (1876–1948), named as the Quaid-i-Azam (Great Leader) by his followers.

REVIVALISTS AND REFORMERS: WALI ALLAH, AL-AFGHANI, AND SYED AHMED KHAN

The scattered nature of Muslim communities and their preference for land and turning into rural clusters worried several metropolitan Muslin intellectuals during the Late Mughal era. Also, Muslim scholars such as Shah Wali Allah of Delhi (1703–1764) were deeply perturbed over the lax behavior of the ruling elite and their courts. To him, only an energized Muslim political authority strongly built on purist traditions could protect Muslims against internal and external threats, especially when Gujarat, Punjab, and central India witnessed regional assertion and displayed strong religious identities.[1] Such deliberations on India, itself falling victim to domestic instability and European colonialism, let the sons and descendants of Shah Wali Allah debate the very status of the subcontinent as a land of peace or a home of warfare. Thus the questions about Islam in south Asia also hinged on India's own characterization and its plural demography. Like Spanish Muslims during the Expulsions and Inquisition who were confronted with the imminent fall of Granada, Wali Allah's disciples in Delhi also feared an approaching twilight on Muslim India unless some political and theological retrieval could hold it at bay.

The debate about India, itself deemed to have been lost to the British and to regional forces that seemed indifferent if not totally hostile to Muslim community interests, assumed a greater intensity during the nineteenth century. Muslims like Shah Abdul Aziz (1747–1823) were conscious of the past history and endowed with a reassured belief in their own creed. He was also exasperated, however, by the dismal political and economic affairs of Muslims all around. He was the son of Shah Wali Allah and an eminent scholar in Delhi, declaring India to be a House of Warfare (*Darul Harb*), where peace could be established only if Muslims undertook a substantial Islamization of their lifestyles. Aware of the Mughal Emperor's abysmal dependence on the East India Company's largesse, and of the shifting loyalties of other regional warlords, this leading scholar was on friendly terms with British officials such as Sir Charles Metcalfe, the powerful British resident in the Mughal capital.[2] It is important, however, to state at the outset that the Muslim thought processes and activism in India were a twin-pronged initiative focusing on revivalism and reformism. The revivalists, through seminaries and educational efforts, sought a back-to-roots movement, whereas modernists desired the same goal but urged for assimilating modernity and westernization, thus forming what is known as Islamic modernism. This ideological divide, although often blurred, persists even today in south Asia and is not unique to the Muslim culture.

A leading Muslim intellectual of early activism was Syed Jamal-ud-Din al-Afghani (1838–1897). He witnessed the consolidation of the Raj, the pervasive sense of loss among Muslims, and a split within the ruling elite. His travels and conversations are reflected through a reconstructive discourse, displaying both revivalist and modernist strands. His subsequent visits to the Middle East and lectures on revitalizing Islam, not merely as a theology but also as an empowering political creed, won him students and followers in Egypt.[3] One of his notable disciples was Muhammad Abduh (1849–1905), who traveled with him to Paris. Together, they published an Arabic magazine, *Urwatul Wussqa*, aimed at a Muslim regeneration but with greater introspection regarding Pan-Islamic bonding. Al-Afghani had been disappointed with his visit to the Ottoman caliphate, which he found suffering from serious inertia and capitulation, and his exhortation for reforms caused serious official rebuke from the Caliphate. Al-Afghani and his disciples were anticolonial as well as Pan-Islamists, but they did not decry the educational and scientific achievements of the West. Thus their teachings sought a synthesis without harboring any self-denial as Muslims.

Other than Al-Afghani, the most towering personality of Islamic modernism in India was Sir Syed Ahmed Khan (1817–98), who pioneered various educational and intellectual movements during his long and productive life.[4] A witness to a serious Muslim predicament, especially after the debacle of 1857 and resultant British fury, this native of Delhi engaged in debates and publications addressed both to the British and to Indian Muslims. An untiring person, he saw Muslim reawakening through a rational soul searching and assimilation of Western education and ethics. Other than his writings, translation works, debates, and addresses, Syed Ahmed's greatest contribution was the founding of Mohammadan Anglo-Oriental College (MAO) at Aligarh, which became the Muslim University in 1920 and is viewed as the power engine of demand for Pakistan.[5] A practicing Muslim, who even published detailed Urdu commentaries of the Quran, Syed Ahmed was a reformer, but not strictly in the mode of a revivalist. His aim was certainly at Muslim regeneration through peaceful means, and, relying on modern education and rationalism, he disagreed with an exclusive approach that was being promoted by his contemporaries at seminaries in Deoband and Rai Bareilli.

At a crucial juncture in south Asian Muslim history, Sir Syed Ahmed Khan offered a pioneering discourse on understanding Islamic and modernist traditions. Going beyond the simplified position of positing Islam merely as an alien force in India, or just one of the major components of eclecticism, Syed Ahmed raised substantive issues about "Muslimness," "Indianness," and even Europe-led modernity. Without turning into a rejectionist or assuming the role of an uncritical imitator, he attempted to rationally interpret these three trajectories. In addition, he even laid out some possible alternatives for a collective Muslim renaissance. Thus Syed Ahmed went beyond the usual limits of a critic or an analyst and proved to be an activist. From easy-to-follow Urdu to the documentation of Delhi's historical heritage, from ethics to interfaith dialogue, and from educational reformism to ecclesiastic reformulation, this Muslim rationalist became the flag carrier for Muslim reawakening. Viewing him merely as a dry naturalist, an over-awed proponent of modernization, or a nostalgic but apologetic Islamic reformer is a misinterpretation of his many attributes.[6]

MUSLIM MODERNISTS: SYED AMEER ALI, MUMTAZ ALI, AND OTHERS

Some of Syed Ahmed Khan's contemporaries, in their own ways, prepared the groundwork for reformism by adopting English and Urdu for their writings and by underlining the urgency of modern education, gender rights, and a better understanding on all sides. After 1857 and official retribution, several missionary organizations also felt energized in their evangelical efforts, and a few of them even began questioning the validity of Prophethood and divine origins of Islam.[7] Although the British colonial administration avoided overt patronization of evangelical enterprises, despite sympathies and favorable attitudes at individual levels, Western missionaries knew that many Indians, overwhelmed by the British status and power, might be tempted to convert. Like Africa, Australasia, China, and the Western Hemisphere, colonization by a globalized Europe had offered rare and timely prospects for Christianity in these vast regions, leading to the emergence of pioneer local Christian communities. Within India, however, other than the "Untouchables" and tribals, well-established Hindu, Sikh, Parsi, and Muslim communities resisted conversion, but would benefit from educational and health facilities offered by missionary societies. Many Muslim *ulama* would even hold elaborate and well-publicized debates with their Christian counterparts,[8] although serious

Muslim intellectuals engaged themselves in scholarly works to refute a Western assault on Islam. Among these early Muslim jurists and scholars of Islamic history, Syed Ameer Ali (1849–1928) was a pioneer historian whose *The Spirit of Islam* and *A Short History of Saracens* appeared at an opportune time and have proven to be historical studies of authoritative nature. Written in the second half of the nineteenth century, the books presented the history of Islam and biographical details on the Prophet based on original sources, not only as a rebuttal of Western and missionary scholarship on Islam, but also as a means of empowering an evolving Muslim middle class.[9] Individuals like Syed Ameer Ali had been the beneficiaries of modern education but resented the defensive and apologetic attitudes of some of their fellow countrymen. Ameer Ali later moved to London and carried on with his scholarly and political efforts, including the organization of the London branch of the AIML in 1908.

There was some resistance to reforms and modern education in northern India, but southern regions were quite receptive. Thus cities like Bombay and Madras had a growing number of Muslim middle class professionals. As a result of the Mughal decline, many seminaries and *ulama* in northern India lost their financial backing and thus opted for rejection or isolation, whereas in the south, their counterparts had, for a long time, fended for themselves and were not keen on seeking official patronage. For instance, in Bombay, Justice Badruddin Tyabji (1844–1906) established the Anjuman-i-Islam School in 1876, aimed at imparting modern education, and today his association is still operating several educational institutions. He was one of the earliest Muslim leaders to advocate women's education and perhaps the first Indian Muslim to send his daughters abroad for advanced studies. In urban Punjab, several Anjumans, including the Anjuman-i-Islamia in Lahore and Amritsar, opened schools for young men, whereas Anjuman-i-Himayat-i-Islam (AHI) pioneered schools for both girls and boys in central Punjab.[10] The annual sessions of the AHI played a leading role in creating cultural consciousness among Muslims in Lahore, Amritsar, and Gujranwala. A young Muhammad Iqbal (1875–1938), the future poet-philosopher of Muslim India, started reciting poems at the AHI's annual sessions, and the cadres of Muslim Leaguers during the 1940s came from similar urban middle class backgrounds.[11] The Foreman Christian (FC) College, dating from the 1840s, is the oldest institution of its kind, imparting modern education in Punjab, and it owes its formation to the American Presbyterians.[12] Government College Lahore was founded in 1864 as a premier institution. Punjab University, Aitchison College (Chiefs College), and Mayo School of Arts—all located in Lahore—were founded during the subsequent decades. The Anjumans also opened up Islamia Colleges in Lahore and Amritsar, and the Islamia College in Peshawar and Mohammadan Anglo-Oriental (MAO) College in Lahore were founded by charity organizations to answer the growing demand for modern education among younger Muslims.

Missionary women had initiated some *zenana* work (for women inside homes), but they largely focused on health matters and subsequently on education. The nineteenth-century Muslim and Hindu reformers had dexterously prepared groundwork for education, and primary schools for girls began to appear soon after 1857. The earliest contributions in this area were by Maulvi Mumtaz Ali (1860–1935), a vocal advocate of Muslim women's rights, who authored a persuasive book, *Huquq-un-Niswaan* (Rights of Women), and led a debate on this topic. Maulvi Mumtaz Ali was a contemporary of Syed Ahmed Khan and believed in the complete equality of men and women. *Huquq-un-Niswaan* was so revolutionary in its innovative and bold approach that even Syed Ahmed tried to dissuade Mumtaz Ali from publishing it, lest it should cause serious opposition to him. As a matter of fact, Syed Ahmed himself was an ardent supporter of women's rights, as is evident from his incomplete commentary on the Quran. He had to reportedly abandon its completion because of pressure from some orthodox *ulama*. In return, they agreed to lend their support for his MAO College at Aligarh. Owing to a passionate conviction for gender empowerment, Maulvi Mumtaz Ali published his volume and helped many future reformers in their efforts. He argued his case for gender equality on the basis of the Quran and Hadith, something unthinkable in those days when women of all persuasions remained totally homebound. Maulvi Mumtaz Ali also published an Urdu magazine, *Tehzeeb-i-Niswaan*, devoted to education and gender issues under the editorship of his wife, Muhammadi Begum. After her death, their daughter assumed responsibility for its publication.[13] Similarly, Sheikh Abdullah, another early Muslim reformer, advocated women's education and established a women's school in Aligarh, which subsequently was elevated into a full-fledged college and is currently a constituent of Aligarh Muslim University.

The reformist efforts of Abdul Latif and help for Syed Ahmed from wealthy Muslim Bengali families reaffirmed the desire among many Muslims for transregional alliances. Some of the educated Muslim families such as the Mians in Lahore and Suhrawardies in Bengal pioneered sending their women to schools. These early role models helped overcome existing prejudices against women's education among urban groups.[14] Efforts for universal education by Muslim pioneers in Punjab, such as Mian Muhammad Shafi (1869–1932), were quite significant, as he sent his own daughters to the institutions of higher learning and encouraged their participation in active politics in the decades preceding Partition. Some contemporary newspapers such as *Paisa Akhbar* of Maulvi Mahbub Alam and *Sharif Bibi*, edited by his daughter, Fatima Begum, encouraged Muslim parents to educate their daughters, even though elsewhere in India women's participation in education and professions remained miniscule until Partition.[15] The Urdu renaissance at Lahore, which began in the late nineteenth century, not only created several literary masterpieces in fiction, poetry, drama, history, and journalism, but also helped sustain an urban and self-confident Muslim community in northern India.

REVIVALISTS AND IDENTITY FORMATION

Despite some inroads made by modernists in urban areas, most of the Indian Muslims were either rural peasants or artisans. There was also a rather small class of landowning elite. As a result, the evolution of the Muslim middle class remained slow and disparate.[16] Academic institutions and the Urdu press duly germinated visible self-awareness on belonging to a separate Muslim community; although a major impetus is also owed to the revivalists, who had themselves been influenced by Shah Wali Allah's teaching and, after the debacle of the Jihad movement in 1831 and of the Faraidhis, focused on seminary-based instruction. The Jihad movement was led by Sayyid Ahmed Barelwi (1786–1831), a pupil of Shah Abdul Aziz, who, on his return from Makkah and Medina, was determined to expel the British from India.[17] Sayyid Ahmed Barelwi's Islamist movement was, in fact, known as Tehrik-i-Muhammadiyya. His closest associate was Shah Ismail (d. 1831), a grandson of Shah Wali Allah, who shared Ahmed's puritanical and activist program. After gathering some devout followers, he undertook a long and arduous march toward the trans-Indus regions. They first wanted to liberate the Indus Valley from the Sikh rule before embarking on the East India Company. Thus, in their march toward Peshawar, they avoided the Lahore kingdom of Ranjeet Singh and instead undertook a circuitous journey through Sindh, Balochistan, and the Pushtun tribal belt. These Mujahideen initially gained victories over the Sikh troops and for a time held control of Peshawar, but desertions and betrayals by some local influential people resulted in their expulsion from the Peshawar Valley. In 1830, they finally reached Balakot, a town in the hilly region of lower Hazara and, after a decisive battle in 1831, both the Jihad leaders and several of their followers were killed by Sikh troops. The Jihad movement failed to dislodge the Sikhs for logistical and technical reasons, and Sikhs as well as the British were able to contain it by portraying Jihadis as intolerant Wahhabis, who had been indoctrinated by the teachings of the Arab revivalist, Muhammad bin Abdel Wahhab (1703–1787). Over the next several decades, the Jihad movement[18] operated in the mountains of Swat and tribal territories straddling the Indo-Afghan borders. The British had to resort to frequent military campaigns to counter their local support among the Pushtuns.[19]

In Bengal, another contemporary Muslim scholar, Haji Shariat Ullah (1781–1840) had launched his Faraidhi movement among peasants and weavers by urging them to focus on *fards*, the fundamental practices and beliefs in a purist tradition. Like Shah Wali Allah and Sayyid Ahmed Barelwi, he insisted on discarding innovations (*bidaa*) and exhibited strong anti-British sentiments. After his death, his mission was continued by his son, Dudhu Mian (1819–1862), who transformed the movement into an active defiance by refusing to pay taxes and by simultaneously resisting Hindu landowners. For a while, the Faraidhi movement tried to wrest land for landless Muslim peasants and built up a case of Muslim solidarity, yet it was soon realized that the simple defiance would not be helpful either against an entrenched Raj or well-established *Bhadralok*. The Faraidhis followed an early model of Political Islam based on pamphlets, politicization, institution building, and the print industry, combined with a zeal for cultural redefinition. Like Mujahideen, they represented a small-town Muslim Bengali consciousness, which displayed explicit "orthodox" imprints of a peaceful nature.[20]

Witnessing the apparent invincibility of the Raj, especially after 1857, and motivated by a keenness to reinvigorate the Muslim masses during a period of introversion, several Muslim *ulama* attempted to organize seminary-based instruction. Like the reformists, they sought Muslim welfare as the ultimate ideal to be achieved through rigorous education, yet this education was totally different in its emphasis, medium, and syllabi. Without rejecting Jihad as an ideology altogether, they believed that the Muslim masses had to be made aware of their own Islamic heritage in Urdu and Arabic before any activism could be undertaken. Like the Arya Samaj among Hindus, they believed in Islamization of Indian Muslims through a planned organizational work where seminaries and their alumni would play a mainstream role. One doctrinal group among these revivalists, however, emphasized a purist and exclusive approach by viewing Sufi saints and their shrines as nonproductive and fatalistic. On the contrary, the other strand took saints and shrines as intermediaries between the Creator and humanity and thus followed a syncretic form of religion. From among the Indian Muslims, the seminary at Deoband—Madrassa Darul Uloom—postulated a back-to-roots, literalist, and purist version of Islam. According to this school of revivalism, a strong disavowal of modernity could hasten their way back to the re-creation of a lost Islamic glory. The founders and leaders of the Deoband seminary combined faith and politics and sought Islamic revival in a more activist form, stopping short of an open Jihad or militarist defiance of the Raj.[21] The generations of *ulama* trained at Deoband established similar regional seminaries all over India, incorporating Deobandi curriculum and, over successive decades, ushered in religiopolitical parties, including the Taliban. The Deobandi Islam gradually gained greater experience in institution building, publications, and training future clerics, who would follow a strict and purist version of Islam, often erroneously identified as Wahhabi Islam. Their connection with the movement in Arabian Najd and Hejaz had been quite limited; they were instead motivated by the internal dynamics and challenges of south Asian politics.

Soon after the formation of the Darul Uloom at Deoband in 1867, another seminary was established again in the UP, at the town of Rai Bareilli, which, unlike its counterpart at Deoband, sought a possibility of Muslim regeneration in the mystical traditions of Islam. Positing Sufi *saintsas* intermediaries between the Creator and the people, the mentors and future generations of alumni situated their kind of Islamic ethos within a syncretic Indian culture. Most of the south Asian Muslims have been and are followers of Sufi traditions, which is where the Brelvi approach has remained ascendant. This is not to suggest that Sufi Islam is totally apolitical and shuns political activism, especially when it comes to basic creed, including an unflinching respect for the Prophet. The Brelvi Islam in the subcontinent revolves around certain Sufi orders and involves periodic rituals and, unlike Deobandi articulation, allows devotional music and dance at the shrines or before a living saint. Brelvi Muslims outnumber other purist groups, yet they do not enjoy the level of institutional framework and rigor that characterize their Deobandi counterparts, and thus they remain segmented.

After World War I, the Deobandi *ulama* formed the Jamiat-i-Ulama-i-Hind (JUH) in 1920. It espoused Pan-Islamic sentiments and evolved during an activist phase in the Khilafat movement in British India.[22] Sharing platforms with the Indian National Congress, these *ulama* advocated independence for India while simultaneously subscribing to a Pan-Islamic identity. Some of them formed parties such as Ahl-i-Hadith and Tabligh, purported to energize marginal Muslims to more rigorous version of Islam, and intentionally avoided involvement in politics. Whereas the Indian National Congress (INC) and the AIML mostly remained dormant during the 1920s, the politicization generated by the Khilafat movement and the Montague-Chelmsford Reforms of 1919 regionalized the Indian political spectrum because some residual powers had been shifted to provincial assemblies.[23] During the 1920s, many ideological and regional parties offered various political programs. Other than the JUH, the Communist Party of India, Hindu Mahasabha, Akali Dal, Majils-i-Ahrar Islam, Krisha Projak, Tehreek-i-Khaksar, the Punjab National Unionist Party, and the Red Shirts (Khudai Khidmatgar) variably jostled for parallel objectives through populist politics. Led by charismatic personalities, many of these parties convened periodic rallies; distributed publicity literature; held parades of their uniformed volunteers; and, in Muslim cases, sought their roots from the era, when Indian Muslims had been perturbed over the political fate of the Ottoman Caliphate.[24] These regional and religiopolitical parties used various cultural and national symbols derived from areas such as religion or ideology, history, territory, economy, and politics to spearhead their causes. Thus the AIML, the party eventually to advocate the case for Pakistan in the 1940s, had to compete against a wide spectrum of forces in its early career and mostly remained an organization of Muslim modernists.

THE ALL-INDIA MUSLIM LEAGUE, MUHAMMAD IQBAL, AND M. A. JINNAH

The AIML, founded in 1906, is credited to have led the campaign for Muslim interests in British India until 1940, when it began advocating for a Muslim state. Led by lawyers and reform-minded Muslims, it played a vanguard role in politicizing south Asian Muslims, who accounted for one-fourth of the total Indian population. These Indian Muslims, from the historic Khyber Pass to the borders of Myanmar, made up the largest Muslim community in the world and were divided into several ethnoregional groups. Compared with an equally diverse Hindu population, however, Muslims were still a minority and, in most cases, were economically and politically underprivileged. The INC included a small sprinkling of Muslim elite, but the party increasingly came under the dominant influence of Hindu leaders such as B.G. Tilak, who gained further momentum after the division of Bengal into two administrative units in 1905. INC's agitational politics coincided with the British promises for constitutional reforms, enabling some modicum of Indian participation in local affairs. Amid fears and expectations, the Muslim professional elite, joined by some landed groups, met Lord Minto in 1906, seeking safeguards for their community in the forthcoming reforms. Their successful lobbying guaranteed them separate electorates, ensuring adequate Muslim representation on elected local bodies. It also made them conscious of their collective need to create a regular party to operate both as a pressure group and an effective watchdog. It is understandable that the pioneering efforts for Muslim political configuration—like the modernist and revivalist articulations—had their roots in Muslim minority provinces where there was a greater sensitivity toward demographic and other imbalances. At places like the UP and Delhi, these Muslim elite, confronted with the majority forces espousing Hindi and the redirection of Indian politics toward the Hindu majority, defined Muslim separatism.[25]

The AIML received an impetus in 1913 when M.A. Jinnah (1876–1948) joined the movement. Jinnah believed in closer cooperation between the two Indian political parties and because of the efforts of this secular barrister the parties agreed to a common formula. The Lucknow Pact of 1916 ensured demarcation of seats for Hindus and Muslims on provincial legislatures and ushered in a period of cooperation that ended two decades later when the INC, after its major electoral successes in 1937, tended to ignore the AIML. The formation of the INC-led ministries in several provinces and their unilateral policies only increased the Hindu-Muslim divide in British India. While Mahatma Gandhi (1869–1948) led the noncooperation movement during World War II, Jinnah, now called the Quaid-i-Azam (Great Leader), busied himself in the reorganization of the League by building alliances with the regional leaders. In 1940, at its annual meeting in Lahore, the League determined to pursue the objective of political sovereignty, which soon came to be known as the demand for Pakistan. The British preoccupation with the war and the exacerbation of interparty differences not only increased communal tensions but also further popularized the demand for a separate Muslim state.

Jinnah was a liberal Muslim who espoused unity, equality, and independence for Indians over and above their ethnic or religious identities and, for a long time, strove for Hindu-Muslim unity to gain independence.[26] During the 1920s, in the wake of changing political alliances and competition among various communities, Jinnah was disheartened by the INC's Nehru Report of 1928, which refused to address prevalent Muslim under-representation in education and the professions. After the failure of the Round Table Conferences in the early 1930s, Jinnah had decided to practice law in London, but he was soon prevailed upon by friends like Muhammad Iqbal and Liaquat Ali Khan (1896–1951) to return to India to lead the AIML in its struggle with the British, INC, and the revivalists. The Muslim revivalists, despite several available forums and imbued with liberationist enthusiasm, lacked any tangible program to resolve the Muslim situation and vacillated between regional and unitary solutions. Muhammad Iqbal, the visionary poet and philosopher, had been seeking a Muslim renaissance and, despite his aversion to territorial nationalism, felt that the Indian Muslims needed to obtain sovereignty as a precursor to an intellectual and cultural rebirth.[27] To him, it was only through their political representation that they might retrieve a needed sense of community, in addition to finding a synthesis between their own glorified traditions and an overpowering modernity. Iqbal's ideas had begun to receive a wider audience since his address to the annual session of the AIML at Allahabad in 1930. His exhortations for a political redefinition and cultural self-awareness were made through empowering literary writings both in Urdu and Persian. His was a message offering greater hope for many Muslims in an intricate and multicultural subcontinent that was gradually edging toward an imminent independence from Britain. Choudhary Rahmat Ali (1895–1951), a Pan Islamic student and thinker at Cambridge, in one of his monographs in 1933, suggested the creation of several Muslim states in consonance with Muslim demography in various parts of India.[28] For the Indus Valley, he recommended Pakistan, comprising Punjab, Afghania (Frontier), Sindh, Kashmir, and Balochistan. His *Now or Never* also proposed a separate state each for Muslim Bengalis [Bengalistan], and the Nizam's state of Hyderabad was to be reorganized as Osmanistan.[29] Although not formally adopted by the AIML until the early 1940s, the Pakistan idea caught on with the public imagination, and during the elections of 1946, it became almost a consensual creed for most Indian Muslims.

In spite of preeminent leaders such as Jinnah and Iqbal guiding the AIML, the party, for a long time, consisted of elite from mainly Muslim minority regions such as the UP, Madras, and Bombay, until it became an organization of the masses during World War II. Its ideological rivals included revivalists such as the JUH, along with the regional contenders like the Unionist Party in Punjab and Red Shirts in the Frontier. The JUH and its various regional and smaller partners did not trust modernists, and their idealization of a modern Muslim territorial state, nor did they trust the Islamic credentials of these leaders.[30] The Unionist Party combined Muslim, Hindu, and Sikh landlords in Punjab and had been formed in 1924 within the Punjab Assembly by Sir Fazl-i-Husian (1877–1936), an astute politician who had tried to help Punjabi Muslims by forging cross-communal alliances.[31] At his death in 1936, Sikandar Hayat Khan (1892–1942) led the organization, and after the electoral victory of the group in 1937, became the premier of Punjab. Sikandar Hayat signed an agreement with Jinnah in 1937 at Lucknow, pledging his support for the AIML.[32] Upon Sikandar Hayat's sudden death in December 1942, Khizr Hayat (1900–1975), a Muslim Unionist from Khushab, became the premier of Punjab and began to resist AIML's demands for amalgamating the Unionist Party into the former.[33] The Jinnah-Khizr rupture became serious after 1944, and a mass boycott in 1947 eventually led to the end of the Khizr ministry, as the Punjab Assembly now had the League majority.

In the NWFP, the AIML had been weaker because of the charisma of Khan Abdul Ghaffar Khan (1890–1988), a Khilafatist who combined Pushtun nationalism with the Islamic concept of general welfare and public service.[34] He also aligned himself with the INC and always kept distant from the AIML. Abdul Ghaffar Khan had formed the Red Shirts in 1929, which sought pride in social service and pursued Gandhian politics of nonviolence. His brother, Doctor Khan Saheb, became chief minister in the province, owing to a slight majority in the assembly but, like Khizr Hayat, he faced mass defiance organized by League supporters. The INC-Red Shirt ministry continued for some time despite public agitation. There were League-led petitions against it, but the final decision about the future of this province was left to a referendum. Held during the stormy days of the transfer of power, the referendum sought the opinion of the Frontier people on their choice between India and Pakistan.[35] The Red Shirts were not clear on their future course of action and mostly boycotted the polls. On the contrary, AIML's slogan for a separate Muslim state had already become quite popular among Pushtuns and other Muslim population groups in the NWFP. The Referendum of 1947, in view of mechanisms agreed on for all of India, did not allow any secession to form an independent ethnic state and thus paved the way for province's integration into Pakistan. Despite the boycott by some Red Shirts, the vote for Pakistan was quite decisive in 1947.[36]

The newly formed province of Sindh, separated from Bombay in 1936, had inherited active party politics revolving around landed and urban personalities. The AIML was able to make an entry into the provincial legislature, and as early as 1940, led by G.M. Syed (1904–95), the Sindh assembly had already voted for "Pakistan" long before it became the mainstay of constitutional and political negotiations between the Indian leaders and colonial administration.[37] In Bengal, the AIML was able to project itself as the main guardian of Muslim cultural and economic interests, and it became a utopia worth achieving.[38] Led by a veteran Muslim Leaguer, Huseyn Shaheed Suhrawardy (1892–1963), Bengal initially tried to seek independence; but like Punjab, its demography pushed it toward partition between India and Pakistan. Finally the eastern regions separated from West Bengal, forming the eastern wing of the young Muslim-majority state.[39] A referendum in some Muslim-majority districts in Assam also affirmed overwhelming support for Pakistan, and thus East Bengal combined with Sylhet became East Pakistan. The Indus Valley, including various administrative regions in Balochistan, was designated as West Pakistan, and M.A. Jinnah became the first governor-general of Pakistan on August 14, 1947. Liaquat Ali Khan, Jinnah's close confidante, took over as the first prime minister. The fifth largest state in the world had come into existence but was already divided into two disparate wings separated by more than 1,000 miles of Indian territory. Pakistan was officially inaugurated by Jinnah and Mountbatten on August 14 at Karachi, amid the world's largest migration and growing mistrust between two young nation-states. The AIML had delivered the country nine years after Iqbal's death and seven years after the Lahore Resolution, which had envisioned territorial redefinition of Muslim majority regions in British India. This process appeared smooth and steady, yet it was paved with serious challenges and concerns as a new state embodying disparate geographical and cultural realities rose like a phoenix from the ashes of the Raj.

NOTES

1. Shah Wali Allah undertook the translation of the Quran into Persian so that the Indian Muslims could follow their religious precepts more closely instead of depending on Arabic, which was not their mother tongue. His own writings, sermons, and correspondence with the Muslim elite of the time catapulted him to a preeminent status and, in a way, he became the fountainhead of Muslim revivalism in India. For more on Shah Wali Allah, see A. D. Muztar, *Shah Wali Allah: A Saint-Scholar of Muslim India*, (Islamabad: National Commission on Historical and Cultural Research, 1979); J.M.S. Baljon, *Religion and Thought of Shah Wali Allah Dihlawi 1703–1762* (Leiden: Brill, 1986).

2. William Dalrymple, *The Last Mughal: The Fall of a Dynasty, Delhi, 1857* (London: Bloomsbury, 2006), pp. 33, 64. Much to the annoyance of several traditional *ulama*, his other brother, Abdul Qadir, had translated Quran into Urdu so that more Indian Muslims could understand and follow the religious text.

3. For details on his life and achievements, see Nikki R. Keddie, *An Islamic Response to Imperialism: Political and Religious Writings of Sayyid Jamal al-Din al-Afghani* (Berkeley: University of California Press, 1968).

4. Hafeez Malik, *Sir Sayyid Ahmad Khan and Muslin Modernization in India and Pakistan* (New York: Columbia University Press, 1980).

5. For a study of early Aligarh graduates, see David Lelyweld, *Aligarh's First Generation: Muslim Solidarity in British India* (New Delhi: Oxford University Press, 2003) (reprint).

6. For more on him, see S.M. Ikram, *Modern Muslim India and the Birth of Pakistan* (Lahore: Institute of Islamic Culture, 1995).

7. For a comprehensive treatment of this subject, see K.K. Aziz, *Britain and Muslim India: A Study of British Public Opinion vis-à-vis the Development of Muslim Nationalism in India, 1857–1947* (London: Heinemann, 1963).

8. Avril Powell, *Muslims and Missionaries in Pre-Mutiny India* (London: Curzon Press, 1993).

9. Syed Ameer Ali, *The Spirit of Islam* (London: Christophers, 1922); *A Short History of the Saracens: Being a Concise Account of the Rise and Decline of the Saracenic Power and of the Economic, Social and Intellectual Development of the Arab Nation* (London: Macmillan, 1924).

10. Ahmad Saeed, *Islamia College Ki Sadd Sala Tarikh*, (Urdu), Vol. I (Lahore: Research Society of Pakistan, 1992); *Anjuman-i-Islamia Amritsar, 1873–1947*, (Urdu) (Lahore: Research Society of Pakistan, 1986).

11. David Gilmartin, *Empire and Islam: Punjab and the Making of Pakistan* (London: I.B. Tauris, 1988).

12. For its history and the early U.S.-south Asian relations in commerce, education, culture, and politics, see Iftikhar H. Malik, *U.S.-South Asia Relations, 1783–1940: A Historical Perspective* (Islamabad: Area Study Centre, 1987).

13. The literary and social efforts of Syed Mumtaz Ali and his family played a pioneering role in increasing educational and intellectual awareness among Muslims in the subcontinent. His son, Syed Imtiaz Ali Taj (1900–70), is known as one of the most distinguished Urdu playwrights. His gifted wife, Hijaab, established her own distinct literary profile and continued to work for women's education.

14. Two autobiographical works in this area could offer useful information on gender education among *ashraf*. Jahan Ara Shahnawaz, *Father and Daugh-*

ter: A Political Autobiography (Karachi: Oxford University Press, 2002) (reprint); Begum Shaista Ikramullah, *From Purdah to Parliament* (Karachi: Oxford University Press, 1998) (reprint).

15. Fatima Begum (1890–1958) was an educationist and from her early life pursued an active political career in Punjab and NWFP. In 1947, she was one of those women from the AIML who had courted arrest while demonstrating against the Unionist cabinet in Punjab. She also undertook welfare work in Bihar in 1946 after the anti-Muslim riots in that province.

16. For more on this subject, see Aziz Ahmad, *Islamic Modernism in India and Pakistan, 1857–1964* (London: Oxford University Press, 1967).

17. This Jihad Movement had its origins in the regions adjoining Delhi and had no direct contacts with the Wahhabis in Arabia, although Sayyid Ahmed had spent some years in the Hejaz. The Jihad movement went on for quite some time in the tribal regions long after the Revolt of 1857 amid an official British propaganda of maligning it as a Wahhabi trajectory. W.W. Hunter's book created even more attention on this movement and was used to present his advocacy of perennial Muslim hostility to the British. See W.W. Hunter, *The Indian Musalmans: Are They Bound in Conscience to Rebel Against the Queen?* London: Trubner, 1871. Shah Abdul Aziz provided moral support to Sayyid Ahmed, who was his disciple and, in the same way, supported his nephew, Shah Ismail and his son-in-law, Abdul Hayy, in their efforts to undertake Jihad in India. These three leaders of the movement spent time in Bengal and built linkages with the activists in Calcutta, Chittagong, Noakhali, and Jaunpur. "The *Jihad* failed, but the enthusiasm which was generated was not confined to Delhi." Ikram, p. 12.

18. Some of the Muslim rebels and sepoys involved in the Uprising of 1857 called themselves Mujahideen—the holy warriors. William Dalrymple, "The Last Mughal and a clash of civilisations," *New Statesman*, October 16, 2006, pp. 34–36.

19. Some authors see parallels between this Tehrik-i-Jihad and the post-9/11 resistance in the tribal regions. They also tend to seek greater alliances between the Jihad leadership in India and the Wahhabis in Arabia, which remains rather contentious. See Charles Allen, *God's Terrorists: The Wahhabi Cult and the Hidden Roots of Modern Jihad* (London: Abacus, 2007).

20. A pertinent study on the subject throws light on the appropriation of a broader "Muslimness." See Rafidddin Ahmed, *The Bengal Muslims, 1871–1906: A Quest for Identity* (New Delhi: Oxford University Press, 1988).

21. For more details, see Barbara Metcalf, *Islamic Revival in British India: Deoband 1860–1900* (Princeton: Princeton University Press, 1982); Muhammad Qasim Zaman, *The Ulama in Contemporary Islam: Custodians of Change* (Princeton: Princeton University Press, 2002).

22. Indian Muslims were worried about the possible abolition of the Ottoman Caliphate after its defeat during World War I and wanted to maintain it as a major symbol of the world's Muslims.

23. For an interesting commentary on this premise and subsequent developments, see M. Yunas Samad, *A Nation in Turmoil: Nationalism and Ethnicity in Pakistan, 1937–1958* (New Delhi: Sage, 1995).

24. During this period of political and economic decline, many Muslims especially in India, viewed even a weakened Ottoman Caliphate as a historic vestige for the Muslim world and were concerned that the Greek irredentism and the Allied invasions would debilitate it once and for all. They were equally perturbed over the future of the Holy Places in that Arabian Peninsula, which now lay unprotected because several chieftains were jostling for power. The movement for the preservation of Caliphate and Holy Places attracted Muslim attention in India and was led by several Pan-Islamists. The Ali Brothers, Hakim Ajmal Khan, Khan Abdul Ghaffar Khan, Saifud Din Kitchlew, Mukhtar Ansari, and several others led the Khilafat movement, which became a Hindu-Muslim mass mobilization owing to Gandhi's entry in 1919. For more on Khilafat, see Gail Minault, *The Khilafat Movement: Religious Symbolism and Political Mobilization in India* (New Delhi: Oxford University Press, 1999); M. Naeem Qureshi, *Pan-Islam in British Indian Politics: A Study of the Khilafat Movement, 1918–1924* (Leiden: Brill, 1999).

25. Francis Robinson, *Separatism among Indian Muslims: The Politics of the United Provinces' Muslims, 1860–1923* (Cambridge: Cambridge University Press, 1993).

26. For an early and fluent biography, see Hector Bolitho, *Jinnah: the Creator of Pakistan* (Karachi: Oxford University Press, 2006) (reprint).

27. Muhammad Iqbal, *The Reconstruction of Religious Thought in Islam* (London: Oxford University Press, 1934).

28. K.K. Aziz, *Rahmat Ali: A Life* (Stuttgart: Franz Steiner, 1987).

29. Choudhary Rahmat Ali, *Now or Never* (Cambridge: University of Openness Press, 2005) (reprint).

30. The JUH leaders such as Husain Ahmad Madani and Abul Kalam Azad favored the Indian National Congress style of composite nationalism. For such views, see Maulana Abul Kalam Azad, *India Wins Freedom* (Delhi: Orient Longman, 1988); Mushirul Hasan, *Nationalism and Communal Politics in India, 1916–1928* (New Delhi: Manohar, 1979); *Legacy of a Divided Nation: India's Muslims since Independence* (London: Hurst, 1997).

31. See Azim Husain, (ed.), *Mian Fazl-i-Husain: Glimpses of Life and Works, 1898–1936* (Lahore: Sang-e-Meel Publications, 1993).

32. For more details on him, see Iftikhar H. Malik, *Sir Sikandar Hayat Khan: A Political Biography* (Islamabad: National Institute of History and Culture, 1985).

33. For details, see Ian Talbot, *Khizr Tiwana: The Punjab Unionist Party and the Partition of India* (Richmond: Curzon, 1996).

34. For more on him, see M.S. Korejo, *The Frontier Gandhi: His Place in History* (Karachi: Oxford University Press, 1994).

35. For further details, see Sayed Wiqar Ali Shah, *Ethnicity, Islam and Nationalism: Muslim Politics in the North-West Frontier Province* (Karachi: Oxford University Press, 1999).

36. For documentary and related details, see Saleem Ullah Khan (ed.), *The Referendum in N.W.F.P. 1947* (Islamabad: National Documentation Centre, 1995).

37. Later on, G.M. Syed became a symbol of Sindhu Desh, or an independent Sindh. For more on him, see M.S. Korejo, *G.M. Syed: An Analysis of His Political Perspectives* (Karachi: Oxford University Press, 2000).

38. Taj Hashmi, *Pakistan as a Peasant Utopia: The Communalization of Class Politics in East Bengal, 1920–1947* (Boulder: Westview, 1992).

39. Tazeen M. Murshid, *The Sacred and the Secular: Bengal Muslim Discourses, 1871–1977* (Calcutta: Oxford University Press, 1995).

7

Pakistan: Establishing the State, 1947–1958

Pakistan, like many other postcolonial states, has faced recurring problems of governance when a consensus-based political system needed for a cohesive nationhood has often appeared distant. The frequent military takeovers and the separation of East Pakistan as the sovereign state of Bangladesh in 1971 have been the symptoms of this malaise. More than six decades after its independence, Pakistanis largely share a sense of common nationality, use Urdu as a national language, and have been economically interdependent, owing to the historical and ecological features of the Indus Valley regions. Ethnic and regional tensions along with dissention between religious elements and their modernist counterparts, however, have kept the country engaged in a long-drawn ideological debate. Despite serious economic, structural, and geopolitical handicaps that the country has been faced with since 1947, its record in institution building, economic performance, and a frontline role on international affairs remains quite significant. In 1947, British withdrawal from the subcontinent took place in a hurried manner that only added to communal riots among Hindus, Muslims, and Sikhs, in addition to unleashing the world's largest migrations across the new borders. The young states of India and Pakistan were born in an atmosphere of mutual suspicions and disputes over boundaries, assets, and the future status of religious minorities left on both sides.

FORMING THE STATE

Among several serious challenges facing the young Muslim country was its geographical division into two wings, separated from each other by 1,100 miles, whereas the partition from India itself proved a volatile affair. Both India and Pakistan were witnessing the world's largest migration, with 14 million people on the move by all kinds of means. Most of them undertook land routes and fell vulnerable to organized attacks leading to indiscriminate massacres, gang rapes, and kidnapping. The division of Punjab—the most pluralistic and equally contested province of British India—occurred amid massive crimes against innocent people committed by communalist criminals. The hapless refugees moving on foot or on the trains were routinely attacked, while groups, whose hatred toward people not belonging to their own religious communities knew no bounds, kidnapped thousands of women. Atrocities happened on all sides, but given the fact that more Muslims were on the move and came from far away places across India, their journey toward Pakistan was proportionately often more traumatic. According to some scholars, 1 million Muslims lost their lives and about 50,000 women were abducted, of whom only 8,000 were ever recovered. About 10,000 non-Muslim women were abducted during this communal frenzy and 6,000 were recovered through subsequent investigations.[1] Eight million Muslims came into Pakistan, whereas around 5 million refugees destined for India left their homes in what became a predominantly Muslim country. In several cases of communal mayhem, even babies and elderly people were not spared. The birth of two sovereign states accompanied ethnic mayhem, communal discord, and large-scale bloodshed that, even after so many decades, continue to underpin bitter memories on all sides.

Karachi was chosen as Pakistan's new capital where M.A. Jinnah (1876–1948), known as the Quaid-i-Azam or Great Leader, was sworn in as the first governor-general and Liaquat Ali Khan (1893–1951) was elevated to prime minister. Pakistan's first constituent assembly consisted of 69 members who had been elected in 1946 during the British era and was destined to formulate constitutional and other needed legislation for the new country. Still, it would take Pakistan another nine years to develop its constitution. In the meantime, the India Act of 1935 operated as the interim constitution for the new country. Karachi, a former fishing village on the Arabian Sea, had been an important commercial and strategic port because of its proximity to the Gulf and because it was connected with the Indus Valley through a railway network. Still, it was located away from the hinterland within the western wing while East Bengal was hundreds of miles away, wedged between the Gulf of Bengal and India. Within a few weeks of independence, Karachi became a populated city, with large numbers of Muslim refugees. Karachi lacked the civic and administrative infrastructure to house the uprooted millions, but the government, as well as the native Sindhis, afforded land and hospitality to these refugees who were called *Muhajireen* (immigrants). With better educational skills and professional acumen, many of these immigrants became the earliest kingpins of the new country, although Punjabis still accounted for the bulk of armed forces and the police. The western wing, in terms of geography, size, and ethnicity, was more pluralistic than East Bengal, a delta land mostly consisting of Bengali-speaking Muslims and a small proportion of Urdu-speaking Muhajireen.

In the summer of 1947, many Hindus and Sikhs left Punjab for India while Muslims from Indian Punjab and other distant provinces of India chose to move westward. Soon cities like Lahore, Multan, Gujranwala, Lyallpur (Faisalabad), Rawalpindi, and Sialkot turned into major urban sprawls with overflowing refugee populations. Besides Sindh and Punjab, East Bengal also received a large stream of refugee population, many of them non-Bengalis, and the country's first priority was the settlement of these 8 million people. Their distribution to various towns and subsequent land allotment of the evacuee property helped them move out of the temporary tent townships that had come about in the wake of Partition, but their trauma would take many more efforts to redress. Jinnah, himself 72 and frail as a result of chronic bronchitis, moved across the provinces to personally supervise refugee settlements at a time when many princely states, including Kashmir, turned out to be sore points in the emerging Indo-Pakistani relations.[2]

The departing British rulers had advised 565 princely states in India to seek union with one of the successor states, keeping in mind their territorial location and demographic realities. Three princely states posed a formidable challenge to India-Pakistan relations at their very inception.

The princely state of Jammu and Kashmir, known for its natural beauty and strategic location, equaled the United Kingdom in size, with 86,000 square miles of immensely scenic landscape featuring tall mountains, lush valleys, and mighty rivers including the Indus system. With an overwhelmingly Muslim majority, Kashmir enjoyed historical and commercial ties with the areas now forming Pakistan. The state was wedged in between Pakistan, India, and China, and all three coveted its natural and strategic potentials. As the ruler dithered on the future of this princely state, many Kashmiri Muslims rose in rebellion and, by October 1947, were able to wrest northern and western territories from his control. They were helped by Pakistani Pushtun tribal volunteers, whose steady advance worried Prime Minister Jawaharlal Nehru of India. Amid greater suspicion between the two neighbors accompanied by a traumatic communalism gripping south Asia, the new armies of India and Pakistan were reluctantly dragged into a war over Kashmir. Negotiations for peace between the political leaders on both sides only added to a military stalemate until the newly formed United Nations was invited to resolve the thorny issue. Several resolutions later and more wars during 1965, 1971, and another armed rebellion in the 1990s, the Kashmir dispute still remains unresolved. Its borders are the most fortified in the world, with the Himalayas and Karakorams having been transformed into a high-altitude battleground.[3] More than anything else, the dispute over the future of Kashmir has spawned discord between India and Pakistan, in addition to a severe sense of alienation among the Kashmiri Muslims, who find themselves in a political dead-end.[4]

Other than Kashmir, the state of Hyderabad in southern India posed some friction in Indo-Pakistani relations. Here the local majority population was Hindu, but the ruler was a Muslim prince who desired to remain independent. In this case, Nehru sent in troops, which annexed the state that equaled France in territory and had been sovereign for more than two centuries. Many Muslims from Hyderabad found refuge in Pakistan, though Pakistan never laid any claim to that territory. These demographic and political developments seriously impacted relations between Delhi and Karachi. The third princely state to underpin the contentious relationship was Junagarh, which bordered India and Pakistan and was located in the southernmost part of the Indus basin. Hindus held a majority in this princely state, which was ruled by a Muslim Nawab, who desired to join Pakistan. Ill feelings between India and Pakistan were not due only to communal riots and disputes over princely states, disputes also occurred over the distribution of monetary and natural resources between the two successor states to the British Raj. Many Pakistanis believed that Indian leaders at large were not happy with the evolution of Pakistan and were intent on scuttling it at its birth. Delhi's procrastinations over releasing funds to Karachi and the stoppage of water into irrigation canals by the Punjab government on the Indian side seemed to affirm Pakistani suspicions about India's reluctance in accepting the existence of a new state on both borders. After the demarcation of boundary lines, especially to the west, several water works located upstream on the rivers had been ceded to India, enabling it to control and limit the water supply into the irrigation system downstream to the Indus Valley. Mahatma Gandhi's fast unto death persuaded the Indian government to release some overdue assets to Pakistan, but only after having damaged trust on Pakistani side.

CENTRAL AUTHORITY AND PROVINCES

Divided into two wings, Pakistan included five administrative units or provinces, four of them within the western wing and a more homogenous East Bengal accounting for the fifth province. As mentioned previously, East Bengal was predominantly a Bengali-speaking region of smaller size, but with slightly more inhabitants than its western counterparts. In the western wing Punjab retained a visible presence in country's civic and military sectors. Still a predominantly agrarian heartland, it depended on the water flow from the canal head works now mostly left behind in India by the departing British authorities. Compared with East Bengal, Sindh, the North-West Frontier Province (NWFP), and Balochistan, however, the province of Punjab (also known as West Punjab) became the powerhouse in the new country, whereas other units desired equal political powers, development funds, and cultural safeguards. Punjab's healthier economy and an edge over other provinces in services evinced suspicions that, in view of a lack of a proper constitutional framework, increased over subsequent decades. The adoption of Urdu as the national language in 1947 did not cause any major resentment within the western wing, but numerous East Bengalis registered a sense of cultural alienation.

The hold of Punjabi politicians in league with the Urdu-speaking immigrants (*muhajireen*) only exacerbated fears of "a Punjabi domination," because most of the civil service came from these two ethnic groups, whereas the armed forces were dominated by the Punjabis at all levels. Balochistan, accounting for 43 percent of Pakistan's territory, was not a province in the early decades, and excluding a smaller area under the British control, the rest of the region was divided among several princely states with the Khan of Kalat holding a nominal primacy over all of them. Other than Kalat being the largest in territory, Makran, Las Bela, and Kharan were the princely states that wanted to join the new state, but the Khan of Kalat's brother and a few other individuals desired complete independence. Negotiations between the Khan and Karachi went on for a year until the state was integrated in Pakistan during the summer of 1948. Ten years later, Pakistan purchased the fishing village of Gwadar from the Sultan of Muscat (Oman) for 3,000,000 pounds. In northern Pakistan, the princely states and partially autonomous regions such as Hunza, Nagar, Chilas, and Gilgit joined Pakistan, following an armed resistance against the Maharaja of Kashmir, who viewed these vital regions as integral part of the state of Jammu and Kashmir.[5]

Because of the disparate nature of Pakistani administrative and political realities and the fear of its disintegration owing to internal unevenness and a possible Indian invasion, successive regimes in Karachi opted for centralizing politics. Such policies, however realistic they might have been, evolved without an accompanying participatory politics, especially when the country lacked a constitution for almost a decade. Pakistan's political parties such as the Muslim League were weakened as their top leaders held political offices and provincial and ideological groups formed their own parties, pulling the new country toward newer directions. Ethnic parities such as the Awami League or National Awami Party demanded more rights for smaller provinces whereas religiopolitical parities, including the Jamaat-i-Islami and Majlis-i-Ahrar, advocated Islamicization of the country.[6] Pakistan's formation as a predominantly Muslim country was not sufficient enough for such ideological groups who demanded its holistic sociopolitical reorientation. But they were not the only ones who sought a systemic change; even the ruling political and civil elite soon began to seek out legitimacy and national cohesion through a selective use of Islamic ethos. Jinnah had been a secular man who believed in equal citizenship for all and completely opposed establishing theocracy, but his death on September 11, 1948 made ethnic and ideological tensions within the country quite sharp.

Comprised of several provinces and territories, and divided into two separate wings, Pakistan's one-house parliament was expected to frame the constitution and laws to run the country, in addition to creating a shared sense of common nationhood. Including the Prime Minister Liaquat Ali Khan, the entire cabinet came from the assembly, which hindered its operations. Imbalances among the constituent units, contentions over the distribution of assets, political offices, and jobs were soon to surface, making governance a testing issue. As long as Jinnah was alive, he could persuade and even pressure regional leaders toward greater mutual accommodation, but after his death, the lack of consensus on the distribution of political power and economic resources often turned controversial. Even a unifying force such as Islam or shared history in the preceding centuries in India could not override personal and ethnic rivalries, and the matter became more challenging when Pakistan did not have a constitution for the first full decade. The Constituent Assembly passed various resolutions and white papers, including the Objectives Resolution of 1949 and the One-Unit Scheme. An agreed upon constitution, however, could not emerge until 1956 and that, too, was scuttled by the army.[7] Dismissals of provincial governments in the NWFP, Sindh, and East Pakistan in the early years did not help create a harmonious atmosphere, nor did the amalgamation of all West Pakistani provinces and regions into One Unit present any solution to a dichotomous relationship between the two major wings of the country. After the adoption of the One-Unit Scheme, Pakistan's western wing was designated as West Pakistan, whereas East Bengal came to be known as East Pakistan.

Tensions between East and West Pakistan were rooted in cultural and economic factors, and a lack of constitutional framework. At another level, relations among the provinces within West Pakistan were often characterized by mutual suspicions, and whenever the central government failed to create balanced and acceptable mechanisms, many ethnic politicians (including their Bengali counterparts) blamed Punjab for monopolizing powers. With politicians usually proving vulnerable to ministerial offices and the country lacking a constitutional consensus, civil servants assumed a mainstream role in the national affairs. Their power increased to such an extent that in 1953, the elected government of Khwaja Nazim-ud-Din (1894–1964) was dismissed by Ghulam Muhammad (1895–1956), the governor-general of Pakistan, who blamed the former of incompetence. Ironically, Ghulam Muhammad was a former civil servant who, like many other colleagues, had risen to the highest offices of the land until he had the temerity to dismiss the elected cabinet. He soon dismissed the Constituent Assembly as well, and both of his verdicts were strangely upheld by country's Supreme Court under "the law of necessity," whereby a strong executive could undertake such measures in the larger interests of the country. The idea of One-Unit was, in fact, linked to Ghulam Muhammad's centralizing tendencies as it owed to the salience of bureaucracy in country's political structures, and was seen as an antidote to vocal East Bengali politicians seeking more powers and resources for their province. In fact, East Pakistan had been the country's most populous region, accounting for 56 percent of the total population. Its leaders agonized over Punjab's salience in Pakistan.[8] The Muslim League, which had triumphantly fought for Pakistan, was not unable to guide the country toward a cherished parliamentary form of government, nor did it succeed in keeping its senior leaders from hankering after public offices. The provincial elections of 1954 proved a death-knoll for the Muslim League and heralded the ascendance of regional and ethnic parties, who, in most cases, pursued their own parallel political programs. In their opposition to the Muslim League controlled by Punjabi politicians, these regional parties had produced a common electoral front called the United Front, but their own squabbles only encouraged centrist forces such as the bureaucracy and military. The country was being run by senior civil servants who held vital positions and, given the discord with India over Kashmir, Pakistan's security imperatives allowed a major share of budgetary allocation for its Army.

1956–1958: CONSTITUTIONALISM OR BUREAUCRATIC CENTRALISM

After Ghulam Muhammad, Iskander Mirza (1899–1969) emerged as the new governor-general of Pakistan in 1955, and his rise was owed to political intrigues that arose from self-seeking elements within the government. Iskander Mirza had been a former civil servant who had served in the tribal region of the NWFP, and he was adept at manipulating the local elite for specific objectives. He had replaced a politician as the governor of East Pakistan and was able to ease out an ailing Ghulam Muhammad to become the governor-general of Pakistan. Mirza was helped by senior civil servants and had significant support from General Ayub Khan (1907–1974), the commander-in-chief of the Pakistani army and a close ally. Within a short span of time, four coalition governments had come into existence in the Center, but they failed to make their mark, as the power concentrated with the executive—the governor-general—who ruled the country like the British viceroy and sought legitimacy from the India Act of 1935. In 1956, Pakistan's second Constituent Assembly was able to form a constitution that defined Pakistan as an Islamic Republic and opted for a parliamentary form of government under a president whose powers included the nomination and dismissal of the prime minister. The prime minister was to represent the majority party in the National Assembly, a unicameral parliament elected by the population, whereas East and West Pakistan were to enjoy parity in representation in the central government. This last principle had been rooted in the One-Unit Scheme, which, through a centralized formula, had amalgamated all four units into a single province of West Pakistan. The idea of federalism had spawned this constitution, which had taken so many years to germinate, yet the debate had often been characterized by dissention rather than dialogue. The country opted for the federal system but also made a conscious decision to refer its laws to classical Islamic sources such as the Quran and the Prophetic traditions. In other words, Islam was seen both as a homogenizer for the state and a means of legitimizing power sharing. The proposed constitution of 1956 allowed a multiparty political culture and adult franchise for all Pakistanis, and its Islamic orientation definitely showed the primacy of religiopolitical elements that had been demanding Islamization of Pakistan since 1948. Although all the clerics (*ulama*) and a sizable number of Pakistanis desired an Islamic republic, their own ideas about the nature and composition of such an ideal system remained hazy and even contradictory. The literalists demanded a puritanical form of government, whereas the Sufis were satisfied with certain Islamic and spiritual features, but the modernists desired a more mundane and accountable order. The importance given to army generals, bureaucrats, and even of clerics did not bode well for secular elements who still cherished the Jinnahist vision of a progressive Pakistan based on equal citizenship and a world apart from theocracy.

Even before the implementation of the Constitution of 1956, the powerful organs of state struck in October 1958 and barricaded the emerging electoral politics that banked on the new constitutional framework. Iskander Mirza, in collaboration with General Ayub Khan, imposed martial law in the country on October 7, 1958, accusing politicians of incompetence in coming to terms with Pakistan's dire political and economic problems. In the name of a stable and reformist administration, Iskander Mirza assumed absolute power as the president of the country, abrogated the new constitution, banned political activities, and asked General Ayub Khan to run military courts to try hoarders and other corrupt elements. Iskander Mirza, a close associate of Ghulam Muhammad and an immensely westernized bureaucrat, did not have any political following, nor did he enjoy the formidable position that accrued to Ayub Khan owing to his uniform. Mirza soon found himself outwitted by the general, who refused to accept this duality. On October 28, 1958, he assumed the leadership of the country and exiled Mirza to London. Ayub Khan, as will be seen in the next chapter, promised cleansing of the administration and shoring up the country's defenses; and his 10-year rule, despite some significant economic growth and liberal policies, turned out to be a trendsetter for his other successors in uniform who have been ruling Pakistan for most of its history.

FOREIGN RELATIONS

Pakistan's location in the vital strategic regions of western and Southeast Asia amid a heightened global Cold War was also significant because of its own security demands emerging from its difficulties vis-à-vis India. The country's security needs, threat perceptions about India especially over the disputed territory of Kashmir, and the westernized mindset of its civil and military elite allowed it to develop closer relationships with the United States and other Western powers. By virtue of their significance as two of the earliest states to gain independence, Pakistan and India competed to gain global allies, and this feature of their otherwise conflict-ridden relationship persists even today.

Since 1947, Pakistan's foreign policy has been focused on three trajectories, which also reveal the three concurrent ideological strands among its elite. By virtue of history and geography, Pakistan has been an important south Asian nation that has always felt separated by an indifferent India between its two wings. The massive refugee influx, the stoppage of canal waters after the boundary disputes, Delhi's reluctance to share assets, and India's control over Kashmir and other princely states transformed it into a foe in the common Pakistani imagination. Indians have also harbored skeptical, ambivalent, and even hostile views about the rationale and political career of Pakistan, usually seeing it as an adversary. It is true that Afghanistan was the only country in the United Nations that had objected to Pakistan's entry into the world body, but India-Pakistan relations were never going to improve after the sordid events of 1947.[9] India's justification for sending troops into the Kashmir Valley was rooted in the Maharaja's signing of an Instrument of Accession with New Delhi in October 1947 after a tribal attack from the west. Circumstances such as the revolt within Kashmir before India's Partition, the arrival of private militias and soldiers from India and Pakistan to support their respective countries, and the timing of the signing of the Instrument, however, still remain contested. Kashmir led to the first Indo-Pakistan war, which ended in early 1948 when the United Nations (UN) intervened. Kashmir was partitioned into Pakistani-controlled Azad Kashmir and the Indian-controlled Kashmir, which included Jammu and Ladakh. The UN, through various resolutions, urged for plebiscite so as to let Kashmiris decide their future, but the plan remained unimplemented. Pakistanis have held all along that Kashmir, being a Muslim majority region, would vote for accession to Pakistan and would accuse Indian leadership of dithering on the issue of self-determination for Kashmiris. India justifies its control of Kashmir on the basis of the Instrument of Accession, and during the 1950s and 1960s, it would demand the withdrawal of Pakistani troops from Azad Kashmir.[10] Although UN observers continue to monitor the Line of Control dividing two parts of the former princely state, various special UN arbiters in the past failed to break this Indo-Pakistani logjam, which eventually led to outright hostilities.

Pakistan has always maintained good relations with Iran and the People's Republic of China, and despite various regional and global upheavals, these neighbors in the west and north have usually been supportive of a stable and peaceful Pakistan. Afghanistan, as mentioned previously, had its own ambitions on Pakistani territory, although more Pushtuns live on this side of Afghan-Pakistan borders than in Afghanistan, and over the years have become stakeholders in the Indus Valley nation. Throughout the 1950s and later, Pakistan allowed transit facilities for goods to this land-locked country and has often provided financial assistance for various development projects.[11] In the early decade of its existence, Pakistan formed closer relationships with Nepal and Sri Lanka, although the turbulent nature of Indo-Pakistani bilateralism prevented closer regional cooperation within south Asia.

Pakistan's second important trajectory in foreign relations has been with the United States and other North Atlantic powers with which it sought closer economic and military ties.[12] The United States was seen as a supporter of newly independent democracies and its military, political, and economic assistance was in great demand among Pakistani elite. Pakistan's breakthrough came with the visit by Prime Minister Liaquat Ali Khan and his wife in 1950 to North America, where he introduced this Muslim nation as an aspirant of democracy and progressive nomenclature.[13] The American Cold War imperatives and search for allies after the Chinese Revolution and the Korean War brought countries like Pakistan, Iraq, Iran, and Turkey in alliance with Washington. Growing economic and military exchanges were soon followed by Pakistan joining two important U.S.-led alliances, assuming that such a relationship would shore up its own regional security objectives. In 1954, Pakistan joined the SEATO (South-East Asian Treaty Organization), where it developed relationships with many Australasian nations. In 1955, Pakistan became an active member of the Baghdad Pact or CENTO (Central Treaty Organization), which had been the brainchild of people like Allan Dulles and John Foster Dulles, who deemed such military and strategic alliances as necessary roadblocks to a feared expansion of communism.[14] Pakistan's closer ties with Washington and its regional allies helped train its own military and civil elite, along with raising the country's global profile, although it stymied the evolution of a more nonaligned foreign policy. For instance, in 1956, many

Pakistanis were furious over the Israeli-British-French attack of Egypt, but Karachi avoided revoking these treaties and, in the same manner, the military coup in Pakistan in 1958 was quickly accepted as a new political reality in a friendly country. Pakistan's third trajectory in forging closer sociopolitical relationships was aimed at the Muslim nations in Asia and Africa. Here, Pakistani leaders recognized religious commonalities in addition to seeking moral and political support in their contest with India. Some nationalist leaders such as President Gamal Nasser of Egypt were critical of Pakistan's close alliance with the United States, as were the post-1958 leaders of the ruling Baath Party in Iraq; but among other nations, including those in Southeast Asia, Pakistan was viewed with respect and affection. Pakistan's stance on decolonization and solidarity with the Palestinians have been two persistent features of its foreign policy.

NOTES

1. M. Rafique Afzal, *Pakistan: History and Politics, 1947–1971* (Karachi: Oxford University Press, 2001 p. 21. For further details, see Gyanendra Pandey, *Remembering Partition: Violence, Nationalism and History in India* (Cambridge: Cambridge University Press, 2001); Urvashi Butalia, *The Other Side of Violence: Voices from the Partition of India* (London: C. Hurst, 2000).

2. For more on Jinnah, see Stanley Wolpert, *Jinnah of Pakistan* (New York: Oxford University Press, 1984); *Shameful Flight: The Last Years of British Empire in India* (New York: Oxford University Press, 2006).

3. Many of the United Nations resolutions demanded a plebiscite of Kashmiri people to determine their future vis-à-vis India or Pakistan, but India's resistance to such a plan in view of its fears of Kashmiris overwhelmingly opting for Pakistan prevented this vote. Both countries contested the mechanisms and modalities of the proposed right of self-determination, and other regional developments also overshadowed the UN resolve to implement its resolutions, although its observers have been monitoring the Line of Control on both sides since 1949. Thus Kashmir remains one of the oldest disputes in UN history.

4. For further details, see Alistair Lamb, *Kashmir: A Disputed Legacy, 1846–1990* (Hertingfordbury: Roxford Books, 1991); Victoria Schofield, *Kashmir in the Crossfire* (London: I. B. Tauris, 1996).

5. During the 1870s, the British had strengthened their hold on Gilgit so as to ward off any feared Russian attack on India and established an administrative agency in the Karakoram town. On the eve of independence, the Kashmiri state troops led by Brigadier Ghansara Singh were challenged by the local Muslims who, in defiance, raised the Pakistani flag and asked Karachi for a formal accession. It was on November 16, 1947 that Pakistan officially

accepted Gilgit Agency's formal request and sent its officials to administer the region.

6. In 1952–1953, these parties and their other allies spearheaded a campaign in Punjab, demanding the exclusion of Ahmadis from being defined as Muslims. The Ahmadis are a messianic movement established by Mirza Ghulam Ahmad (1835–1908) in Punjab who, to the chagrin of other Muslims, viewed himself as the Promised Messiah. Demonstrations by religiopolitical parties soon became intertwined with the contemporary political factionalism where politicians such as Mumtaz Daultana tried to create problems for Nazim-ud-Din. The prime minister refused to budge and instead imposed martial law in Lahore, although demands persisted for the removal of Ahmadi Foreign Minister Zafrullah Khan. Two decades later Pakistan's National Assembly declared Ahmadis (Qadianis) to be a non-Muslim group owing to their specific views on the finality of Prophethood.

7. The Objectives Resolution was a policy statement on the ideals and directions of the would-be constitution. Among many of its recommendations, it stipulated an Islamic orientation of the political framework. Passed under the stewardship of Liaquat Ali Khan, it was destined to precede future constitutions of the country.

The One-Unit Scheme was mostly pioneered by the Punjabi politicians who sought unification of four regional administrations in the western wing into a single political unit. It also sought parity with East Pakistan in the allocation of political seats and financial assets. For non-Punjabis, this idea proved anathema and was eventually rescinded in 1970.

8. Although Ghulam Muhammad was succeeded by Iskander Mirza as the fourth governor-general of Pakistan, Liaquat Ali Khan's assassination in October 1951 had been followed by several prime ministers until October 1958 when the military formally took charge of the country. Nazim-ud-Din, Mohammad Ali Bogra, Ismail Chundrigar, Huseyn Suhrawardy, Chaudhr Muhammad Ali, and Firoz Khan Noon were all prime ministers of Pakistan within five years and often lost their offices to shifting alliances and gubernatorial unilateralism. There is a concurrent list of several provincial politicians who held ministerial offices at varying times, and some of them became quite adept in forging alliances and coalitions.

9. The Kabul regime protested Pakistani control of the Pushtun tribal regions in the NWFP by backing out of its early covenants with the British Raj. Afghan support for factious elements within these regions was perceived in Pakistan as a destabilizing ploy by "Kabul+Delhi axis." Afghan dependence on Pakistani communication and transport networks, however, along with the greater integration of Pushtuns within the Pakistani economy, gradually lessened the threat of secession.

10. Pakistanis would challenge India's legality on allowing the ruler to decide the future of the states, which the latter did not permit in similar cases such as Hyderabad and Junagarh where rulers wanted to remain independent or join Pakistan. Pakistanis would also suggest simultaneous withdrawal of troops from both sides to let the neutral observers operate the interim administration until the UN-led plebiscite was complete. For more on various views including the demand for a united and free Kashmir, see, Raju G. C. Thomas (ed.), *Perspectives on Kashmir: the Roots of Conflict in South Asia* (Boulder: Westview Press, 1992).

11. Other than common religion, shared ethnicity and history, many Afghans have been seasonal emigrants to Pakistan along with their herds, and this has been happening since time immemorial. These migratory Ghilzai tribes seek pastures in the Indus Valley and come down the mountains during the harsh winters of Afghanistan. After the Soviet invasion in 1979, millions of Afghan refugees sought shelter across Pakistan and many of them continue to reside here.

12. For the pre-1947 relationship between the United States and the subcontinent see, Iftikhar H. Malik, *U.S.-South Asian Relations, 1940–47: American Attitude towards Pakistan Movement* (Oxford: Macmillan-St. Antony's Series, 1991).

13. For his speeches and statements during this historic visit, see Liaquat Ali Khan, *Pakistan: The Heart of Asia* (Cambridge: Harvard University Press, 1950). For the earliest work on Pakistan, see Richard Symonds, *The Making of Pakistan* (London: Faber and Faber, 1950).

14. For further details, see Robert J. McMahon, *The Cold War on the Periphery: The United States, India and Pakistan* (New York: Columbia University Press, 1994).

8

Military Takeover and the Separation of East Pakistan, 1958–1971

Led by General Ayub Khan (1907–1974), the military coup in Pakistan on October 28, 1958 proved to be a turning point in the country's history and also a new threshold in the civil-military relationship. Given wider acclaim as a revolution by Ayub Khan himself and projected as a protest against politicians accused of incompetence and corruption, this military takeover happened at a time when U.S.-Pakistan relations were strong, whereas Indo-Pakistani relations remained turbulent. Despite Ayub Khan's efforts to induct an indirect system of democracy, questions about the legitimacy of his rule, rifts between West and East Pakistan, and polarization between modernist Pakistanis and their conservative counterparts led by religious scholars (*ulama*) continued unabated. The military's role had changed from its previous indirect player as a powerful factor in Pakistani politics during the parliamentary era of 1947–1958 to a flagship position that, over successive years, became deeply entrenched along with raising serious issues about the viability of a political culture led by the army. Ayub Khan's era was said to be a decade of development, but its unpredictable nature, as well as its reluctance to engage Pakistani dissenting and pluralistic politics only aggravated East-West tensions. As a consequence, Pakistan underwent a tumultuous partition in 1971, as the issues of governance remained largely unresolved in a military-led centralized system. In recent years, however, there has been a growing interest in studying Ayub Khan's role as one of the modernizers in the postcolonial societies such as Pakistan. After the death of Pundit Jawaharlal Nehru in 1964, Ayub Khan was often seen as one of the preeminent statesmen in Asia.

WHY THE ARMY?

When the military formally overtook the reigns of power, many Pakistanis welcomed the change assuming it would bring about a positive transformation; others remained skeptical but waited to form their opinion. During the last five decades, the army has been at the helm of the country's affairs, vacillating between full control to partial withdrawal; and ordinary Pakistanis, as well as academics, have been raising issues about the reasons and results of military rule. During the 1950s and 1960s, several nations in Africa, Asia, and Latin America had come under military control; and in all these cases the generals promised reforms, economic development, responsive political systems, and a transparent governance. For a while, they were welcomed by the Western governments because they offered stability and order, and even several scholars supported the military takeover.[1] In successive decades, when military regimes failed to deliver and instead exacerbated ideological and economic schisms, civic groups, analysts, and academics grew critical of military authoritarianism. With the end of the Cold War in 1989, the sentiments for full-fledged democratization became more popular, although many countries including Pakistan were still bedeviled by political and ideological challenges, and generals would often offer promises for new order.[2]

There are several views about the military's persistent ascendance over Pakistan's political and economic structures and institutions. Traditionally, the evolution of Pakistan and its location in two distant and disparate regions had resulted in some skepticism regarding its viability. These feelings increased when the country lacked proper leadership after the death of its founder, M. A. Jinnah. Comparison with India remained a hallmark of such analysis, as Pakistan was often seen as the *other* of a democratic and secular India, although both countries had inherited similar pluralistic cultures and structures. Nehru and the other founding fathers ensured a systematic formation of the Indian Union through a secular and participatory constitution, reorganization of the constituent states. and reliance on well-developed political parties such as the Indian National Congress. Delay in formulating a constitution, misplaced focus on personalities instead of institutions, and preference for security instead of nation-building, however, all combined to weaken Pakistan's fragile political culture. In a power vacuum, generals and bureaucrats became the arbiters, with politicians becoming their junior and even dependent associates.[3]

The elite pursuit of state building, even at the expense of nation building, may explain the primacy of bureaucracy over political and other civic institutions such as the judiciary and the media. As the strongest arm of the bureaucracy, the army was a beneficiary as well as a concerned spectator over squabbles among the politicians, although on occasions, it never hesitated in exploiting these dissentions. Pakistan's army chief, General Ayub Khan, as is affirmed in his autobiography and other contemporary writings including the papers released by the U.S. Government, had been party to several important decisions and developments in the country since he became the commander-in-chief in 1951. His strong inclinations toward the United States and the latter's need to include the Muslim nation in its global strategy of combating communism brought more arms and clout for the Pakistani army. Ayub Khan, while leading troops in East Bengal, had used his indirect influence vis-à-vis the politicians, and following his handling of the Rawalpindi Conspiracy case in 1951, established himself as the paramount power within Pakistani political spectrum. The conspiracy was attributed to a few senior military officials and their leftist allies who were alleged to have plotted to bring about a military coup to establish a socialist republic in the country. The conspiracy came to official notice when an insider confided with the authorities, allowing Prime Minister Liaquat Ali Khan (1896–1951) and the army chief to undertake preemptive measures. Ayub Khan tried the military elements through special army courts and jailed them for extended terms, as well as ensuring that the army officials followed a strict British model of staying away from political activities. In fact, he himself was planning on taking over power and redirecting Pakistan's political fortunes even long before he formally assumed control on October 28, 1958.[4] Ayub Khan had become a defense minister in 1954 and thus held an important position on the cabinet and surely bided his time.

The primacy of Pakistani generals within the country's political culture is owed, among other factors, to the Cold War imperatives of successive U.S. administrations that desired a strategic ally in the two vital Asian regions bordering China and Soviet Central Asia. Concurrently, Pakistan needed arms and economic assistance from Washington at a time when the former colonial power had been seriously weakened and India refused to budge on Kashmir. These mutual priorities were underwritten by the Western orientation of Pakistani civilian and military leaders who preferred closer alliance with the North Atlantic powers.[5] This security relationship, however, prevented an open debate on democracy and foreign policy in the country and led to enduring imbalances in its political economy.[6] Even after more than six decades, Pakistan's political culture remains fractured, and its development sector inclusive of education and health stays meager compared to a large-scale defense expenditure including an unaudited nuclear sector.

It may be easier for generals to take over power, but it is always difficult to "ride down the tiger," as their personal and sectional interests become entwined with their country's infrastructure.[7] Although the army remained an unchallenged force in Pakistani domestic and foreign policies, it added to a greater sense of deprivation among the politicians and general population outside Punjab, as most of the personnel and senior military officials hailed from this province. Since the British ruled in India, the military recruitment was confined to certain areas and groups designated as "martial races" by the colonial administrators, allowing a lion's share to Punjabi Muslim and Sikh peasants. In 1947, Pakistani civil and military sectors were heavily Punjab-dominated and the army generals assumed a leadership role in country's politics, often in league with the Punjabi politicians. As a result, a grave sense of alienation arose among East Bengalis and other provinces in West Pakistan. Over successive decades, Pakistani armed forces have tried to recruit non-Punjabis, and among the higher ranks there are more Pushtuns and Urdu speakers now than there were two decades back.[8] More than the air force and navy, it is the army that has been at the forefront of the country's political economy, as the other two branches of the military have often been viewed as more professional and even nonpolitical. Simultaneously, within the army, it is the senior generals or corps commanders who have been making several significant decisions on areas such as the change of government, foreign policy, nuclearization, and budgetary allocations. The army has a strong tradition of top-down command and upholds decisions reached by generals including the imposition of martial law, conducting war with India, or monitoring situations Pakistan-Afghan borders.

GENERAL AYUB KHAN, 1958–1969: A DECADE OF DEVELOPMENT OR DISCORD?

Muhammad Ayub Khan, subsequently to be known as field marshal and president, was born in a scenic village of Rehana in the North-West Frontier Province (NWFP) on May 14, 1907. His father was a retired junior official from the British Army and, despite a meager pension and large family, sought excellent education for his children. In 1922, he sent Ayub Khan to Aligarh to pursue higher studies at the well-known institution founded by Sir Syed Ahmed Khan, the great Muslim benefactor. Here Ayub Khan proved his academic and athletic acumen, and immersed himself in the British, south Asian, and Muslim political undercurrents. While pursuing his graduation, he was selected for a direct army commission by General Skeen, the adjutant-general of British Indian Army, who visited Aligarh looking for prospective Indian cadets. Ayub underwent training both in India and then at Sandhurst and afterwards served during World War II on the Burma front. At independence,

Ayub was a senior official of the Boundary Force commanded by General Rees and that had come in for some criticism as a result of large-scale communal killings in Punjab during the migrations of 1947. After independence, Ayub Khan was stationed in East Bengal in January 1948 and lobbied hard to consolidate the Pakistani defense establishment at a time when money and weaponry were scarce. During his command in East Bengal, Ayub Khan learned more about politicians such as H. S. Suhrawardy, Fazlul Haq, Muhammad Ali Bogra, Nazim-ud-Din, and Nurul Amin and subsequently developed fraternal relationship with Ghulam Muhammad, Chaudhari Muhammad Ali, and Iskander Mirza. These three men were destined to play a pivotal role from 1951 to 1958 as the chief executives of Pakistan, ensuring the primacy of bureaucratic, authoritarian rule.

In 1950, Ayub Khan returned to Rawalpindi, which served as the general headquarters for the newly established Pakistan Army and through Iskander Mirza, the defense secretary, came closer to Pakistan's ruling circle. Upon the death of the two other senior generals in an air crash, Ayub Khan was appointed as the commander-in-chief in January 1951, which allowed him to divide his time between Karachi and Rawalpindi, with occasional visits to East Pakistan. He soon developed relationships with most West Pakistani politicians. As mentioned previously, he quashed the Rawalpindi Conspiracy that was attempting to overthrow the existing regime, which endeared him with Prime Minister Liaquat Ali Khan and the Americans. After the prime minister's assassination in October 1951, Ayub Khan witnessed the weakening of political culture as a result of petty squabbles over power sharing, while the Constituent Assembly failed to produce a constitution. He claimed to have agonized over the state of affairs and even drafted a political plan for his country while on a visit to London in 1954.[9] Soon the general was inducted into the cabinet, although in view of Iskander Mirza's ambitions, he remained cautious in dealing with the latter. Mirza had assumed the presidency of the country and thus enjoyed powers to appoint and dismiss prime ministers, as well as military chiefs.

In his memoirs, Ayub Khan claimed to have been deeply disturbed over the political instability in the country and was even urged by prominent people such as the Aga Khan and Begum Ranaa Liaquat Ali Khan to take charge of the country. Pakistan's armed forces, as in some other postcolonial states, were seen as the most disciplined and modern segments that could usher a new era of stability, as well as helping the United States in its global containment of communism. General Ayub Khan developed a friendship with Allen Dulles, the head of the Central Intelligence Agency (CIA), and through him was able to forge links with John Foster Dulles, the U.S. secretary of state. With these contacts and American military assistance, Pakistan, prodded by the general, agreed to join Southeast Asia Treaty Organization (SEATO) and Central Treaty

Organisation (CENTO). By the summer of 1958, Ayub Khan was finishing his second term as the army commander and, despite maintaining amicable relations with Iskander Mirza and Prime Minister Firoz Khan Noon, was unwilling to retire. Mirza allowed him another extension for two years in June 1958 on the understanding that the general would stand by the president in any new political development. By that time, Mirza had become quite unpopular among Pakistani politicians and other concerned citizens who accused him of manipulation and personal aggrandizement. With Ayub secure for the next two years, an insecure Mirza had become dependent on the former's support, although he did not have any of his own constituency in the country or in the military. Mirza, driven by his whims and insecurity, decided to impose martial law on October 7, 1958 and asked General Ayub Khan to arrest politicians and to hold military courts to prosecute hoarders and smugglers. Only three weeks later, Ayub Khan overtook an isolated Mirza and assumed all powers as the chief martial law administrator. Since the imposition of martial law on October 7, Mirza had dismissed the central and provincial governments, abolished all political parties, and abrogated the constitution by putting the entire responsibility of government's incompetence on to the politicians.[10]

In general, Pakistanis welcomed Ayub Khan, as they expected stability and systemic overhaul. Also, the press had been put under stringent control, so dissent, if any, was not well known in the country. He promised not to retain martial law "a minute longer than is necessary."[11] Ayub Khan was a well-built man of towering height, and his order carried authority. Soon the country seemed to be moving forward, especially when it came to matters such as prices of goods, the competency of the lower courts, and the general behavior of junior bureaucrats. Ayub Khan appointed 30 expert commissions and committees to recommend specific reforms in every major sector of national life. His Land Reforms Commission, the Law Reforms Commission, and the Press Commission received significant public attention. Ayub Khan implemented first-ever land reforms in Pakistan, which limited landholding while ensuring security for landless peasants. The reforms also banned forced labor and tried to consolidate land for small landowners under a new settlement plan. The big landlords were allowed to keep a maximum of 500 acres of irrigated or 1,000 acres of arid land; the rest was to be distributed among the peasants. These reforms could not be fully implemented, as the general soon required the support of local intermediaries for his own political system; thus Pakistan's feudal families remained powerful, both locally and nationally.

Ayub Khan's political reforms reflected his own strong reservations against politicians as he tried to control them through a number of restrictive measures including disqualifications and detentions. Eventually, however, he needed their support when, in 1962, he finally lifted martial law and implemented a constitution of his own choice. This constitution introduced an indirect system of government in which voters would elect councilors, who, besides running the local government, would also form an electoral college to elect the president. Initially, there were 80,000 such "basic democrats"; the number was subsequently increased to 120,000. The two separately elected assemblies were to run both East and West Pakistan; the power remained with the president in the central government and the governors of the two provinces. The Constitution of 1962 had a strong presidential writ and disallowed universal franchise to elect even an otherwise powerful president. If the president were to become incapacitated, the speaker of the National Assembly—the single-house parliament for the entire country—was to succeed him. The constitution did not resolve Pakistan's age-old problem of power sharing between the central government and the provinces, nor did it allow adult and direct franchise. Instead it opted for greater centralization, which for a pluralistic country created ill feelings. Its recommendations on seeking guidance from Quranic sources on Islam, despite a preference for more mundane solutions, did not suggest any tangible connection between politics and religion, nor did it offer any durable balance of power between the two.

The advice and groundwork for Ayub Khan's political ideas came from various sources, although two of his cabinet ministers played a pivotal role, and both were westernized lawyers who shared a strong skepticism about public opinion. Putting aside the Law Commission's recommendations for an empowered parliamentary system, Manzur Qadir and Zulfikar Ali Bhutto only refurbished the general's preferences for strong central government over and above democratic prerogatives. Qadir was a British-trained lawyer whose keen intellect had impressed Ayub Khan when he appointed him as his foreign minister. Qadir devoted his energies in persuading the general not to place any significant trust in the masses, although the latter often talked of "the genius of the people." In the same way, Zulfikar Ali Bhutto, a young Oxford-trained Sindhi lawyer, proved to be an ardent loyalist to the extent of calling the general a new Saladin and often counseled for an elitist system. Youthful Bhutto was the commerce minister and was soon to emerge as a charismatic foreign minister who made his name by concluding border agreements with China.[12] Ayub Khan was resentful of print media and through his information secretary and confidante, Altaf Gauhar, introduced various bans and restrictive measures. Earlier, he had assumed control of three independent newspapers owned by the Progressive Papers Limited, as he was sensitive to their criticisms. In the same vein, he ensured full control of radio and television stations while establishing special prizes and advantages for proregime writers.

Despite his dictatorial tendencies, Ayub Khan envisioned a modern future for Pakistan. Owing to his military training, he was unable to see the pluralistic and diverse nature of human civic relations and held his belief in the transformative potentials of official institutions. It is true, however, that planned industrial development along with the induction of the Green Revolution, brought about through mechanized agriculture, transformed the Pakistani economy, although the common belief in the trickle-down effect of such growth was somewhat displaced. Floods in East Pakistan and a greater burden on West Pakistani economy often led to more foreign borrowing, although schools, family planning clinics, electrification of villages, and development of road infrastructure all improved under Ayub Khan. By the time Ayub Khan, at the behest of his advisors, sought to celebrate "the decade of development," however, he appeared more solitary while sitting at the apex of a system that was tailor-made to suit his own temperament and personal requirements rather than resolving the age-old issues of governance. By 1968, he was more or less on his own, as his former allies such as Bhutto had either left the government and had become his vociferous critics, or had been overtaken by more opportunistic allies within the fold of his Pakistan Muslim League. In 1965, Ayub Khan contested presidential elections, counting on the loyalty of a small electoral college, often propped up by the civil servants. His opponent was Miss Fatima Jinnah (1893–1967), the widely respected, veteran Muslim Leaguer and a founder of Pakistan who was known as *Mather-i-Millat* or Nation's Mother. It was only through the manipulation of his two governors—Muhammad Amir Khan and Abdul Monem Khan in West and East Pakistan, respectively—that Ayub Khan carried the day. Even before the elections, Miss Jinnah and her supporters faced serious official restrictions on public rallies or in reaching out to the electors through the print media. Ayub Khan's opponents rallied around Miss Jinnah, although the official machinery ensured the general's victory. Despite a docile National Assembly full of Ayub Khan loyalists, a passive judiciary, and a pliant media, a serious legitimacy crisis lingered on.

Other than his notorious electoral bout with Miss Jinnah, Ayub Khan's own untenable position became more apparent when, after the Indo-Pakistani War of 1965, many Pakistanis felt betrayed by the performance of their country's leadership. Averse to official propaganda and despite a valiant fight by the soldiers, the leadership of the country and its armed forces appeared inchoate much to the chagrin of the public. This dismay was exploited by Bhutto who had been dismissed by the general in 1966 and had not forgiven his former patron. In 1967, Bhutto formed the Pakistan People's Party (PPP) and promised the fulfillment of basic needs of ordinary Pakistanis, through his espousal of Islamic socialism. He was joined by Asghar Khan, a former air chief; and soon disgruntled politicians, especially from East Pakistan, took to the streets seeking the ouster of the general and demolition of his centrist political system. Ayub Khan had already imprisoned Sheikh Mujibur Rahman (1920–1975) of the Awami League in January 1968 on allegations of conspiring with India, which only made this Bengali leader even more popular in his native province. A former student leader and a follower of Suhrawardy, Rahman had become the leader of the Awami League, founded in East Pakistan in 1949. More like Bhutto, he was prone to verbosity and emotional outbursts, which only widened the chasm between the country's two wings. Through his Six-Point agenda, he demanded more political and financial autonomy for East Pakistan and thus became the symbol, as well as the symptom, of East Pakistani political disillusionment. For West Pakistani generals and politicians, his six points were nothing short of complete secession, as he demanded a separate constitution, currency, taxes, trade and foreign policy, all autonomous of the central government. Ayub Khan, himself ill-disposed during those months, failed to curb the discontent that soon began to claim human lives as a result of clashes with the police. As a last resort he invited all politicians for a round-table conference in Rawalpindi, but the talks failed because the general was unwilling to bow to the demands for universal empowerment, provincial autonomy, and free elections. In the meantime, a demoralized Ayub Khan became confined to a small coterie of advisors while General Yahya Khan (1917–1980), the new commander-in-chief, ensured the isolation of a marooned president.[13] Eventually, on March 25, 1969, Ayub Khan abdicated in favor of a formidable Yahya Khan instead of bequeathing powers to the speaker of the National Assembly, as had been promised in his own constitution.

FOREIGN RELATIONS DURING THE 1960s

At the official level, Pakistan's closer relationship with the United States remained sacrosanct for quite some time, although the coup in Iraq in 1958 and an unquestioned American assistance for Israel underpinned several anxieties among concerned citizens.[14] In the same vein, Pakistanis felt that U.S. support for Pakistan did not extend to pressuring India to relent on Kashmir, but the government remained steadfastly aligned with Washington. Yet this bilateralism on the part of the United States was to prove shaky because of developments such as the Pakistani decision to close down Budaber Air Base near Peshawar, which the United States had been using to fly U-2 planes to spy over the Soviet Union and for which Moscow had even threatened Pakistan with dire consequences. Moreover, in 1962, India and China went to war over an unresolved boundary dispute, which, for many Pakistanis was an opportune time to seek concessions from New Delhi on Kashmir. Yet Ayub Khan disallowed any such adventurism, as he was dissuaded by the Kennedy Administration, as well as by his own cautious disposition, although he did not harbor any high opinion of India's defense potentials. Nehru had pursued neutrality and nonalignment as the cornerstones of his policies, but amidst a debilitating war with China, he sought immediate help from Washington and

Moscow, who for their own reasons helped India but not without accentuating anxieties in Pakistan.[15]

Pakistan had started to negotiate with Beijing over the border demarcation in 1959 and talks were carried on by Bhutto after he became the foreign minister. Pakistan and China finalized the demarcations while Indo-Chinese tensions were quite high, and Washington did not appreciate its ally's growing relationship with Beijing. Ayub Khan, confronted with a hostile India, an indifferent Afghanistan, and an unfriendly Soviet Union, could not afford one more antagonistic neighbor to the north. Soon after the presidential elections of 1965, Ayub Khan undertook a high-profile visit to China and Prime Minister Chou En-lai escorted him to several Chinese cities where numerous vital agreements in the areas of trade and defense were finalized. The Johnson Administration was highly critical of Pakistan, but over the decades Sino-Pakistani relations have worked in favor of the United States; as in 1971, interestingly, Pakistanis facilitated normalcy in Sino-American relations by acting as interlocutors. Chinese military and diplomatic assistance for Pakistan has been vital, especially in the latter's relationship with India. China has also helped build Pakistan's Karakoram Highway, which passes through its northern areas and connects with Sinkiang province. Chinese help in Pakistan's nuclear program and more recently in the development of Gwadar as a deep seaport has earned respect for Beijing within Pakistani society. China, especially during the years of its international isolation and limited foreign exchange reserves, also duly benefited from its multiple relations with Pakistan. While establishing stronger ties with the northern neighbor, Ayub Khan also tried to allay Soviet reservations and doubts regarding Pakistan in view of Karachi's abiding relationship with Washington. After his visit to China, Ayub traveled to Moscow and held talks with Soviet leaders, although New Delhi remained a far more significant priority for the Russian leaders.

Pakistan's relationship with India has been a constant priority and a difficult process for both nations owing to the issues rooted in the dissolution of the British Raj. The Kashmir dispute and contentions over water resources have led to a history of hostility that had been further compounded as a result of the first Indo-Pakistani war of 1948. Ayub Khan, while building up a stronger defense, also sought political support from Western allies and Muslim nations and tried to woo China while simultaneously attempting to neutralize Russia. In the meantime, he maintained close contacts with Nehru, expecting a breakthrough on divisive issues. Pakistan was deeply concerned over the fact that three of its rivers either originated in India or flowed through Indian territory. Given the location of several waterworks in India and past stoppage by the latter, Ayub Khan sought some tangible mechanism to manage water resources with New Delhi. Eventually, owing to arbitration by the World Bank, the Indus Basin Treaty was finalized in 1959, which, to a great extent, resolved this thorny issue, although territorial disputes remained unaddressed. In addition to Kashmir, the undemarcated region of the Rann of Kuchch in the lower Indus delta created serious tensions between the two countries that finally led to a limited military showdown in April 1965. Here, Pakistani soldiers performed rather well despite logistical handicaps, although the issue was subsequently resolved through external arbitration. It was mainly Kashmir and a host of other factors, however, that led to the Indo-Pakistani War of September 1965. The Indian defeat by the Chinese and the Pakistani performance in Kuchch had encouraged certain elements among the ruling Pakistani elite who felt that India would never agree to a political solution to the issue of Kashmir. The failure of direct and UN-led negotiations only encouraged such a hardened attitude, whereas within the Valley of Kashmir a growing disenchantment with Delhi was perceived as a full-fledged defiance by the Muslim Kashmiris against Indian control. Amid exaggerated expectations and unanalyzed repercussions, Pakistani authorities encouraged infiltration into Kashmir, which became quite visible in the summer of 1965, although Rawalpindi kept attributing the incursion to the Kashmiris themselves. Finding itself in a quandary, India under Prime Minister Lal Bahadur Shastri decided to undertake a frontal attack on Pakistan, which resulted into India's advances in Punjab and Sindh. Pakistani generals, to a large extent, were caught unaware, although the soldiers and the nation put up a bold resistance and were able to thwart Indian excursions. The 17-day war exhausted both nations as a UN-led ceasefire managed the cessation of hostilities on September 23. Moscow offered its arbitration to both Ayub Khan and Lal Bahadur Shastri by inviting them to Tashkent in early 1966, where protracted negotiations finally led to a peace treaty. Accordingly, the troops were withdrawn to their prewar positions, prisoners were exchanged, and both countries agreed to pursue negotiations encompassing various divisive issues. The Tashkent Treaty, however, failed to resolve the Kashmir problem, and distrust continued between the two nations, with their mutual contacts reduced to a minimum.

GENERAL YAHYA KHAN (1969–1971) AND THE SEPARATION OF EAST PAKISTAN

The Tashkent Treaty was followed by the sudden death of Prime Minister Shastri on his way back to India and Bhutto's exit from Ayub Khan's cabinet. At the same time, serious questions arose among many East Pakistanis about their own vulnerability in security areas, as the war had been mainly fought in the western regions.[16] East Pakistanis felt that the regime was mainly interested in protecting the western wing and had left them on their own, although China had raised some morale-boosting statements. Yet East Pakistan lacked any ability to withstand an Indian attack. In addition, East Pakistanis were dismayed over a continued centralization of power and resources that seemed to be mostly reserved for their counterparts in West Pakistan. Ayub Khan's own political structure disappeared with his downfall when an ailing president lost control and General Yahya Khan was able to manipulate political instability to obtain his own ascension to power. Born in Peshawar in 1917 of Persian ancestry, Agha Muhammad Yahya Khan had been commissioned into the Indian army in 1938 and soon rose to senior ranks. As Ayub Khan's confidant, he gained further power when the field marshal tended to the affairs of state and Yahya Khan was elevated to the command of the Pakistani army in 1966. Earlier, he had headed the commission that chose the site of present-day Islamabad as the new federal capital and also enjoyed closer rapport with U.S. officials.

Yahya Khan had begun to increase his own influence during 1968–1969 when an isolated Ayub Khan faced a formidable mass mobilization, and the former differed with the president on using force against public demonstrations. After making Ayub Khan abdicate his powers, Yahya Khan and his junta tried to pacify the public by undertaking several measures. Through a Legal Framework Order, which was announced on March 30, 1970 and was presumably the handiwork of G. W. Choudhry, a Bengali academic, Yahya Khan promised countrywide elections to be held in October 1970 on the basis of a universal adult suffrage. The proposed National Assembly was to consist of 313 members with seats allocated according to the population of each federal unit. Yahya Khan had done away with the One-Unit for West Pakistan and, more in keeping with the pre-1955 era, Pakistan again consisted of the provinces of East Pakistan, Punjab, Sindh, NWFP, and Balochistan along with special seats for tribal regions. Thus the National Assembly was meant to have more representation from East Pakistan (162), followed by Punjab (82), Sindh (27), NWFP (18), Balochistan (4), and the tribal regions (7). In addition, 13 seats were reserved for women, with 7 of them allocated to East Pakistan. Provinces were to have their own respective regional assemblies, although the constitution for the country was to be formulated afresh by the National Assembly within 180 days. While imposing martial law in the country in 1969, Yahya Khan had abrogated Ayub Khan's constitution of 1962, and a new constitution was to be worked out by the proposed assembly.

Some members of Yahya Khan's junta were close to Zulfikar Ali Bhutto but held serious reservations against Mujibur Rahman's Six Points and hoped for a mixed verdict in the elections. The national and provincial elections held in October 1970 were contested by 25 parties fielding 1,570 candidates for 300 seats and proved to be a major spectacle, as this was the first time that a universal adult franchise was being exercised by Pakistanis. The results astounded everyone, as Rahman's Awami League emerged as the single largest winning party by acquiring 167 seats out of 169, whereas in West Pakistan

Bhutto's PPP mustered majority seats (81) in Punjab and the NWFP and thus emerged as the largest political bloc. Elections in East Pakistan were held at the time of major floods and cyclones, and resentment against the central government had been further hyped in the electoral campaign mounted by the Awami League. Yahya Khan and his close military associates such as Generals Abdul Hamid, A. Peerzada, Muhammad Umar, Tikka Khan, Yaqub Khan, and others held talks with Rahman regarding the possibility of toning down his Six Points; Bhutto used his position in the west to his maximum advantage, creating serious doubts among the Awami Leaguers about the future political dispensation.[17]

March 1971 turned out to be crucial. It appeared that the proposed convention of the National Assembly in Dhaka was already at an impasse on the nature of future relations between the central government and East Pakistan. The generals wanted to keep the entire leverage with them, whereas a victorious Rahman sought to implement his own agenda, and an equally ambitious Bhutto refused to accept the role of a minority opposition leader. After a serious deadlock developed, the generals lost their patience, and orders for the arrests of Rahman and his close associates were given followed by a military crackdown on the Awami Leaguers all over East Pakistan.[18]

After unleashing the armed forces on the Awami Leaguers, Yahya Khan, his close military associates, and Bhutto flew out of East Pakistan on March 26 amid the chaos, civil war, and bloodshed that grew by each passing day. The junta believed that their strong-arm tactics would succeed in containing the growing separatist tendencies among Rahman's supporters, but they underestimated the cost and its impact on East Pakistanis, as well as the campaign India was planning to undertake to partition Pakistan. Led by Mrs. Indira Gandhi, the Indian government began receiving political refugees from Bangladesh, allowing them to form a Provisional Government of Bangladesh in exile. The Indian government also offered moral, financial and technical support to the rebels. As the civil war became a protracted affair, the rebels organized themselves into militant groups such as Mukti Bahini who were trained and equipped by the Indian troops, themselves encircling East Pakistan.[19] The Nixon Administration favored Yahya Khan's regime and was critical of Indira Gandhi for her closer alliance with Moscow, yet other than supportive statements and some token gestures, Washington shied away from undertaking any substantive steps. Pakistan had, in fact, arranged Henry Kissinger's secret visit to Beijing, which had ushered in a détente in Sino-American relations, and Washington was equally concerned about political instability in Pakistan, which would allow a more pronounced role for the Soviet Union in the Indian Ocean.

Pakistani authorities, however, found it difficult to quell public defiance, which had the full support of India, which was determined to seek a pound of flesh from its neighbor. Earlier, India had even banned civil flights between

West and East Pakistan over its own air space, making travel between the two wings nightmarish. Logistically, it became even more difficult for Pakistani troops and supplies to reach a battle-weary East Pakistan. Confrontation between the Awami League and Pakistani army became a civil war, with some elements in East Pakistan supporting the latter, although most of the public was distressed by the military operation, which went on for months. With Pakistan in a precarious position and using the pretext of refugee presence on its soil, Indian troops entered East Pakistan where a demoralized Pakistani army waited for some clear guidelines from Rawalpindi. Yahya Khan and his junta opened the western front in November 1971, but half-hearted operations did not deter India from seeking complete control of Dhaka and the surrender by Pakistani troops headed by General A. K. Niazi.

After the ceasefire was signed on December 16, 1971, East Pakistan became Bangladesh. In West Pakistan public furor over defeat and separation knew no bounds. People blamed the generals, Indians, and the United Nations for their humiliation and defeat; and Bhutto, who had been delivering fiery speeches at the UN, was flown back from New York to head a crestfallen populace. Both Pakistan and the young state of Bangladesh continued on, reliving memories of a turbulent past while feeling unsure of an uncertain future. During the closing days of 1971, killings, destruction, migration, refugee camps, and a sense of helplessness and anguish characterized life both in the Indus Valley and the Gangetic Delta.

NOTES

1. For instance, see Samuel Huntington, *Political Order in Changing Societies* (New Haven: Yale University Press, 1968); *Changing Patterns of Military Politics* (New York, Free Press, 1962).

2. One of the major voices for this new beginning was the Japanese-American scholar who thought that the world was heading toward liberal democracy and similar economic order based on mutual dependence. See Francis Fukuyama, *The End of History and the Last Man* (London: Hamish Hamilton, 1992). For his more recent work, see *After the Neocons: America at the Crossroads* (London: Profile, 2006).

3. Lawrence Ziring, *Pakistan: The Enigma of Political Development* (Boulder: Westview, 1980); Khalid B. Sayeed, *Politics in Pakistan: The Nature and Direction of Change* (New York: Praeger, 1980).

4. Other than some senior military officers, it involved several intellectuals and literary figures. For further details on the events and developments including the trial and conviction, see Hasan Zaheer, *The Times and Trial of the Rawalpindi Conspiracy, 1951* (Karachi: Oxford University Press, 1998).

5. For further details on British and American influences on Pakistani defense planning, equipment and personnel, see Stephen Cohen, *The Pakistan Army* (Berkeley: University of California Press, 1984).

6. Ayesha Jalal, *The State of Martial Rule: The Origins of Pakistan's Political Economy of Defence* (Cambridge: Cambridge University Press, 1990).

7. For this perspective supported by various case studies including Pakistan, see Christopher Clapham and George Philip (eds.), *The Political Dilemma of Military Regimes* (London: Croom Helm, 1985).

8. For more on this subject, see Brian Cloughley, *A History of the Pakistan Army: Wars and Insurrections* (Karachi: Oxford University Press, 2006).

9. Muhammad Ayub Khan, *Friends Not Masters* (London: Oxford University Press, 1967), pp. 186–190.

10. *Dawn* (Karachi) October 9, 1958.

11. Ayub Khan, p. 86.

12. Altaf Gauhar, *Ayub Khan: Pakistan's First Military Ruler* (Lahore: Sang-e-Meel Publications, 1993), pp. 26–31.

13. Ayub Khan believed that political instability had been caused by economic factors, and the criticism of the celebrations of "the Decade of Development" only strengthened his belief. He finally gave way, however, to political talks with politicians who now agreed on his ouster and the restoration of an unfettered democracy, as well as the dismantling of the One-Unit scheme. Herbert Feldman, *From Crisis to Crisis. Pakistan 1962–1969* (Karachi: Oxford University Press, 2001), pp. 249–251.

14. After the coup led by military generals who had overthrown the monarchy, Iraq pulled out of the Baghdad Pact or the Central Treaty Organisation (CENTO). Iran, Turkey, and Pakistan remained aligned with the United States in this alliance.

15. For further details, see Neville Maxwell, *India's China War* (London: Cape, 1970).

16. It is interesting and revealing to read Ayub Khan's diary entries and notes on contemporary events and personalities. These have been published only recently. Craig Baxter (ed.), *Diaries of Field Marshal Mohammad Ayub Khan, 1966–1972* (Karachi: Oxford University Press, 2007).

17. For a political and chronological account see, Rounaq Jahan, *Pakistan: Failure in National Integration* (New York: Columbia University Press, 1972).

18. For more details, see Hasan Zaheer, *The Separation of East Pakistan. The Rise and Realization of Bengali Muslim Nationalism* (Karachi: Oxford University Press, 1994).

19. For further details on the domestic and regional aspects of the crisis, see Richard Sisson and Leo Rose, *War and Secession: Pakistan, India, and the Creation of Bangladesh* (Berkeley, University of California Press, 1990).

9

Zulfikar Ali Bhutto, Pakistan People's Party, and the Military Regime of General Zia-ul-Haq, 1972–1988

As Pakistan "sleepwalked into war with India" in 1971, its civil conflict in the eastern wing turned into a full-fledged separatism aided by the neighboring country, and the war situation on the western front was not that encouraging either.[1] The Pakistani public, fed on exaggerated lies of a victorious army on both sides, agonized over the surrender of December 16, which resulted in the loss of the majority province and turned more than 90,000 Pakistani soldiers into prisoners of war. Antagonism toward an alcoholic General Yahya Khan (1917–1980) and his junta knew no bounds among the civilians and the junior commissioned officers, ensuring the return of Zulfikar Ali Bhutto (1928–1979) from New York to head a tottering administration and partitioned nation. Zulfikar Ali Bhutto, a mercurial politician with degrees from Berkeley and Oxford, hailed from a Sindhi feudal family, whose personal brilliance contrasted with his unscrupulous zeal for power and penchant for revenge. In Pakistan reams have been written about this charismatic politician who is seen by his followers as the most gifted statesman after Jinnah, but to his opponents, he remains an egoist whose own ambitions for power facilitated the military operation in East Pakistan. His critics accuse him of refusing to share power with Mujibur Rahman (1920–1975) whose Awami League had gained an absolute majority in the elections and deserved to form the civilian government in

Pakistan as laid down in Yahya Khan's Legal Framework Order. To these critics, Bhutto's own designs converged with the sectional interests of the generals who wanted to deny Rahman his due and did not seek a political solution to Pakistan's predicament. Instead, through a disastrous military strategy, he caused humiliation and the partition of Pakistan. Bhutto's supporters credit him with the re-creation from ashes of a "new Pakistan" and with ensuring its survival against odds. They accuse the military of transferring the responsibility for its own defeat to Bhutto, who was eventually hanged by the former on April 4, 1979, following his deposition by General Zia-ul-Haq (1924–1988) two years earlier. Bhutto's mystique and legacy outlive him, and he's now joined by his daughter Benazir Bhutto (1953–2007), after a heroic and tragic struggle to lead the Pakistan People's Party (PPP). With the death of Benazir, the Bhuttos have attained an almost sublime status in public memory.

In fact, the history of Pakistan all through the 1970s and ever since revolves around the personalities and ideologies of two men, who are poles apart in every aspect of their lives and legacies. Bhutto, a westernized civilian prime minister, believed and practiced populism, whereas Zia-ul-Haq, a military man, sought his legitimacy from Islam. Both adversaries ruled the country using authoritarian methods and met unnatural death, yet their legacies continue to polarize Pakistanis even several decades after their departure. Bhutto was born in Larkana in 1928 and was the son of Sir Shahnawaz Bhutto (1888–1957), who had been the *diwan* (prime minister) of the princely state of Junagarh and ensured good education for his promising son. Bhutto lands extended all the way into India, and the younger Bhutto went to Berkeley in 1948 while still holding an Indian passport. His foray at Oxford at Christ Church and the bar-at-law from Lincoln's Inn were followed by legal practice in Karachi where he moved among the westernized circles of the then national capital and came to be known as an enthusiastic party man.[2] His affinity with Iskander Mirza (1899–1969) through a family connection eventually landed him a ministerial position by which the lawyer came into closer contact with General Ayub Khan (1907–1974). The general put Bhutto in charge of commerce, although Bhutto is known to have harbored higher ambitions, which later materialized with his elevation to the post of foreign minister.[3] Bhutto sought a father figure in Ayub Khan and often lavished him with unique compliments, although they were to part ways soon after the Tashkent Treaty of 1966. By that time, Bhutto had established for himself a niche in the public imagination, especially at a time when Pakistanis were disenchanted with the United States and looked toward Mao's China to counterbalance their dependence on Washington.[4] Negotiations with Beijing had begun in 1959, but it was Bhutto's good fortune that they matured during his tenure as foreign minister. His well-publicized visits to China, portraits with Mao Tse-tung, Chou El-lai, and other Chinese revolutionaries created an aura of a defiant

Bhutto who, despite his daredevil modernism, also represented Sindhi Sufi and folk traditions.

Some of Bhutto's contemporaries blame him for leading an otherwise cautious Ayub Khan on the warpath over Kashmir in 1965, so as to claim political mileage for himself.[5] Bhutto lost favor with Ayub Khan soon after the Tashkent Treaty, although the general, as is evident from his *Diaries*, had developed serious reservations about his foreign minister, and his sacking only helped Bhutto gain further public support.[6] Bhutto was widely received in Lahore and Karachi after his dismissal, and his emotional speeches brought him closer to his admirers. The stories of a "sell-out" at Tashkent by Ayub Khan and amassing of wealth by his sons and family added to a pervasive public dismay with the general. In the meantime, Bhutto turned himself into a populist by promising empowerment of ordinary masses and turned "bread, clothes and shelter" into the basic creed of his campaign.[7] Bhutto's espousal of Islamic socialism fit well with similar contemporary Arab thought and carried a tinge of anti-Western ideology besides applause for China, reverberating an ambivalent form of anticolonialism. Such an ideology sought nationalization of big industries to eradicate financial monopolies of the "twenty-two families" and promised land reforms. Imbued with such ideas, many progressive urban Pakistanis joined hands with Bhutto and finally, in 1967, the PPP was founded, advocating the mentioned creed and promising liberal and progressive agenda. Soon the tricolor of the PPP appeared on shops, houses, and lorries all across West Pakistan, although it did not make any headway in East Pakistan, where this reception was reserved only for Rahman and his advocacy of maximum autonomy.[8]

Bhutto's hour came with his leading role in anti-Ayub mass campaign that had begun from the university campuses and engulfed the entire country, seeking to overhaul the system by overthrowing the general. In the meantime, Bhutto developed closer associations with senior military commanders such as S. Peerzada, Tikka Khan, and Gul Hassan who were to form the inner group in Yahya Khan's junta. In the elections of 1970, Bhutto did not win any seats in East Pakistan, nor did Rahman make any headway in West Pakistan, and this widening provincialization of Pakistani politics required corresponding political and constitutional measures. But the top leaders, like those in British India during 1947, were driven by their hardened attitudes and were less amenable to conciliation while pursuing their parallel agendas, which left little space for hope. Army operation in East Pakistan, both volatile and unnecessary, only worsened the situation, leading to disastrous results for all. At this stage, Bhutto had been sent to New York to plead the case for Pakistan in view of India's invasion of Pakistani territory. The United Nations might have undertaken some ameliorative steps, but sympathy for Bengali sentiments overrode such a possibility, and Bhutto's emotion-ridden speech and walkout from the hall did not attract any major international peace initiative to salvage a united Pakistan. A rudderless country simmered under the tutelage of incompetent generals driven by some fantastic but impractical ideas and thus was soon divided, allowing Bhutto to return to Pakistan as a redeemer.

BHUTTO'S ADMINISTRATION

After his assumption of power in December 1972, Bhutto became the first-ever civilian martial law administrator of Pakistan for the next four months and justified this position on two grounds: providing continuity from the retired Yahya Khan, and undertaking some emergency measures for the restoration of normalcy in the country. During this period, Bhutto retired several senior military officials, placed some curbs on the bureaucracy, and implemented his policy of nationalization. Bhutto's preoccupation at that stage seemed to have been mainly to send the army back to the barracks so that the electoral institutions could function more smoothly. At the same time, however, he was concerned that Pakistan's defenses needed a major moral and technical boost and sought to significantly increase the military budget. His other challenges were to find a synthesis between Islam and nationhood, as well as formulating a new constitution. All these objectives were huge, but given the contemporary mass-based goodwill, Bhutto was able to make some headway, although his personal insecurity and authoritarianism often alienated him even from his closer friends.

Under Bhutto's program of nationalization, 30 industries including the banks and insurance companies were selected for takeover by the state, and more were to come from the textile sector and rice husking. Bhutto implemented some land reforms as well by limiting the holdings to 150 acres of irrigated and 350 of acres of nonirrigated land, although landowners were allowed to disperse their assets among family members to avoid official appropriation. Exemptions were also made for people owning tube wells and tractors so as to provide incentives for mechanized agriculture. These measures did not result in any radical change in landholding patterns, however, as most of the feudal population had become PPP members and sat in the assemblies ensuring minimum impact on their political and economic powers. Like Ayub Khan's land reforms of 1959, Bhutto's measures shied away from holistic transformation, although it is true that peasants and landless *haris* across the Indus Valley viewed Bhutto as their main benefactor. In addition, Bhutto introduced some reforms in labor laws that were certainly short of being radical and disappointed some of his socialist supporters.

The PPP had its roots among the ordinary masses, but its leadership was often in the hands of the feudal elements, although a small middle class also subscribed to a new distribution of wealth and resources in the larger interests of the country. Bhutto seemed to speak for the masses, yet he gradually came to depend more on his landowning associates. Factionalism within the PPP, for instance, in the Punjab owing to groups led by middle class urban leaders such as Hanif Ramay and Shaikh Rashid, were largely sidelined by landowners such as Ghulam Mustafa Khar and Nawab Qureshi, whereas in his native Sindh, the Talpurs and Makhdums ran the roost much to the discomfort of the emerging lower middle class. Bhutto's alignment with the landed influential citizens, especially in Sindh, soon turned into a serious ethnic issue between the native Sindhis and the Urdu-speaking Muhajireen. Geared by genuine desire to help underdeveloped areas, Bhutto had encouraged special legislation in Sindh, allowing positive discrimination. The process began in July 1972 with the induction of Sindhi as the second major language of the province followed by implementation of a quota system. Accordingly, the province was divided into rural and urban constituencies, with 60 percent of seats in the educational and professional institutions along with a similar ratio of jobs in the official sector being reserved for rural areas, whereas 40 percent of the same were allocated to urban dwellers. These measures caused major resentment among the largely urbanite Muhajireen, who felt that their cultural and economic rights had been usurped to appease the rural communities. Bhutto's takeover of major financial concerns and industries, promulgation of quota system to help rural population, and greater recognition of Sindhi language deeply infuriated the Muhajireen. Soon the PPP was confronted with a Muhajir-led backlash in Karachi, Hyderabad, and Sukkur where most of the Urdu speakers had been based. A few years later, the resentment led to the formation of the Muhajir Qaumi Movement (MQM). The riots in Karachi only increased the Muhajir-Sindhi chasms with repercussions for the entire country in decades to come. The distrust of the PPP among the Urdu speakers knew no bounds and still remains a major fact of life in urban Sindh, as ethnic lines remain vividly drawn.[9]

Bhutto held contradictory views about the armed forces. On the one hand he wanted them to emerge as a formidable force to ensure Pakistan's security vis-à-vis India and the western frontiers, but on the other hand, he expected the generals to be subservient to the civil authorities. Bhutto's trusted man, General Tikka Khan, was redesignated as the chief of army staff instead of the erstwhile commander-in-chief, and likewise his counterparts from the navy and the air force attained new titles. Bhutto held the office of defense minister and also appointed a head to oversee the three chiefs along with liaising with the political authority.[10] The major issue confronted by Bhutto at the time was the repatriation of 93,000 Pakistani prisoners of war (POWs)from Indian detention. This could not happen, as per conditions by Indira Gandhi, until and unless Pakistan recognized the sovereignty of Bangladesh. Soon after the fall of Dhaka, Pakistan tried to deter foreign governments from recognizing the independence of Bangladesh and in several cases broke diplomatic relations with those who developed ambassadorial contacts with Dhaka. Bhutto had released Rahman from a Pakistani jail soon after assuming power yet was under strong domestic pressure not to acknowledge the separation of Bangladesh, especially when most of Pakistani military perceived it as an Indian ploy to humble their country. Bhutto was aware that without negotiations with India, Pakistan would not be able to retrieve its occupied territories, nor could it make any headway on POWs.

After some exchanges and external persuasion, both Indira Gandhi and Zulfikar Bhutto met in Shimla in July 1972 to hammer out a new agreement. Victorious Indians were definitely not in a mood to offer many concessions to a weakened foe, nor were they prepared to show any accommodation on the age-old issue of Kashmir. At times, it appeared that the Indo-Pakistani talks, watched by the entire world with both expectation and fear, would flounder and south Asia would be back to saber rattling, but then both leaders met privately without any advisors. Their meeting resulted in an agreement stipulating the withdrawal of troops from the forward positions, a new line of control in divided Kashmir, and cessation of hostilities and propaganda on both sides. In addition and very significantly, Bhutto was able to acquire Indira Gandhi's willingness to hold bilateral negotiations on all outstanding issues including Kashmir, as this was inserted as a crucial clause in the Shimla Agreement. For Bhutto, the agreement was a major achievement; but for his opponents, especially from Jamaat-i-Islami, it was a humiliation, although ordinary people welcomed peace in the region, thereby raising the possibility of repatriation of the POWs.[11] In reference to the recognition of Bangladesh, Bhutto was certainly on the horns of a dilemma, as he could not openly defy the domestic reservations regarding partition of the country. He found a solution to the problem, however, by holding a summit of the Islamic countries in Lahore in February 1974, to which President Rahman was formally invited as the head of the sovereign state of Bangladesh. Soon Pakistani soldiers were repatriated, although many outstanding issues, such as the Bengalis left in Pakistan and the Urdu-speaking Pakistanis (also called Biharis) in Bangladesh, proved formidable. In addition, Bhutto resisted President Rahman's demand for the trial of about 100 senior Pakistani military officials for committing human rights violations, and his resistance was applauded by senior military officials.

Bhutto had replaced General Gul Hassan Khan with General Tikka Khan as the army chief, and this entire episode was accomplished in a rather dramatic way in light of fear of a possible reaction from Hassan's colleagues.[12] Upon Tikka Khan's retirement, Bhutto opted for General Zia-ul-Haq as the next chief of army staff, although he was considerably junior to several other colleagues; but given his religiosity and an apparently apolitical disposition,

Bhutto viewed him as nonthreatening. In fact, General Haq eventually turned out to be Bhutto's nemesis, for he overthrew Bhutto in 1977 and then hanged him two years later over some trumped-up charges of a political murder. The manner in which Hassan had been replaced, did not sit well with many senior generals who remained skeptical of Bhutto's actual intentions about the army's possible role within the country. Despite the generous inflow of Chinese weapons, however, Bhutto was aware of serious Indo-Pakistani military imbalances in conventional areas, and given the U.S. reluctance to offer full diplomatic and logistical assurances to Islamabad, he sought help from China and the Muslim nations. The Islamic Summit was certainly a turning point in defining Pakistan as an important actor in west Asian affairs besides absorbing Pakistani labor in the oil boom in the Middle East. The relationship with the Muslim world stood him in good stead when he needed funds and support to initiate Pakistan's nuclear program soon after the nuclear test by India in 1974. Here, Bhutto once again exhibited leadership, and by congregating Pakistani scientists and building an infrastructure, he initiated Pakistan's search for "credible deterrence" against any future security threat. This entire process happened at a time when most of the Western powers had become critical of nuclear proliferation. Pakistan pursued its nuclear research despite North Atlantic pressure and justified its stance on the basis of India having led the new arms race in the region.

Bhutto had been quite active on the foreign front. He ensured a closer relationship with China and often displayed solidarity with the Afro-Asian world, although his decision to pursue a nuclear program and exit from the Commonwealth did not sit well in Washington and London. Bhutto worked in close cooperation with the Shah of Iran and tried to cultivate friendly relations with Kabul, where, in 1973, King Zahir Shah had been overthrown by his cousin, Sardar Daud Khan, who often issued statements critical of Pakistan. Daud Khan was known for his pro-Moscow leanings, and his interest in Pakistani tribal Pushtun regions alerted Bhutto of any external interference in northwestern Pakistan. Pakistan's relationship with Washington nosedived in 1977, however, when confronted with protests by opposition groups over allegations of rigged elections, Bhutto suspected covert American support of his critics. Using Henry Kissinger's critique of the Pakistani nuclear program, Bhutto, in some of his public speeches, expressed his disenchantment with U.S. policies. He was fond of making long speeches interspersed with a mixture of Urdu, English, and Sindhi, much to the enjoyment of the masses who relished his blunt language and wry sense of humor. Such events not only displayed Bhutto's unbound energy but engendered a great trust in pubic sentiment for him. His populism might not have been sufficient enough materially for ordinary Pakistanis, but it certainly increased their self-esteem. In many cases, his economic policies only added to the miseries of the ordinary citizenry, as the growth rate had been slackened owing to nationalization, but his relationship with the population never faltered.

Bhutto's patronage of regional languages and the folk cultures of Pakistan led to the founding of several academies and museums that preserved and celebrated Pakistan's regional folk heritage. In the same manner, Bhutto personified a Sufi version of life by promoting Pakistani cotton clothes, folk music, and regional dances, which the public embraced. This touch with the common people, however, did not stop Bhutto from seeking vengeance from his antagonists, as he was not accustomed to burying the hatchet. The discovery of some weapons in the Iraqi embassy in Islamabad on February 10, 1973 eventually led to Bhutto's dismissal of provincial governments of Balochistan and the North-West Frontier Province (NWFP), which were, in fact, coalitions formed by Abdul Wali Khan's National Awami Party (NAP) and some other religiopolitical groups. The PPP did not have any visible presence in these two provinces, and sacking of the governments led by the opposition only weakened the political processes in the country. Prodded by the paranoid Shah of Iran, Bhutto feared that the NAP harbored pro-Moscow elements who wanted to destabilize Pakistan and Iran. He thus took an extreme step culminating in insurgency in Balochistan. Bhutto had already used troops in Karachi to quell riots over the Urdu-Sindhi controversy in 1972, and now he engaged them in fighting the Baloch nationalists who began receiving arms and help from a number of sources including Kabul and Moscow. Bhutto's reluctance in accepting any counter view and his retaliatory disposition would often cause several unintended crises that further isolated him from the armed forces, political groups, and even some of his early close PPP associates who complained of mistreatment. An embattled Bhutto gradually came to depend on the Federal Security Force (FSF), a parallel militia force, and turned toward the landed elite in the forthcoming elections.

THE CONSTITUTION OF 1973

Bhutto might have faltered in several areas, yet among his several contributions, the formulation and promulgation of the Constitution of 1973 has been a landmark achievement of the PPP administration. As mentioned previously, Bhutto ran the government for the first four months enjoying unquestionable powers, and that is when he implemented new labor laws, inducted nationalization, introduced his package of land reforms, and retired the junta. In addition, he tried to systemize the induction, training, and job allocation of senior civil servants in an attempt to strengthen his political hold over the bureacracy.[13] In April 1972, an interim constitution of 290 clauses and seven sections, all covering the legislative, judiciary, and executive branches of government, was implemented in the country, and the National Assembly began debating its merits and possible amendments in successive sessions. The members of the National Assembly had been elected in 1970 and came from the four provinces and tribal regions, although each province had its own separate provincial assembly and cabinet headed by a chief minister. While the National Assembly worked to amend the interim constitution into a long-awaited national document, Bhutto held the office of the president, which again granted him significant powers like his predecessors. The PPP regime had antagonized the Jamaat-i-Islami (JI), National Awami Party (NAP), and some sections of the Muslim League; yet these opposition groups, sensitive to the urgency of the time, joined together under the leadership of the Pir of Pagara, an influential spiritual leader from Sindh. This coalition was named the United Democratic Front, which, despite dissention over developments in Balochistan, still cooperated with the PPP in finalizing the document that came to be known as the Constitution of 1973 and was implemented on August 14, 1973 amid great fanfare.

The constitution stipulated a parliamentary form of government under an empowered prime minister. The president headed the state but held only ceremonial powers, as in India. In an indirectly elected system, the president was bound to the advice offered by the prime minister. Parliament was to consist of two houses: the upper house, Senate, was to ensure equal representation for all the regions, whereas the lower house, National Assembly, was to be elected for five years on the basis of population and would consist of 200 MNAs. The majority party in the lower house, elected through universal franchise for all citizens above 21, was to form the central government, and the provinces followed the same organization. The constitution also guaranteed independence of the judiciary and the media. Specific clauses such as Article 6 defined any defiance or transgression of the constitution to be treasonous. To many observers this was to ward off any future military adventurism, although the pliant courts had often legalized such takeovers, as they did Ayub Khan's coup under "the law of necessity." The parliamentarians wanted a national constitution to codify their preferences for a civil government and, as per Article 153, formed a Council of Common Interests to resolve interprovincial disputes. The constitution upheld the erstwhile tradition of naming the country officially as the Islamic Republic of Pakistan, where laws repugnant to classical Islamic sources were to be avoided. This Islamic orientation of the national document was quite visible in February 1974 during the Islamic Summit in Lahore and became more apparent in the subsequent debates in the parliament.[14] The constitution allowed amendments, but only if the measures enjoyed the support from two-thirds of the legislators. The Constitution of 1973 can be characterized as a resilient document that has withstood several amendments over the subsequent decades when regimes, both military and civil, sought legitimacy for their specific administrative and political policies.

As of 2008, the constitution has added 17 amendments—in most cases offering blanket protection to various executive and administrative measures. In 2000, General Musharraf's coup was legitimized by Pakistan's Supreme Court, which also allowed him to amend the constitution—a rare precedent in the country's history where a single individual, and an official employee, could introduce amendments into this vital national document.

THE PAKISTAN NATIONAL ALLIANCE MOVEMENT AND MILITARY COUP OF JULY 1977

After the constitution was approved, Bhutto assumed the prime ministership and carried on until early 1977 when, in accordance with public demand, elections were planned for the country. Earlier, Bhutto had appointed Rafi Raza, a PPP leader and lawyer-minister, to head his election campaign. On January 7, 1977, he announced that the election would be held in March. Despite all the desertions from the PPP owing to authoritarianism and unpopular military operation in a restive Balochistan, people expected Bhutto to return with a clear majority. But surrounded by some sycophants and vulnerable to his self-centered disposition, Bhutto mainly sought pliant candidates for the central and provincial assemblies, some even enjoying covert support from the intelligence agencies. On January 11, nine opposition parties in Pakistan decided to form a united front called the Pakistan National Alliance (PNA) and determined to disallow an easy majority victory to the PPP. Preelection distrust and recriminations soon turned into a violent polarization as PNA leaders refused to accept the election results announced on March 7. According to these results, the PPP had won 155 of the 200 total seats for the National Assembly, with the PNA having won 36. Each group obtained 58.1 percent and 35.4 percent of the total votes, respectively. The PNA, already fuming with anti-Bhutto sentiment, accused his government of massive rigging. The postelection PNA rallies demanding high-level inquiry, new polls in several constituencies, and disqualification of some MNAs soon turned into an anti-Bhutto campaign dominated by religiopolitical parities such as the Jamaat-i-Islami (JI), Jamiat Ulama-i-Islam (JUI), and Jamiat-i-Ulama-i-Pakistan (JUP). These parities had mutual doctrinal differences yet demanded Islamization of the country, which soon became the common cry of their demonstrations.[15]

Within a few weeks, 200 demonstrators were killed in Lahore, Karachi, and several other towns by the security forces. The situation appeared to be getting our of control when a panic-stricken Bhutto, in late April 1977, imposed martial law in Karachi, Hyderabad, and Lahore.[16] Still, the demonstrations went on unabated, and efforts to resolve the PPP-PNA deadlock, despite input from some Arab arbiters, failed but not without further politicizing senior army commanders. On July 5, General Zia-ul-Haq took control of the country through a coup, annulled the election results, and put Bhutto, some PPP stalwarts, and the entire top PNA leadership under house arrest in Murree and Abbotabad. In his speech to the nation, Zia-ul-Haq explained his reasons for the coup code-named "Fairplay," but promised to conduct free elections to restore power to the elected representatives. On August 2, 1977, Maulvi Mushtaq Hussain, the chief election commissioner, even announced the polling schedule, followed by the release of Bhutto and other leaders from their detention. It appeared as if the masses were still with Bhutto because it took his procession 10 hours to cover just a few miles between the Karachi train station and his home in Clifton. A vast sea of people turned up to welcome him. Similar other mass rallies in support of Bhutto in Rawalpindi, Lahore, and Multan led Zia to a serious review of his entire game plan. Now apprehensive of a reinvigorated Bhutto, the general feared for his own safety and, along with his junta, decided to stay on at the helm of affairs by holding the entire political process in abeyance. Bhutto's second arrest soon followed and a case was made against him for ordering the murder of a political opponent through his FSF. The criminal case was upheld by the superior courts and, after a conviction, he was quietly hanged in the Rawalpindi Jail on April 4, 1979.

THE ZIA-UL-HAQ ERA: 1977–1988

Dissolution of the Bhutto government by martial law and his own tragic end through a criminal case not only added to political instability and disillusionment within the country, but allowed the Pakistani army to gain power over all other institutions. Policies inducted by General Zia were not only authoritarian; they also led to further sectarian and ethnic fragmentation of the society, with democracy, women, and minorities being the major losers. A country, otherwise endowed with hard-working people and unbound resources, definitely deserved better life than what its ruling elite had subjected it to. Zia's 11 years turned out to be the worst era for civic institutions and was further pushed toward religious intolerance and political expediency. Questions still abound about Bhutto's failure to establish proper governance in Pakistan despite a sought-after opportunity afforded to him after the tragic events of 1971. His personal insecurity, authoritarian temperament, and lack of accommodation for counter views did not help his otherwise genuine concern for the primacy of ordinary people and civic politics in the country. His confrontational politics with the opposition, feuds with the Baloch leaders, and dependence on feudal families only aggravated his isolation, and the age-old structural anomalies within the Pakistani system remained unattended. The traditional preeminence of the army did not take too long to return, especially when crestfallen generals had been amply provided by Bhutto and were eventually used against his own political opponents, allowing them a central role that only emboldened them to overthrow one more regime.

General Zia-ul-Haq, or General Zia as he was known, came from a modest middle class background. He was born on August 12, 1924 in Jullundur (now in Indian Punjab) and attended St. Stephen's College in Delhi. During World War II, he obtained commission in the British Indian Army and, after the creation of Pakistan, benefited from rapid promotion. Bhutto appointed him as his army chief, bypassing several other senior generals, believing that the latter would not pose a threat to him. Zia, with his humility and personal piety, was the antithesis to the flamboyant Bhutto and thus was able to win over many middle class Pakistanis, as well as the foreign visitors who were always impressed by his unassuming personality.[17] He was certainly a cunning person, however, who knew how to pursue his own interests ruthlessly and whose rule proved to be the longest in Pakistan's history. General Zia's ruling military junta included his close associates such as Generals K. M. Arif, Faiz Ali Chishti, and Akhtar Abdur Rahman who were born in Jullundur and whose family backgrounds were similar to Zia's.[18]

SOVIET INVASION OF AFGHANISTAN

Zia's global isolation was over the moment the Soviet Union invaded Afghanistan in December 1979, and Pakistan emerged as the frontline state during this intense phase in the Cold War. His selective Islamization, execution of Bhutto a few months earlier, and other human rights violations through the military courts were all forgotten. The Western powers, conservative Arab states, and China rediscovered Zia as a courageous ally who could stand up to a superpower. The Carter Administration offered $400 million in assistance to Pakistan to shore up its defenses and fledgling economy, but Zia rejected the offer by calling it "peanuts." Under President Reagan, Pakistan was offered even more substantial assistance, and the CIA began to equip and train the Afghan resistance known as Mujahideen, or the holy warriors. Zia's Sunni Islam proved an asset, as it shared anti-Soviet sentiments at a time when the American presence had completely disappeared from the region following the Imam Khomeini-led revolution in Iran in February 1979. The CIA, in fact, through its Pakistani counterpart—the Inter-Services Intelligence (ISI)—ran the biggest covert operation in its history, which involved Afghans from among the refugee camps in Pakistan and their contacts within the country.[19] Pakistanis had provided shelter and local hospitality to 4 million Afghan refugees out of humane considerations, and cities like Peshawar and Quetta soon were overcrowded with the refugee population. In addition to countless displaced people and their cattle causing serious strains on the Pakistani economy and ecology, the country had to face the Soviet wrath in the form of public rebuke and intermittent bomb blasts. These blasts and selective killings were attributed to KHAD (a secret service-like organization), the Afghan secret agency, which operated as the Soviet surrogate and tried to pursue counterinsurgency in Pakistan. The Afghan war increased Zia's global stature, however, and brought in funds and goodwill as well. By that time, Pakistani expatriates in the Persian Gulf had begun to send their remittances, which also greatly helped the Pakistani economy. In addition, despite occasional criticism in the Western newspapers of Pakistan's antidemocratic policies and its secret nuclear program, the Reagan Administration ensured material and diplomatic support to Zia in fighting a proxy war against "the evil empire."

Zia knew that even with all the Western support for his foreign policy, he could not evade the serious issue of legitimacy and, like Ayub Khan, tried to introduce a controlled form of select democracy. Most of the politicians, especially from the PPP, had already been either imprisoned or were in exile, so Zia planned for a pliant parliament. His first experiment was in the shape of a nominated assembly called Majlis-i-Shoora or Advisory Council, which included only his nominees but, as a matter of fact, it was his stop-gap arrangement, constantly challenged by civic groups. In 1981, several anti-Zia parities formed the Movement for Restoration of Democracy (MRD), which was brutally suppressed by Zia, especially in Sindh during 1983, yet the demands for democratization and restoration of the Constitution of 1973 refused to wither away. Zia's use of intelligence agencies against democratic elements and their public floggings could not suppress the movement until the military dictator was compelled to announce nonpartisan elections in 1984. Earlier, he managed a fraudulent referendum seeking his own selection as the president for five years in view of his plan to Islamize the country's administration. Here again bureaucracy, secret agencies, and the Jamaat helped him in a campaign that suffered both from lack of transparency and a very low turnout.[20]

Elections were held as promised but not from the party platforms, and the new assemblies were convened. In early 1985, however, Zia demanded that the assemblies validate all the ordinances and laws that he had implemented in the preceding eight years. He threatened the assemblies with dissolution if they refused to give him blanket approval of all his past actions and policies. The assemblies complied through passage of the Eighth Amendment. It not only indemnified his past actions and deeds but also allocated more powers to his office including a vital authority to dismiss the prime ministers and assemblies. Thus the entire parliamentary character of the constitution was changed to suit General Zia, and Prime Minister Mohammad Khan Junejo (1932–1992) was made totally dependent on the general-president. When Junejo, a mild-tempered Sindhi politician, tried to assert his autonomy, he was dismissed while on his return from an official visit to east Asia in June 1988. Zia planned on a new and more submissive parliament, but he was killed in an air crash on August 17, 1988 along with the U.S. ambassador and several other senior generals. They had gone to Bahawalpur to examine the performance of a new American tank that Pakistan was considering for its troops. The presidential C-130 came down soon after its takeoff and even after two decades, the cause of the crash has remained elusive. Zia's sudden death opened a new avenue for democratic forces in Pakistan, but his legacy has continued to dictate political events and ideological conflict in the country. Zia's Afghan policy had been successful, although he died a few months before the last Soviet troops left Afghanistan, followed by the demise of the Soviet Union itself.

General Zia's long 11 years in power marginalized constitutional politics and will be remembered as the most testing time for Pakistani democratic forces. Other than suppressing the PPP and such other forces, Zia put curbs on the media, arts, literary works, and all related areas of public life by using Islam as the rationale for Pakistan. Women were asked to stay indoors and, in their public role, were advised to cover the head and pursue a more segregated life.[21] Offices were urged to establish places and times for prayers, the government took it upon itself to collect charity—*zakat*, and democracy was posited as a Western, non-Islamic concept. There was a time when Zia even harbored the role of a spokesman for the whole Muslim community and visualized Pakistan as an Islamic utopia. The rules that he implemented in the name of Islamic Sharia were mostly controversial and harsh and only aggravated the human rights situation in the country. Lashing and stoning were decreed as Islamic punishments under a series of laws called the Huddood Ordinances, which also made a woman's testimony worth only half that of a man's. These laws also did not clearly differentiate between rape and adultery, and even a victim who became pregnant was often penalized as a criminal. Soon Pakistani jails were full of women who, after being abused, had been abandoned by their male relatives. Men accused these women of immoral behavior, although their actual grievances might have been of a totally different nature. Pakistani women, who after a protracted struggle, had obtained certain civic rights in the 1960s, now experienced serious regression in the name of *Chaadar* and *Chaardiwari* (strictly domestic and segregated role) idealized by some conservative Muslims that disallowed any public space and personal enhancement. Pushed against a wall, many urban women were left with no option but to organize themselves into groups to articulate their resistance and were helped by civil society that agonized over such segregationist laws, which seriously affected the media, women, and minorities.[22] In the absence of democratic and participatory institutions and owing to the proliferation of arms from neighboring Afghanistan, cities like Karachi became volatile. Ethnic militants from among the MQM and their Sindhi and Pushtun counterparts engaged in random and selective killings.[23] Criminalization of ethnicity occurred while tensions between Sunnis and Shias increased all through the 1980s. Pakistanis agonized over a series of volatile conflicts happening across the urban centers that seriously impacted economic growth and destabilized national harmony. Such acute problems did not bode well for the 1990s when another short democratic era dawned on the country's horizons.

NOTES

1. Ian Talbot, *Pakistan: A Modern History* (London: Hurst, 1998), p. 202.

2. For his early encounters with the Karachi feudal and westernized elite, see Sherbaz Khan Mazari, *A Journey to Disillusionment* (Karachi: Oxford University Press, 2001).

3. He held on to his beliefs firmly and promoted his interests firmly within the ministerial circles, often lacking trust in many around him. Lawrence Ziring, *Pakistan in the Twentieth Century: A Political History* (Karachi: Oxford University Press, 1997), pp. 274–276.

4. Anwar H. Syed, "Z. A. Bhutto's Self-Characterizations and Pakistani Political Culture," *Asian Survey*, XVIII, December 1978.

5. It is suggested that Pakistanis like Bhutto underestimated Indian retaliation and encouraged infiltration into Kashmir. For this view, see Altaf Gauhar, *General Ayub Khan: Pakistan's First Military Ruler* (Lahore: Sang-e-Meel Publications, 1993), pp. 204–205.

6. Craig Baxter (ed.), *Diaries of Field Marshal Mohammad Ayub Khan, 1966–1972* (Karachi: Oxford University Press, 2007), pp. 3, 15, 29, 33.

7. For an interesting biography of Bhutto, see Stanley Wolpert, *Zulfi Bhutto of Pakistan* (New York, Oxford University Press, 1993).

8. For further details on the PPP, see Philip E. Jones, *The Pakistan People's Party: Rise to Power* (Karachi: Oxford University Press, 2003).

9. As also seen in neighboring India, such official efforts for positive discrimination, where origins become more important than the merit, often prove controversial and must be handled rather carefully.

10. Hasan-Askari Rizvi, *The Military and Politics in Pakistan, 1947–1997* (Lahore: Sang-e-Meel Publications, 2000).

11. The Jamaat-i-Islami (JI) mistrusted Bhutto and was also critical of Indian control of a major section of Kashmir. The JI had supported the military operation in East Pakistan, and many of its members had been killed by Mukti Bahini; thus any compromise on Kashmir and East Pakistan was a serious betrayal.

12. For further details, see Gul Hassan Khan, *Memoirs of Lt. General Gul Hassan Khan* (Karachi: Oxford University Press, 1993).

13. For more on Pakistani civil service and occasional reform measures, see Charles H. Kennedy, *Bureaucracy in Pakistan* (Karachi: Oxford University Press, 1987).

14. In fact, within two weeks of the summit, several clerics led by the Karachi-based religious scholar Maulana Yusuf Binouri, formed an alliance of

ulama demanding exclusion of Ahmadis from Islam. Formed by Mirza Ghulam Ahmad (1835–1908) this messianic sect had been often challenged by the traditional Muslim groups, and agitation against them had even led to the imposition of martial law in Lahore in the early 1950s. This demand was revived with new vigor and, with a nod from the regime Pakistani National Assembly, in 1974, declared Ahmadis as non-Muslims, because of their nonbelief in the finality of the prophethood of the Prophet Muhammad.

15. In their parlance, it was called the implementation of *Nizam-i-Mustafa*, or the Prophetic order and was meant as a rebuke to Bhutto's liberal lifestyle.

16. To win over conservative support, Bhutto soon closed down liquor shops, banned gambling, and declared Friday to be the weekly holiday, but these measures only emboldened his opponents.

17. Shahid J. Burki, "Pakistan Under Zia, 1977–88," *Asian Survey*, XXVIII, October 1988.

18. Although Arif and Chishti have offered their detailed accounts of the 1977 coups and subsequent details, Rahman was killed with Zia in the same air crash near Bahawalpur on August 17, 1988.

19. George Crile, *My Enemy's Enemy: the Story of the Largest Covert Operation in History. Arming of Mujahideen by the CIA* (London: Atlantic Books, 2003).

20. In popular parlance the referendum was known as rig random.

21. For his curbs on civil liberties, the press, and literary activities, one may refer to three articles written by Zubeida Mustafa, Asif Farrukhi, and Kishwar Naheed that appeared in the country's leading newspaper on Zia's death anniversary. "Books," *Dawn* August 19, 2007: http://www.dawn.com/weekly/books/books4.htm.

22. For further details see, Iftikhar H. Malik, *State and Civil Society in Pakistan: Politics of Authority, Ideology and Ethnicity* (Oxford: St. Antony's-Macmillan, 1997) (especially Chapter 7, pp. 139–167).

23. On ethnic violence see, Malik, pp. 168–256; and, Feroz Ahmed, *Ethnicity and Politics in Pakistan* (Karachi: Oxford University Press, 1998).

10

Democratic Decade, 1988–1999: Benazir Bhutto and Nawaz Sharif

General Zia-ul-Haq's death in an air crash on August 17, 1988 removed a whole group of senior military commanders from the political map and ushered in a new era of democratic restoration characterized by several elections and civilian regimes. Structurally weak and featuring petty rivalries, these regimes were more often dismissed by generals who enjoyed an indirect role in routinely forming and dissolving such governments. Thus during the next decade, Benazir Bhutto (1953–2007) was twice chosen prime minister as the head of her Pakistan People's Parity (PPP). Mian Nawaz Sharif (1950–) also obtained the same high office twice, but neither of these post-1947 Pakistani politicians could complete their five-year terms. They were often accused of incompetence and corruption, and some of their political opponents even encouraged the generals to oust the governments and elected assemblies. Since August 1988, Pakistan has held six elections: 1988, 1990, 1993, and 1996, 2002, 2008. In addition to the two-term prime ministerships of Bhutto and Sharif in the 1990s, the country was administered by three interim prime ministers who were appointed by the presidents and the army chiefs to run the administration and conduct elections. During the 1990s, Pakistan enjoyed more civil freedoms, although many of the restrictive laws imposed by Zia remained intact. In addition, ethnic issues and disorder continued to bedevil

Karachi, whereas intelligence agencies such as the Inter-Services Intelligence (ISI) proved almost untouchable and played a controversial role in domestic and regional politics. Pakistan's relations with the United States also cooled as a result of the American rebuke over Islamabad's nuclear program. At the same time, however, Pakistanis noticed some progress toward an overdue normalization with India. Finally, on October 12, 1999, the curtain on the second administration of Nawaz Sharif was drawn when the agitated military colleagues of General Pervez Musharraf (1943–) dismissed the prime minister through a military coup, and once again the country came under the strong purview of the khaki forces.

BENAZIR BHUTTO AND THE PPP GOVERNMENT, 1988–1990

General Zia's authoritarianism and selective use of Islamization were meant to offer him legitimacy, especially after the country's lackluster economic performance resulting from a hasty nationalization under Zulfikar Ali Bhutto. In addition, Zia felt that Pakistan's internal roadblocks in achieving national integration might be removed by forging unity through a shared Islamic ethos. Thus the establishment of a penal code, blasphemy laws, and the Federal Shariat Court, and an accent on Islamic economics and modest behavior all aimed at the same objective. Whatever his motive, the fallout from his authoritarianism only accentuated intra-Muslim doctrinal differences causing an unprecedented volatility in the Sunni-Shia relationship. For many civic forces, Zia was pandering to fundamentalist lobbies to shore up his own position, and Afghan resistance only helped further marginalize society's critics. Simultaneously, by suppressing political forces such as the Movement for the Restoration of Democracy, Zia's regime spawned centrifugal and segmented elements that turned Karachi and Hyderabad into a boiling ethnic cauldron. His death thus created an aura of expectations from Benazir Bhutto, who, after her exile in London, had returned to an unprecedented public welcome in 1986 and now waited for her time to enter national politics. Benazir Bhutto had studied in the United States and Oxford and had been on foreign visits with her father including her close observation of the Shimla negotiations with India in 1972. She was in detention along with her mother, Nusrat Bhutto, when her father was being tried by the military regime and was subsequently hanged in April 1979. Benazir Bhutto, after her internment in Pakistan under the military regime, mostly lived in exile while her brother, Murtaza Bhutto (1954–1996), traveled across Europe, North Africa, and Afghanistan seeking support for his Al-Zulfikar, a movement aimed at overthrowing Zia's military regime. The other brother, Shahnawaz, lived in exile until, in 1985, he was mysteriously found dead in a flat in France. Thus

Benazir Bhutto took upon herself the mantle of political opposition to Zia and inherited her father's leadership of the PPP. A former president of Oxford University's Student Union and westernized in her lifestyle, Benazir Bhutto underwent transformation by donning Pakistani clothes and trying to speak Urdu to develop a closer connection to ordinary people. Her return to Pakistan in 1986 raised expectations for a full-fledged restoration of democracy, eradication of authoritarian politics, and a new civic beginning in Pakistan. In her autobiography, she detailed her struggle, as well as her vision, for a progressive society and thus observers waited for a post-1947 generation of leadership in south Asian politics.[1] This anticipation was also fueled by the leadership of Rajiv Gandhi in neighboring India.

After the death of Zia, Ghulam Ishaq Khan (1915–2006), chairman of the Senate, as per the amended constitution, became the president of the country. He decided to hold countrywide elections, allowing full participation to political parties. A lifelong civil servant, Khan had served many Pakistani presidents and had been a Zia loyalist, but he was fully aware that he could not ward off public demands for free elections. In the meantime, Pakistani political parties had been divided into two broad electoral alliances, which also reflected two divergent viewpoints broadly representing the parallel legacies of Zulfikar Bhutto and Zia-ul-Haq. Benazir Bhutto's coalition, called the Pakistan Democratic Alliance (PDA), was dominated by her PPP and included other progressive forces such as Abdul Wali Khan's Awami National Party (ANP). The Islamic Democratic Alliance (IDA or IJI) included certain factions of the Muslim League and several religiopolitical parties. It was headed by Mian Nawaz Sharif, a pro-Zia Leaguer and the chief minister of Punjab. More than this political polarization, Pakistan's constitutional anomalies following Zia's amendments had crucially turned the balance of power in favor of the president who, under Article 58–2B, could dismiss both the parliament and the prime minister. Other than a powerful president, the army chief was another and perhaps the most powerful component of this "troika," where the prime minister was perhaps the third and the weakest partner despite having been elected through universal franchise. Such a structural imbalance was further aggravated by the more intense and often destabilizing role of the intelligence agencies such as the ISI, which, given their high profile and resources because of Afghan resistance, did not want an assertive political authority to run the country.

Despite pervasive goodwill for Benazir Bhutto, official cards were heavily stacked against her, and only an absolute parliamentary majority could enable her to restore the parliamentary primacy and eradicate repressive laws. In addition, Karachi had been restive since the mid-1980s, and the relationship with the Muhajir Qaumi Movement (MQM)—representing the Urdu speakers in urban Sindh—was not going to be an easy proposition for any new PPP regime. After her marriage to Asif Zardari in 1987, Benazir Bhutto became more vulnerable to a storm of criticism because her husband's family did not enjoy a positive reputation, and even foreign correspondents worried about a fall-out from these nuptial bonds.[2] The October 1988 elections were conducted for 207 National Assembly seats (excluding seats for women and Federally Administered Tribal Areas [FATA]) amid great expectations and mass rallies, although the powerful province of Punjab was already under the IJI control, and Sindh had been acutely divided between two parallel ethnic urban and rural groupings. In the same manner, the North-West Frontier Province (NWFP) and Balochistan appeared to give a mixed verdict owing to competitive forces of ethnicity and religion. Polls took place amid acrimonious allegations and the final tally for all the 240 seats showed 108 seats for the IJI, 94 for the PPP, and 32 for the independents. After arbitration by the U.S. Ambassador, Robert Oakley, who sought a compromise from Benazir Bhutto on the continuation of Ziaist foreign policies regarding Kashmir and Afghanistan and the retention of the president and the foreign minister, the PPP leader took her oath as the prime minister on December 2, 1988.

It was not going to be smooth sailing for the new government, as the chief minister of Punjab, Nawaz Sharif, soon began to defy the writ of the federal government in his province. Egged on by his own personal ambitions and assisted by several anti-PPP elements within the government and especially from the intelligence community, Sharif also spearheaded opposition in the National Assembly. Bhutto initially enjoyed the goodwill of her supporters and General Aslam Baig, the army chief, who avoided an open confrontation with her. Yet Pakistan was soon to begin a new era of fractured democracy where more energy was wasted on mutual refutations than on resolving the country's age-old problems of governance.[3] Other than an acute political polarity and structural imbalances, Karachi, Kashmir, and Kabul turned out to be the proverbial straw for a youthful Bhutto, who at 35 had become the first-ever woman prime minister of a Muslim country. Her foreign visits were well received, although for many conservative Islamist groups, her gender often generated some resentment; however, ordinary Pakistanis worried more about their mundane problems than her being a woman. Like Nawaz Sharif and his diehard supporters, Benazir Bhutto did not make any substantial effort to hold extended dialogue with her political opponents, and with the passage of time, many of her own coalition partners in the PDA also moved aside.

The MQM had harbored longstanding reservations about the PPP because of the quota system and the latter being more entrenched among the rural population in Sindh. But the MQM's leader, Altaf Hussain (1953–), and his group of firebrands were not comfortable with the Pushtun, Punjabi, and Baloch communities in Karachi, because other than a changing demography, housing, jobs, transport, and local political power appeared to be slipping away from the erstwhile well-ensconced Muhajireen. Basing its case on Muhajir victimization, MQM ran its own militias and fought running battles in the growingly segregated areas in Karachi, which seriously affected Pakistani economy and morale. While seeking support from the MQM, which held 13 vital National Assembly seats (11 from Karachi and 2 from Hyderabad), Bhutto tried to assuage MQM's apprehensions about her government. The MQM was reluctant to enter in a coalition following heightened tensions with the Sindhi nationalists, as the situation worsened after a bombing campaign in Hyderabad on September 30, 1988 that claimed 200 lives.[4] As a result of the public outcry in urban Sindh, however, both parties gradually grew closer. A 58-point agreement was signed in December 1988 in Karachi between Benazir Bhutto and Altaf Hussain. The agreement angered several Sindhi nationalists, although given the lack of trust between the two parties, there was very little hope of its successful implementation. The IJI led by Nawaz Sharif also began to woo Altaf Hussain, a move mainly intended to destabilize Bhutto. In the meantime, Karachi still suffered from intermittent cases of kidnaps, mysterious killings, and occasional ethnic clashes, which only fueled the IJI criticism of the PPP administration.

The MQM, at one stage, even approached the army chief to intervene in Karachi, which meant that the PPP in Sindh had become one-sided or was incapable of containing violence. The MQM was also demanding repatriation of 250,000 Urdu-speaking Biharis living in camps in Bangladesh since 1971 and who were often referred to as "stranded Pakistanis." Islamabad was reluctant in bringing them to Pakistan, fearing a backlash from the Sindhi population, as most of these Biharis already lived in urban Sindh, and their new arrivals might simply inflate existing ethnic tensions. On May 27, 1989, several civilians and MQM activists were killed in a police shootout in Pukka-Qila of Hyderabad, a predominantly Urdu-speaking area, and Altaf Hussain accused Benazir Bhutto of backstabbing. Such recriminations only hastened secret negotiations between the MQM and Nawaz Sharif, as Bhutto was seen as a common foe. On September 18, 1989, MQM formally aligned itself with the IJI, which had grown into a bigger alliance called the Combined Opposition Parities (COP) determined to bring down the PPP regime through a no-confidence motion in the National Assembly. Bhutto survived the vote but did not make any substantial effort to redirect her energies in building bridges with her political opponents, and thus national politics remained fragile. In the meantime, as subsequently reported by the media, the country's intelligence agencies pursued their parallel activities and further eroded confidence in the youthful prime minister.[5] Bhutto remained busy on foreign tours where she usually derided India for its human rights violations in Kashmir and sought more political and material assistance for Pakistan.

Pakistan and India had been members of the South Asian Association for Regional Cooperation (SAARC), a regional alliance to promote socioeconomic cooperation formed in 1984, and other than these two neighbors, included Bangladesh, Sri Lanka, Nepal, Bhutan, and Maldives. The SAARC held periodic high-profile meetings where attention would remain focused on leaders from the two rival nations, and thus the 1988 summit in Islamabad generated immense global and regional interest in Rajiv Gandhi and Benazir Bhutto. Their resolve to curb political upheavals to establish greater cooperation, however, faltered once they went back to their respective constituencies where intolerant forces and hostile establishments would veto dissolution of a regional cold war. The Indian-controlled Kashmir had been characterized by unrest since 1988 amid a host of longstanding and new grievances against New Delhi that soon turned into a militant defiance. Instead of resolving the issue through negotiations with the Kashmiri leaders and also by holding a meaningful dialogue with Pakistan, India used troops against demonstrations in the valley often causing numerous deaths. Indian authorities believed that they could contain dissent by suppressing it with a brutal force as had been done in Indian Punjab in the 1980s when the movement for an independent Sikh state (Khalistan) was quelled through sheer force. Kashmiris, however, wanted a new beginning in their collective life and refused to be seen as a strategic pawn, which agitated their younger groups who, more like Afghans, wanted to assert their own sovereignty. In this situation, crucial Pakistani political and material assistance helped their rebellion assume more enduring patterns until New Delhi was compelled to deploy more troops. Kashmir once again brought India and Pakistan to a standstill, as their mutual accusations and confrontational postures disallowed a peaceful resolution. Benazir Bhutto, egged on by an eager establishment and tormented by her weakened grip on national affairs, used the Kashmir dispute as a rallying cry, but the issue was to outlive her.

Pakistan had been hosting millions of Afghan refugees while helping the resistance in its war with the Soviets. Concurrently, they held indirect talks with Moscow in Geneva under the United Nations auspices to find a tangible solution to the problem. Finding it a lost and costly campaign, President Gorbachev finally decided to withdraw Soviet troops from Afghanistan, which left the pro-Moscow regime in Kabul in a precarious situation. Headed by Najibullah, a former doctor and head of the KHAD (the Afghan secret service), the regime did not lose its nerve despite its confinement to Kabul with outlying regions mostly under Mujahideen control or held by ethnic warlords. In April 1989, enthused by the Soviet retreat and Najibullah's vulnerability, the nine Mujahideen groups aided by the Central Intelligence Agency and ISI attacked the eastern city of Jalalabad hoping to dislodge the Kabul regime. It turned out to be a rather hasty development and resulted in the rout of several thousand Afghan fighters on all sides. This event not only exposed the intractability of the Afghan situation to outside powers such as Pakistan and the United States, it also added momentum to intra-Afghan discord and tribulations. The refugee population, its economic and ecological costs, and proliferation of arms and drugs all resulted in more discomfort for Pakistan, and an element of exhaustion only added to Islamabad's worries at a time when Washington and other foreign backers decided to leave Afghanistan on its own. In addition, Pakistan's nuclear program came under serious congressional review, which resulted in a demand for a "roll back" amid a threat of complete cessation of aid to Islamabad. Benazir Bhutto could have used the Jalalabad fiasco to establish a fresher perspective on the region, but her reluctance to take on the Pakistan army and the ISI only exposed her own untenable hold on a well-entrenched establishment. She was able to gain some support from President George H.W. Bush in 1989, but Pakistan's domestic and regional problems needed more dynamic and systemic solutions, which were, perhaps, not possible within a fractured political culture.[6] As was expected, Ishaq Khan dismissed Bhutto's government in August 1990, only 18 months after its formation, and charged her with incompetence, corruption, and severe deterioration in law and order.[7] This dismissal did not evoke any major global outcry, as world attention was more focused on the Iraqi invasion of Kuwait and the resultant developments. President Ishaq Khan appointed Ghulam Mustafa Jatoi (1937–), a Sindhi politician, to head the interim government for the next three months until the new elections for the assemblies could be held. Dismay with the Bhutto regime led to continued unrest in all the three Ks (Karachi, Kashmir, and Kabul), and pronounced support from anti-Bhutto forces within the establishment[8] resulted in an electoral rout of the PPP in October 1990.

NAWAZ SHARIF, 1990–1993: MUSLIM LEAGUE IN GOVERNMENT

Sharif, a scion of a Lahore-based Punjabi business family, had come to the attention of General Zia when he needed various political allies across the nation. Sharif's first important cabinet portfolio occurred in the mid-1980s when he became the finance minister in Punjab, aligned himself with the military junta, and eventually landed himself the leadership of pro-Zia Muslim League. After Zia's death, Sharif, by now the chief minister of Punjab, built upon a wave of sympathy for the deceased general in Punjab and used his contacts with the establishment and other centrist politicians to forge the IDA/IJI. Earlier, when the Junejo government had been dismissed by Zia in June 1988, Sharif's own cabinet had been spared and the Punjab Assembly remained intact. With Junejo gone and the rest of the pro-Zia coalition in disarray, Sharif thought he deserved to be prime minister. President Ghulam Ishaq Khan certainly had a soft spot for Sharif, who, unlike Benazir Bhutto, did not seek to change ongoing domestic and external policies.[9] After the elections of October 1988, Sharif further consolidated his own forte in Punjab and engaged in a rather uninhibited contest with Bhutto over all the issues such as the center-province relationship and state of affairs in Karachi. To browbeat Bhutto, he even used the regionalist card by accusing the PPP government of victimizing his native Punjab and allowed his ministers to propagate on such sectional lines. When Bhutto was left out on a limb partly by her own drift and partly by Sharif's machinations, the ambitious Punjabi politician got his chance to further debilitate Bhutto in her native Sindh by forging an alliance with the MQM. The 17-point agreement between Sharif and the MQM had been, according to some reports, facilitated by Ishaq Khan.[10] Failure to dislodge Bhutto through a no-confidence vote, despite a clear majority of the League in the Senate, did not slow down Sharif who heartily welcomed President Ishaq Khan's dismissal of the PPP regime.

Bhutto was critical of the interim regime led by Jatoi and accused it of conducting a witch hunt to establish corruption cases against her family, but a multiparty alliance against her was already well established as Pakistanis went to the polls in October 1990 after a ban on aid imposed by Washington. President Bush Sr., under a congressional requirement known as the Pressler Amendment, had been unable to certify that Pakistan did not possess a nuclear program. Consequently, the economic and military assistance worth $564 million was stopped, along with delivery of 71 F-16 aircraft and their spare parts for which Pakistan had already paid. Amid a wider public disenchantment and hair-splitting among politicians, voters, in general, returned the IJI with a clear majority, enabling Sharif to become the prime minister on November 7, 1990. His alliance had won 105 of the National Assembly's 207 contested seats compared to the PDA's 45. The MQM once again emerged as the majority party in Karachi and an important powerbroker by capturing all the Urdu-speaking constituencies. The PPP was critical of these results and cried foul through its press conferences and special *White Papers*, but that did not stop the IJI from forming a central government and in Punjab while a demoralized PPP stood on the margins.

Sharif promised economic reforms, better power sharing with the provinces, peace in Karachi, and a robust stance on Kashmir and Afghanistan. Given the stoppage of U.S. aid, violence in Karachi, widespread corruption, and tensions with India, Sharif sought help from the International Monetary Fund (IMF) and the World Bank who imposed their own conditions, making basic goods and services rather more expensive for ordinary Pakistanis. Concurrently, in February 1992, Sharif lifted various controls on foreign currencies, mainly to invite more international investments besides pursuing a policy of privatization seeking major funds and efficiency. The Gulf crisis seriously hurt Pakistan, as many remittances by its expatriates dried up. In addition, Pakistan was persuaded by Washington and other allies such as Saudi Arabia to contribute 10,000 troops, which the former did despite serious reservations by General Aslam Baig and ordinary Pakistanis who were deeply resentful of American aid stoppage.

In his election campaign, Sharif had promised systemic Islamization of Pakistan, which had gained him support from religious groups such as the Jamaat-i-Islami now led by Qazi Hussain Ahmad. In May 1991, Sharif, under pressure from his allies for the promulgation of Islamic law (*Sharia*), presented a watered-down resolution in the National Assembly that was resisted by the PDA and MQM and was eventually sent to special committees for their consideration. Crucially, in November 1991, the Federal Shariat Court, while hearing a petition on the country's financial practices, declared interest (*riba*) repugnant to Islam. This injunction also found 20 other federal and provincial laws in the economic sector un-Islamic and sought their prompt removal. Sharif did not want to challenge this verdict directly and instead used some financial institutions to seek a redress from the Supreme Court. He also tried to provide relief to the poor through bigger projects such as the motorways, increase in salaries, and easier bank loans for purchasing smaller yellow taxi cars. Sharif convened a meeting of the Council for Common Interest to resolve tariff and trade issues bedeviling center's relations with the provinces. It was the disorder in Karachi, however, that refused to go away despite the Muslim League-MQM coalition, and daily kidnaps, car thefts, selective killings of civilians, and political opponents intensified civic pressure for a major military operation to arrest the miscreants and confiscate illegal weapons. The IJI-PDA tensions had been escalating by each passing day, with the latter accusing the Sharif government of organized victimization and when a massive scandal involving Punjab officials came into public knowledge, the PPP sent telegrams to Ishaq Khan demanding the removal of the prime minister. Pakistanis came to know of large-scale misappropriation of public funds causing the collapse of Cooperative Societies, which held the deposits worth 20 billion Rupees belonging to ordinary citizens. It appeared that the IJI had been unable to restore public confidence in areas such as the economy and law and order.

The law-and-order situation had been steadily deteriorating in rural Sindh where bandits made the life of ordinary people almost impossible and goods traffic between Karachi and the rest of the country was being seriously affected. As Karachi was already volatile, the news from the interior of Sindh turned equally gloomy. The high-handed policies of Jam Sadiq Ali not only worsened the situation, they also compelled Islamabad to order a military operation. In the meantime, a more vocal print media began to publish stories that corruption and coercion were occurring at the behest of powerful political elements such as the MQM and Irfanullah Marwat, Ishaq Khan's son-in-law.[11]

Pressure for military operation, despite Altaf Hussain's resistance and that of some of Sharif's close associates, continued to build up. The death of Jam Sadiq Ali and the replacement of General Aslam Baig by General Asif Nawaz Janjua in early 1992 followed a military campaign or "Operation Clean-Up" in May 1992. The official pictures of MQM's torture houses, scandalous stories about its leadership, and a general narrative of gun running and organized crimes shocked Pakistanis who felt reassured by the operation that continued even after Janjua's sudden death in January 1993. As a result, Altaf Hussain and many other MQM activists and militants sought asylum in Britain, the United States, and South Africa, and many more went underground or went to Dubai. At the same time, a few MQM activists revolted against Hussain and formed another faction called MQM (Haqiqi), which led to mafia-style running battles between these factions. It appeared that Sharif had failed to address the economic and political situation in the country, nor could he offer some fresher perspective on Kashmir and Afghanistan.

An insecure Sharif and a wily Ishaq Khan soon developed serious personal differences over the appointment of senior judges and military officials. Khan was also incensed over Sharif's rapprochement with Bhutto who had agreed to chair the Parliamentary Committee on Foreign Affairs. Sharif wanted to outmaneuver Khan before the latter could use Article 58–2 (B) for dismissing his government and thus was reluctant to support President Khan in his reelection for another term. Ishaq Khan began to woo Benazir Bhutto who, despite dissuasion from some senior colleagues, was willing to collaborate with the president and wreak revenge on her adversary. Amid these palatial intrigues and machinations, Sharif's government and the assemblies were finally dismissed on April 18, 1993 and the prime minister's last-minute emotional speech a day earlier would not stop Khan from dissolving the second elected regime during his tenure. Sharif, however, decided to file a petition on April 19 with the Supreme Court against his dismissal, and the latter gave its historic verdict three weeks later by restoring the prime minister. A majority verdict with 1 vote in dissent and 10 in its favor visibly shook Khan, but Sharif was equally weakened and the country could not operate smoothly with two antagonists holding top two offices. The new army chief, General Abdul Wahid Kakar, intervened on July 18, 1993 and counseled both contenders to resign so that the country could be run by a new interim administration that would ensure new elections for a fresh start. As was decided, both the president and prime minister resigned and the army invited Moeen Qureshi, a Pakistani expatriate banker, to become an interim prime minister. Wasim Sajjad, the chairman of Pakistani Senate, became the acting president while Qureshi, the former World Bank Executive, selected his team of technocrats and some public figures to give a clean and efficient administration to the country.

BENAZIR BHUTTO, 1993–1996: THE SECOND ADMINISTRATION

Bhutto's victory in the elections held on October 6–8, 1993 was one more chance offered to her by fellow citizens to steer them out of their cycle of governance by consolidating democracy and improving the economy, and this time her position was stronger. Voters did not care that she was a woman. They yearned for some consensual policies on all the challenging issues within and outside the country. A clear emphasis on Islam, the demand for a transparent system, and yearning for tolerant and capable leadership spawned the contemporary political ethos. Moeen Qureshi had provided an example in good governance through transparent administration and freer media, but the technocrat had deeply annoyed many influential Pakistanis by publishing a list of 5,000 loan defaulters and other beneficiaries of unaccounted official largesse, amounting to a massive volume of 62 billion Rupees.[12] This exposé endeared him to the ordinary people, and when he tried to reform the age-old taxation system, he stood in good stead with the public. Earlier, he had suggested a first-ever agricultural tax in the country at the rate of 6 percent, much to the chagrin of landowners, although his removal of subsidies from the basic provisions made life expensive for ordinary people. Many of his critics, including the religiopolitical leaders, accused Qureshi of implementing the IMF-World Bank agenda and serving Western interests, yet people appreciated a visible level of accountability and efficiency.

In the elections conducted by Qureshi-led interim administration, the PPP obtained 86 seats in the National Assembly, Sharif's Muslim League gained 73, and the rest were divided among the ANP (3), Junejo Muslim League (6), and the Jamaat-led Pakistan Islamic Front (PIF) (3).[13] The MQM (Altaf group) had boycotted the elections in protest against the ongoing military operation and also because of its strong reservations against intelligence agencies for allegedly supporting the Haqiqi rivals. Benazir Bhutto's position as the prime minister registered a significant boost on November 13, 1993 when Farooq Leghari (1941–), her PPP colleague, was elected president of the country by gaining 274 votes from the assemblies compared with 168 votes cast for Wasim Sajjad. The latter was nominated by the Sharif-led Muslim League and had been chairing the Senate along with his designation at the acting president after the departure of Ishaq Khan. People now expected Bhutto to lead the nation on all outstanding issues by starting afresh, and analysts expected her to properly govern the nation instead of her familiar outbursts as an oppositional leader. The three K's, however, would again pose formidable challenges, causing her second loss and Punjab, once again, under Chief Minister Manzoor Wattoo, proved the proverbial Achille's heel for her administration. The chief minister in Lahore headed his own section of the Muslim League and resisted pressures and persuasion from Bhutto to join hands with her, but to no avail. Wattoo, however, kept himself confined to Punjab and, unlike Sharif in 1988–1990, avoided a countrywide confrontation with Benazir Bhutto yet caused her nightmares and a grave waste of resources.

Peace in Karachi remained elusive as MQM activists trusted neither the army nor the other two major political parties, and their leaders in exile including an oratory-prone Altaf Hussain, used pamphlets, audiocassettes, and videocassettes to propagate the intensity of state-led violence against fellow Muhajireen. Hussain and his few associates had been awarded British citizenship, but they maintained their involvement in Karachi politics through an efficient system of communications while based in the Edgware suburb of London.[14] Soon Benazir Bhutto's brother, Murtaza Bhutto, decided to return to Karachi in late 1993, which unnerved the former leader and her spouse, Asif Zardari. Murtaza, with his Syrian wife, Ghinwa, viewed himself to be a genuine heir to Zulfikar Ali Bhutto's legacy and justified his case on the basis of exile and personal bereavement. Murtaza was to be another major concern for the prime minister, whose own preoccupation at this stage appeared to be high-profile visits abroad.

In 1994, she was able to persuade the Clinton Administration and U.S. Congressmen to relent in their criticism of the Pakistani nuclear program so as to restore military and technical assistance to her country. This development raised her profile at a time when the Indian military operations across the Kashmir Valley and skirmishes between the two neighbors did not result in any breakthrough in their stalemated relations. Bhutto was, once again, taking a vocal stance on Kashmir but concurrently, under U.S. persuasion, sought normalcy with New Delhi. Political instability in India after the assassination of Rajiv Gandhi in 1991, demolition of the Baburi Mosque in 1992 in Ayodhya, and the posthumous anti-Muslim riots in India dampened hopes for any Indo-Pakistani breakthrough. After the elections of 1996, however, the short-lived administrations of Deve Gowda and I. K. Gujral allowed some optimism as the Indian and Pakistani prime ministers often met under the SAARC's auspices. The situation was soon to change with the formation of government by Ultra-Right Bharatiya Janata Party (BJP), which had been responsible for the demolition of the mosque and was rabidly anti-Muslim. This strong nationalist party conducted India's nuclear tests in early May 1998, followed by Pakistan, but soon began showing interest in friendship with Pakistan.[15]

A factionalist Afghanistan, however, remained a major concern for Pakistan because of the continued presence of Afghan refugees and also because the drug trafficking and Kalashnikov culture linked with the events in the neighboring country began to heavily afflict Pakistan. Divided by rent-seeking war lords—Pushtun, Tajik, Uzbek, and Hazara—regional and ethnosectarian rivalries in the post-Soviet country further decimated hope for peace and normalcy. The downfall of the Najibullah regime in 1992 ushered in another intense phase in the internecine civil war, vetoing a stable and unified administration. In this state of dismay and disunity, some former Afghan students turned to Mullah Omar, a former Mujahid and now confined to teaching at a religious seminary near Kandahar in southeastern Afghanistan. These Afghans had been the graduates of religious schools on the Frontier and mostly came from Pushtun refugee background. Disillusioned by chaos and moral degradation of the warlords, they organized themselves into a puritanical movement called Taliban and began their operation in 1994 until they were able to capture Kabul in 1996. Except for a small Tajik territory under Ahmad Shah Masud in the Panjsher Mountains, they imposed their strict form of religious codes on the society. Many of their former associates—Arab and others—who had fought anti-Soviet holy war (*Jihad*) came back to fight warlords and other miscreants. Osama bin Laden and his followers found a safer sanctuary in Afghanistan at a time when no other Muslim country was willing to give them shelter.

The Bhutto government and the ISI helped the Taliban, as the movement seemed to guarantee peace in the war-torn land, and their Pushtun identity-sharing kinship with the Pakistani tribals won them a soft spot in Islamabad. The Taliban had shown some interest in the Middle East and the United States, although the latter, under pressure from civic groups, would not recognize their puritanical administration.[16] The Taliban ascendancy enthused fundamentalist tendencies in Pakistan, as they were idealized by some similar purist groups on the Frontier. In fact, Mullah Soofi Muhammad led a defiant campaign to implement Islamic laws in Malakand and Swat and named it Tehrik-i-Nifaz-i-Shariat, or the movement for the implementation of Islamic law. The same cleric was subsequently responsible for sending in thousands of Pushtuns into Afghanistan to wage a Jihad against Westerners after the invasion of Afghanistan in October 2001. Also, support for Taliban activated Pakistani Sunni militant groups such as Lashkar-i-Jhangvi and Jaysh-i-Muhammad that soon engaged in the selective killings of middle class Shias, as well as volunteering for the Taliban and Kashmiri activists. Pakistani Shias, accounting for 20 percent of the total population, attempted to counter such Sunni militants by organizing their own group, Sipah-i-Muhammad, which allegedly received support from external Shia groups. Thus during the Bhutto's second tenure, Pakistan became a focal point for Sunni-Shia sectarian dissention, often supported by Taliban, Saudi, and Iranian backers.

Karachi again proved the toughest test for the Bhutto administration, and MQM's absence from electoral politics only added to schismatic patterns. After Murtaza Bhutto's return in 1993, some disgruntled PPP supporters gathered around him, making it difficult for his ailing mother who agonized over the schism between her two eldest children. Zardari and Murtaza never saw eye to eye with each other, as the firebrand Bhutto openly denounced Zardari's domineering influence on his sister. On September 20, 1996, Murtaza Bhutto was killed outside his Clifton residence, and Zardari, police officials, and the Indian intelligence were all blamed for his cold-blooded murder. Volatile feuds among the MQM militants belonging to the Altaf and Haqiqi factions, their encounters with the security forces, and clashes across ethnic lines accompanied by a parallel wave of sectarian attacks made Karachi almost ungovernable. For instance, on February 25, 1995, 25 people were killed by unknown miscreants, and on March 8 two U.S. consulate officials were gunned down on Shahrah-i-Faisal in the broad daylight. After the rape of a Muhajir girl on June 22, rockets were fired at Pakistan Television Centre, and the provincial PPP administration led by the chief minister, Abdullah Shah, sat by helplessly. Between late August and November in the same year, the death toll in Karachi had already peaked to 500. Under dissuasion from the Sindhi nationalists, the PPP would not welcome negotiations with the MQM (Altaf group), which had an upper hand in Karachi's violence and instead left it to the Haqiqi and Rangers to fight it. In December 1995, Nasir Hussain, the elder brother of Altaf Hussain, had been killed, and within two weeks in a revenge attack the brother of the chief minister was gunned down.

Confrontational politics in Karachi and Punjab germinated ill will between President Leghari and Prime Minister Bhutto, although they both belonged to the same party and had shared a common political persuasion. But Leghari became resentful of Zardari's interference in the administration, especially when the latter did not enjoy any positive reputation. Also, both Leghari and Bhutto quarreled over the appointment of senior judges and traded accusations in a variety of areas such as corruption, monopolization of politics, and nepotism.[17] In the meantime on November 3, 1996, the Lahore High Court restored Manzoor Wattoo as the chief minister of Punjab and the PPP candidate, Arif Nikai, had to make way for the former. Zardari would not accept this reinstatement and went to Lahore, apparently to buy the loyalties of many provincial legislators through "horse trading." On November 5, on encouragement from the army and a nod from Sharif, President Leghari dissolved the assemblies, dismissed the Bhutto government, and established a new interim government under the veteran politician, Malik Meraj Khalid (1916–2003).[18] The new interim administration included several public figures such as Mumtaz Bhutto, Zulfikar Ali Bhutto's cousin, and Shahid Javed Burki, a former vice-president of the World Bank. Once again, the new government undertook several measures to restore the economy besides an efficient administration, but its main action was to hold elections within the stipulated 90 days. During its tenure the idea of having an all-powerful national security council consisting of senior politicians and military chiefs was floated so as to avoid intermittent imposition of military rule became the democratic interregnums were proving cyclic, short-lived, and equally controversial. The PPP, however, took the dissolution of its regime to the Supreme Court, challenging presidential order under Article 58–2 (B), although the public usually stood with Leghari's decision owing to widespread disorder and corruption within the country.

NAWAZ SHARIF, 1997–1999, AND THE MILITARY COUP

Within a decade Pakistan was undergoing a third election, and the public at large felt dismayed at the failure of one more semidemocratic phase in the country, which was already under severe external scrutiny for its nuclear program and support for the Taliban and Kashmiri activists. The Supreme Court, in its verdict just four days before the election, upheld the dissolution of the PPP regime by Leghari, which further weakened interest in the elections. An isolated and rather aggrieved Pakistan cast votes in February and expectedly the turnout was not impressive, around 26 percent. Results showed an overwhelming support for Nawaz Sharif's Muslim League (PML-N), which garnered 135 seats in the new National Assembly contrasted with only 19 by the PPP. The MQM was able to retain its 12 urban seats along with 29 seats in the Sindh Provincial Assembly. Even in the Sindhi heartland, the PPP lost many seats to the Muslim League and gained only 36 seats, whereas the ANP emerged as the majority party in the NWFP by winning 31 seats in the provincial assembly.[19] Another new entrant to the political field had been Imran Khan (1952–), a Pakistani cricketing hero and philanthropist who had formed his own Tehrik-i-Insaaf or justice movement to fight corruption and the lack of direction in Pakistani politics. He did not have enough time to organize his party for elections but emerged on the political scene as a moderate reformer.

Sharif formed the government in the wake of goodwill and reawakened optimism as was evident by the sudden upward trend in Karachi's stock market. Sharif was aware that Pakistan's recurrent crisis in government and a faltering economy had been generating several gloomy predictions, and he appealed for an austerity drive while promising to safeguard the country's assets. Pakistan's foreign exchange reserves had been low for quite some time, and there was serious concern about a possible default on loan repayment. On his appeal, Pakistanis donated generous sums to shore up country's dwindling reserves, but gradually systemic malaise began to resurface. Sharif had to tread carefully in his relations with a powerful Leghari who, like Khan before him, desired his reelection at a time when both Leghari and Sharif did not enjoy good relations with Benazir Bhutto. Relations further nosedived in the wake of registration of 18 corruption cases against Bhutto and her conviction by the High Court, followed by Zardari's internment.[20] Bhutto decided to go abroad while investigations continued in Pakistan and Switzerland, tarnishing her image at a time when her second administration had ended so ingloriously. Disappointment with her knew no bounds both inside the country and without, and she found self-imposed exile the best possible escape from this ignominy.

Sharif, aggrieved over sectarian chaos, decided to establish special summary courts to try perpetrators, yet the bomb blasts in Lahore and Karachi along with Sunni-Shia murders kept defying official writ. Other than differences over the formation of these courts—assumed by judiciary as a parallel system—it was the elevation of five judges by the Supreme Court that the seeds for a feud were sown among the three highest offices of the civil administration. An agitated Chief Justice Syed Sajjad Ali Shah had the support from President Leghari, whereas the prime minister saw their objections as an infringement on his own authority. Instigation for rebellion against the chief justice from within the highest echelons of the judiciary became a blatant affair, as Sharif's supporters, including some serving cabinet members, took it upon themselves to harass the Supreme Court. Jumping the security parameters on November 28, 1997, a mob attacked the chambers while the Supreme Court was in session, alarming the entire nation that watched the unruly and traumatizing scenes on their screens. Eventually, the chief justice, losing the confidence of his colleagues, left his office, which proved an unsavory victory for Sharif whose penchant for confrontational politics disillusioned many Pakistanis. On December 2, 1997, President Leghari left office as well, as his relations with the prime minister had seriously deteriorated and, in addition by virtue of the Thirteenth Amendment passed by Pakistani legislators earlier in April, presidential powers to dissolve cabinets and assemblies had been removed. Gone was the controversial Eighth Amendment inducted in 1985 by General Zia to shore up the presidential office. Sharif now was at the apex of his powers and nominated Muhammad Rafiq Tarar (1929–) for the presidency. A retired judge and fellow Punjabi, Tarar was a Sharif loyalist whose election in December 1997 completed the "Punjabisation" of Pakistan with the president, prime minister, and the army chief all belonging to Punjab.

Initially, the army seemed to work in close collaboration with the Muslim League regime and was deputed by Shahbaz Sharif, the chief minister of Punjab and the prime minister's brother, to root out "ghost schools" across the province.[21] In October 1997, Sharif developed personal difference with General Jahangir Karamat, who had publicly supported the idea of National Security Council where senior politicians and services chiefs will confer together to undertake vital decisions on all domestic and external issues. The general's plea was to ward off the possibility of any more military takeovers by institutionalizing its role within the power structure. Sharif viewed in this proposition an extraprofessional role for the armed forces at the sheer expense of civil authority and, amidst a hyped-up furor, compelled Karamat to resign and instead appointed General Pervez Musharraf (1943–) as the next chief of army staff. Pakistan's relations with India witnessed a dramatic change in February 1998, when after people-to-people contacts and informal diplomacy carried out by retired diplomats from both sides, the Indian prime minister, A. B. Vajpayee, undertook a special visit to Lahore. He went to the historic Iqbal Park and, in a speech, reaffirmed India's support for Pakistan's sovereignty, something that generated new momentum in Indo-Pakistani relations, although it was received with cynicism by khaki forces on both sides. The Lahore peace process faced a serious debacle in May 1998 when both countries detonated nuclear devices and then, a year later, fought an undeclared war in the Kargil area of Kashmir. Pakistani troops had been helping the Kashmiri rebels who had captured some peaks on the Kargil Heights at a time when the Indian troops had apparently left them unoccupied. Pakistani generals wanted to use this limited military operation to further pressure India, as the latter faced an insurgency inside the Kashmir Valley, but was unwilling to enter into a serious dialogue with Pakistan. Generals did not take the repercussions of such an adventure into their strategic considerations and, as in 1965, held exaggerated views of India's vulnerabilities in the troubled region. Soon the Indian Air Force began to strafe forward Pakistani positions while its Swedish Bofor guns constantly pummeled Kargil Heights. In the wake of heightened patriotism, BJP threatened Pakistan with dire consequences and was eventually able to benefit from the fallout from this surge. Pakistan withdrew its troops after President Clinton pressured Sharif, who had rushed to Washington for assistance with the worsening situation on the borders. The Kargil campaign not only damaged Pakistan's global profile, but it equally laid bare differences between Prime Minister Sharif and General Musharraf.[22] Both never forgave each other for the humiliation on Kargil.

On October 12, 1999, Sharif surreptitiously tried to replace Musharraf with General Khawaja Ziauddin while the former was still in the air on his way back from a visit to Sri Lanka. Musharraf and his allies viewed this move quite perniciously, and even before the delayed flight could land at the Karachi airport, Musharraf's military colleagues had dismissed the Muslim League government after taking Sharif into custody. Once again, Pakistan came under military rule, with blame being hurled at "inept" politicians, many of whom were certainly willing to work under the general, while the superior judges engaged in their usual business of legalizing the takeover.

NOTES

1. Benazir Bhutto, *Daughter of the East* (London: Hamish Hamilton, 1988).

2. For a critical contemporary commentary on the perks and privileges of the Pakistani elite, as contrasted with the realities of ordinary life, see

Christina Lamb, *Waiting for Allah: Pakistan's Struggle for Democracy* (London: Hamish Hamilton, 1991).

3. Talat Aslam, "Punjab: Clash of the Titans," *Herald*, XX, February 1989.

4. *Dawn* October 2, 1988.

5. General Baig, ISI and the IDA all shared millions of rupees provided by some bankers to destabilize the PPP regime. Revelations about this scandal known as the Mehrangate were made in the mid-1990s and were taken up by the superior judges who failed to reprimand the culprits, although many of them had retired from military services by then.

6. On the role of ISI elements in destabilizing the PPP regime, see Shaheen Sehbai, "The Day of the Night Jackals," *Dawn Overseas Weekly*, June 14, 1989; Iftikhar H. Malik, *State and Civil Society in Pakistan: Politics of Authority, Ideology and Ethnicity* (Oxford: St. Antony's-Macmillan Series, 1997), pp. 99–103.

7. By that time, corruption had become a major issue and the public demanded accountability of the loan defaulters. For details, see *Newsline*, August 1990.

8. Because of a more visible profile of a luxury-loving Asif Zardari, the PPP opponents focused on him and attributed to him several instances of corruption. For details, see *Dawn*, August, 5 and October 12, 1990.

9. In May 1989, Jam Sadiq Ali, a former PPP stalwart from Sindh, returned after spending 12 years in exile in London and was warmly received by PPP supporters. Ali, a ruthless politician with a feudal mentality, soon joined hands with anti-Bhutto forces and grew close to the president. A few months later, Ali was to become the chief minister of Sindh under the IJI government and further discriminated against the PPP.

10. Ian Talbot, *Pakistan: A Modern History* (London: C. Hurst, 1998), p. 306.

11. When the prominent English monthly *Herald* published the stories of organized rape and ransom-taking, the Sindh government proscribed all the copies of the issue. Marwat's gun-toting picture had appeared on the front cover of this widely read magazine. See *Herald*, October 1991.

12. See Zafar Abbas, "Moeen Qureshi and Associates," and, M.S. Ghausi, "The Great Bank Robbery," Herald, September 1993.

13. For an overview of these elections and related issues, see Mohammad Waseem, *The 1993 Elections in Pakistan* (Lahore: Vanguard Books, 1994).

14. In Pakistan cases of murder, torture, and extortions were filed by the authorities against Hussain and his close associates, but they continued to profess their innocence and built up a strong network of international MQM in the Diaspora. Based on a personal interview with Hussain and other MQM leaders in 1997 in London.

15. For more on the BJP and the rise of majoritarianism, see Iftikhar H. Malik, *Jihad, Hindutva and the Taliban: South Asia at the Crossroads* (Karachi: Oxford University Press, 2005).

16. The Taliban are reported to have carried out negotiations with foreign governments and international oil companies given Afghanistan's location and its potential in natural resources that remain untapped. Many companies have been interested in building pipe lines from central Asian sources and desired a peaceful Afghanistan as a transit for oil supplies. People like Hamid Karzai and Zalmay Khalilzad had been in touch with the Taliban during their heyday. For more on the Taliban, see Ahmed Rashid, *Taliban, Islam, Oil and the New Great Game in Central Asia* (London: I. B. Tauris, 2002).

17. Leghari accused Bhutto of pressuring Chief Justice Sajjad Ali Shah through his son-in-law, Pervaiz Shah, who was a PPP minister.

18. Zahid Hussain, "Benazir Bhutto: Fall from Grace," *Newsline*, November 1996.

19. *Dawn*, February 5, 1997.

20. Benazir Bhutto left Pakistan in 1999, although several cases of corruption filed by the Sharif government against her were later quashed by the country's Supreme Court on the basis of flimsy evidence. Zardari, however, remained behind bars until 2004, when Musharraf allowed him to leave the country. The cases against the couple were finally withdrawn by Musharraf in 2007.

21. These schools did not exist at all but were incurring salaries and other maintenance expenses which were being billed to the national exchequer. Mostly they were under control of local influential individuals who through such "schools" found any easy way of receiving development grants from the provincial government.

22. For further details on Kargil and its fallout for Sharif and Musharraf, see Owen Bennett Jones, *Pakistan: Eye of the Storm* (New Haven & London: Yale University Press, 2002).

11

General Pervez Musharraf and Pakistan in the Twenty-First Century

General Pervez Musharraf (1943–) has been widely known in the West for his leading role in the U.S.-led war on terror after the 9/11 aerial attacks on New York and Washington and the Western invasions of Afghanistan and Iraq amid several other significant measures to detain Muslim activists. From his overthrow of the elected regime of Prime Minister Nawaz Sharif through a military coup on October 12, 1999 until the dramatic events of 2001, Musharraf was an unknown military general in a country with which the United States had been allied off and on for its own global policy imperatives. Gradually, patience had run out worldwide with the military and authoritarian regimes, at least among the civil groups, and democracy was seen as the best possible system to guarantee greater space for individual liberties and collective rights. Thus when Musharraf headed Pakistan as the chief executive, he was usually perceived as another Third World dictator in a country that had periodically suffered from such military coups and had been a perennial victim of its inept and equally callous political leaders. Given Pakistan's pervasive problems of governance, a faltering economy, and its location in a rather volatile region, few people wanted to delve into Pakistani affairs or to bail it out from its muddled politics where history had been repeating itself so often. Given the past records of several military dictators in Pakistan and elsewhere, there was little enthusiasm for Musharraf who lived a modern lifestyle, adored Turkey's Mustafa Kemal Ataturk, and wanted to see Pakistan as a progressive society based on interethnic peace, transparent culture, and developing economy. His seven-point formula promised much the same as had his other predecessors, and he criticized politicians who had bled the country with their internecine battles. Like other generals dismissing political regimes, he blamed Sharif, Bhutto, and several others of venality and incompetence and delivered promises for a "new" Pakistan. In the aura of accountability and development, Musharraf created several new commissions and bureaus to recommend new strategies on education, politics, national reconstruction, economy, media, and accountability. It appeared as if more like Ayub Khan, Musharraf visualized Pakistan in his own liberal image without fully comprehending the complexity of a nation-state and the imperatives of a political system, which, unlike a predictable life in military, remains a complex affair.

Born in Delhi and having grown up in the cosmopolitan milieu of Karachi, Lahore, and Ankara, Musharraf joined the Pakistan army's Special Services Group, an elite force not known for brooding over intellectual issues once the orders have been issued by superiors.[1] His colleagues such as Generals Mahmud Ahmad, Usmani, and others had alerted him on Sharif's decision to replace him with General Ziauddin from country's de facto position of the army's chief of staff while Musharraf was still in the air. His plane had very little fuel left but was diverted to some other airport, avoiding Karachi, which, according to the prime minister in Islamabad, would allow his appointee more time to consolidate his position vis-à-vis other powerful corps commanders. The senior generals stood by their chief and took control of the Karachi Airport as the others overpowered the police at the Prime Minister House and Pakistan Television Centre, and soon Musharraf emerged on the national television promising a new beginning. Some Pakistanis, brimming with frustration with an embattled political administration, welcomed Musharraf and accepted his promise to return the country to a transparent system, but the world witnessed this drama unfolding with shock and curiosity.

FROM A CHIEF EXECUTIVE TO PRESIDENT

Amid fears and expectations prevailing in Pakistan, General Musharraf began to consolidate his position in his self-designated office of the chief executive, although Muhammad Rafiq Tarar continued to hold the presidency. Musharraf was the de facto head of state. Tarar, both by his office and disposition, maintained a mere ceremonial profile that worked in Musharraf's favor, especially when President Clinton visited south Asia on March 19–26, 2000. He was reluctant to visit Islamabad and intended to spend more time in India, with only a short visit to Bangladesh. The U.S. President had strong reservations against visiting Pakistan owing to its military dictatorship, and he did not want to be seen with General Musharraf at a time when the world was critical of authoritarian rulers. In Pakistan itself there was strong resentment against U.S. policies as a result of severe sanctions that had been imposed on the country after its nuclear tests in May 1998 amid an undiminished criticism of Islamabad's role vis-à-vis terrorism. Persuaded by his security advisors such as Admiral Brent Snowcroft and General Anthony Zinny, Clinton made a short visit to Islamabad on March 25 where he was received by Tarar. Here he delivered a broadcast to Pakistan, which, in fact, had been earlier recorded in India. His few hours in Pakistan were mainly a token visit given the half-century security-based relationship with Pakistan and did not aim at endorsing the military regime.[2] His was the first-ever visit by a U.S. President to the country in three decades and took place amid fears and concerns, but he did not resolve Musharraf's ongoing isolation from the global scene, as he was constantly shunned by many Western leaders for overthrowing an elected regime. The Commonwealth had also suspended Pakistan's membership for the same reason, and the country, after the coup, felt more isolated and even abandoned at a time when Afghanistan and Kashmir both remained restive.

Clinton's visit to south Asia had been planned for a long time and aimed at establishing closer economic ties with India besides dissuading New Delhi and Islamabad from confrontational politics with nuclear implications. India, faced with a serious defiance in Kashmir, was trying to project Pakistan as a terror-sponsoring state and had even been encouraged by the American threats of 1992 to put Pakistan on a "watch list" of such states. According to Indian diplomats such pressure tactics were necessary to neutralize Pakistan's stance on Kashmir. After the coup, Indian authorities intensified their efforts to deter Clinton from visiting Pakistan, which many analysts found counterproductive, as such a step would have exacerbated Indo-Pakistani acrimonies.[3] Like Musharraf, the Bharatiya Janata Party (BJP) government in India also sought closer relations with Washington, especially after the dissolution of its erstwhile ally, the Soviet Union, and this was the first-ever visit by a U.S. President in two decades. Clinton advised both countries to seek common grounds on Kashmir and other outstanding issues so as to avoid military escalations and pioneered a crucial beginning in political and economic relations between the United States and India.

Despite Musharraf's openness and desire for peace, India itself harbored doubts about his commitment to regional cooperation since New Delhi accused the general of masterminding the Kargil campaign in addition to overthrowing Sharif. The BJP had come into power in India in part because of strong post-1992 patriotism when the forces of Hindu nationalism had visibly increased. Vajpayee's visit to Lahore in February 1998, the nuclear tests in 1998, the Kargil fiasco a year later, and the dismissal of the Muslim League government in October 1999 jolted the spirit of the Lahore Declaration, committing both countries to peace and harmony. The economic and political fallout from these events was certainly more taxing for Pakistan, and its cyclic problem of governance underpinned apprehensions about its territorial integrity at a time when several states had been falling apart.

Many Western regimes and civic groups did not appreciate Pakistani support for the Taliban and Kashmiri militants, especially after the 1998 attacks on the U.S. embassies in East Africa attributed to Al-Qaeda and Afghanistan-based Osama bin Laden. Resentment against the Taliban regime pursuing a restrictive code and its shelter to Al-Qaeda had turned Afghanistan into a pariah state. Since Pakistan was seen as Afghanistan's ally, few Western nations were willing to negotiate with Musharraf. Musharraf's visits to Turkey and a few other Muslim states were meant to establish his credentials as a statesman in his own right, but Western countries usually avoided well-publicized contacts with the military ruler, who had been promising political and economic reforms in the country. In the meantime, Musharraf, like other military rulers before him, tried to contain political opposition while co-opting some willing elements. His National Accountability Bureau, headed by a general, began investigating many politicians, although it purposely avoided civil servants and military officials. Several politicians decided to support Musharraf in lieu of escaping the official wrath on loan defaulting and other serious cases of corruption. Musharraf's promises of restoring the country's plundered resources proved to be a selective campaign and when, like General Ayub Khan, he floated the idea of local government through locally elected councilors, many landed interests joined him.[4]

Musharraf's administration received a major impetus when the Supreme Court upheld cases against the deposed prime minister over his orders to divert and delay the landing of Musharraf's plane in October 1999. Sharif, who was already in a high detention center at the Attock Fort, was given two life sentences in April 2000 for masterminding the plane hijack and terrorism. Emboldened by this verdict and the Court's validation of his coup and, even more crucially, the allowance to change the country's constitution, the General found himself fully reassured. With Benazir Bhutto convicted of corruption charges and already living abroad, her husband languishing in jail over similar charges, and with the Sharif brothers incarcerated, the chief executive planned to remove President Tarar. In May 2000, after Clinton's visit and the judicial verdict, Musharraf announced his decision to hold national elections in October 2002. For a while, Nawaz Sharif's wife, Kulsoom Nawaz, tried to hold rallies across the country seeking public support for her husband besides shoring up an anti-Musharraf momentum. It appeared that the country might be heading toward a new polarization, especially in view of Sharif's convictions, who enjoyed a good rapport with some members of the Saudi ruling family. Through their interventions, in December 2000, Musharraf granted presidential clemency and allowed Nawaz Sharif to go to Saudi Arabia, an exile that suited both Musharraf and the Sharif Family.[5]

With Benazir Bhutto, Nawaz Sharif, and Altaf Hussain all in exile, Musharraf felt more secure at home despite Pakistan's economic travails and political uncertainty, although Western nations still avoided direct parleys with him. In the Western media, Pakistan would often receive negative reportage because of its military regime and Islamabad's soft corner for the Taliban and Kashmiris. In his own interviews and speeches, however, Musharraf presented himself as a clean, straightforward, honest leader who had assumed the stewardship "to put the house in order." His public image showing him dressed in expensive suits while holding Chihuahua dogs and praising secularists like Jinnah and Kemal Ataturk won him plaudits but did not increase Western approval. The BJP-led India soon reassessed its erstwhile denunciatory policy toward Pakistan and decided to hold talks with the general and invited him to a three-day summit. In May 2001, Musharraf accepted Prime Minister A. B. Vajpayee's invitation, which was followed by the "retirement" of President Rafiq Tarar on June 20, although it was widely believed to be a plain "dismissal" of the incumbent. In his subsequent interviews, Tarar called it a dismissal, which only registered mild criticism from Washington and London.[6] On July 14, 2001, Musharraf undertook a state visit to India and was taken to his ancestral home in Old Delhi, followed by the Indo-Pakistani summit in the Mughal city of Agra. Given the longstanding mistrust on both sides interspersed with routine accusations and counteraccusations, it was unrealistic to expect any dramatic breakthrough, although the confrontational rhetoric subsided, and the world eagerly waited more such summits.[7] Musharraf's rather empty-handed return from Agra dismayed Pakistanis who believed that the lack of his democratic credentials had compromised the general's bargaining power with the Indians. Attitudes were soon to change, as 9/11 made Pakistan an important state, and Musharraf assumed the coveted status of a trusted ally as his country was transformed from a pariah to a partner.

9/11 AND PAKISTAN

On 9/11, the United States had been hit quite ferociously and sought revenge from Afghanistan, a country already devastated by the Soviet invasion and the subsequent infighting. The former Mujahideen and their international Muslim backers including Osama bin Laden, who had been Washington's closest allies in fighting "the evil empire," had already parted ways. For Musharraf, 9/11 was a godsend, for the Pakistani army chief was befriended by the Bush Administration and given an opportunity to assume a vanguard role in what was being termed as the "global war on terror." The events of

9/11 signaled an end to Musharraf's marginalization, a fate that befell his predecessor, General Zia-ul-Haq, after the Soviet invasion of Afghanistan in 1979. At that time the United States and other allies used Pakistan as a front-line state against the Soviet occupation of Kabul. Mounting the biggest and perhaps most successful operation in its history, the CIA had flown into Peshawar planeloads of holy warriors such as Osama from all over the world to spearhead a Jihad, but after the Soviet departure in 1989, Afghans were once again left on their own to pick up the pieces.

George Bush, not known for a command over global affairs, could well afford to confuse Musharraf's name during his first election campaign, but now he needed him as a confidant in a loosely defined yet equally pernicious war on terror. Here, once again, the hapless people of Afghanistan were to fall victim to daisy cutters, cave busters, and a sustained military operation that continued unabated, although ironically the Afghans did not cause 9/11. Their crime was the presence of Al-Qaeda on their soil, brought in first by the CIA and other intelligence agencies, and that had now overstayed. Erstwhile Mujahideen and President Reagan's "moral equivalents of our Founding Fathers" were recast as sexist and uncivilized enemies led by one-eyed Mullah Omar who had challenged the super power by hosting the Saudi fundamentalist.

Pakistan's decision to join the Anglo-American alliance intent on undertaking military strikes against Afghanistan was perceived as a less undesirable choice than staying neutral or taking an altogether antagonistic stance against a revengeful power seeking retribution. Indian enthusiasm to offer bases and unfettered support hastened Pakistan's decision, although New Delhi's move might have been geared to put Islamabad in a more awkward position. Musharraf was willing to be co-opted by the United States and was equally persuaded, although the short-term military and economic gains may not have been worth the long-term socioideological cost that might further fragment Pakistan's precarious ethnic pluralism.[8] The Pakistani elite welcomed Colin Powell's apparent support for preventing a de facto role for the Northern Alliance in the future dispensation of Afghanistan, as the former always distrusted these groups. The U.S. secretary of state's rather routine reference to the Kashmir dispute as "the central issue" dividing the two neighbors further placated their worries while raising suspicion in India. Given the fluidity and volatility of the situation so close to Pakistan and the various spillover effects, Pakistan found itself in a dilemma. Many Pakistani liberals were not happy with the Taliban model of Islam and worried about a possible "Talibanization" of Pakistan, especially when many of these fundamentalist groups had enjoyed official support. Several intelligence agencies had, in fact, helped train Jihadi groups that came to be known as military + mullah axis, dating from the Zia era.[9] The Anglo-American invasion of Iraq in light of Israeli campaigns against the Palestinians increased pressure on Musharraf and

Pakistanis, like the rest of the world, desired peace and agonized over the increase in Islamophobia.[10]

Amid this support for Musharraf and his elevation to the status of a dependable ally and global statesman, restoration of democracy as promised by the general became a peripheral issue in U.S.-Pakistani relations. Musharraf was celebrated in the Western capitals and was projected as the embodiment of a modern Muslim ruler who was determined to contain Jihadis and fundamentalist religious seminaries, and was steadfast on fighting Al-Qaeda. In the meantime, the U.S. administration banned various Muslim organizations including the Lashkar-i-Jhangvi, Jaysh-i-Muhammad, and several others that pursued both militant and sectarian agendas in Pakistan. Restrictions on direct money transfers known as the *Hawala* system led to the regularization of currency exchanges, which benefited the Pakistani economy, although only after a serious commercial and economic setback resulting from warfare in neighboring west Asia. In addition, the Bush Administration resumed economic and military assistance to Pakistan, which continued until 2007, when, as in the past, Pakistan once again came under scrutiny and the Congress passed a measure requiring presidential certification offering aid to Pakistan in exchange for the country's full support in the war on terror. Pakistan's economy improved as more Pakistani expatriates sent money home and, amid some reforms in taxation and privatization led by Musharraf's finance minister, Shaukat Aziz, the country began to achieve energized economic growth.

Musharraf's Pakistan may have benefited from some financial improvement, but its chronic problems of governance remained as unresolved as they were when the general took over amid promises of reform and accountability. Issues of poverty and sectarianism were as acute as they had been a decade earlier while Balochistan and Waziristan witnessed an unnecessary bloodshed that could have been avoided through proper political and economic integration. After approval of the crucial amendments in the country's constitution and the election of Musharraf as president through a referendum on April 30, 2002, the general held "sanitized" elections on October 10, 2002. Here the mainstream political parties such as the Muslim League (Nawaz Sharif group) and Pakistan People's Party registered official disapproval, whereas Islamist and ethnic organizations such as the Muttahida Qaumi Movement (MQM) along with the loyalists came to dominate the assemblies. Still, for several months the assemblies could not begin their sessions owing to a lack of consensus and official gerrymandering. The religiopolitical parties such as the Jamiat-i-Ulama-i-Islam or even Jamaat-i-Islami, espousing a purist form of Islamic order, proved to be the main beneficiaries in the elections because of an increased emphasis on Political Islam in the Muslim world, as well as a formidable wave of anti-Americanism. Cobbled together as the Muttahida Majlis-i-Ammal (United Action Forum) (MMA), they assisted Musharraf through a constitutional amendment that not only ratified his presidency while he still held the office of the army chief but also gave a blanket approval to all his previous ordinances. Significantly, this Seventeenth Amendment of 2003 upheld Musharraf's presidential referendum and appropriation of radical powers in his office including the authority to dismiss the prime minister and legislatures. The MMA gradually turned more critical of his stance on the U.S.-led war on terror, but Musharraf felt secure by simultaneously holding on to the two most important offices of the land. In 2004, he contravened his own earlier pledge to give up his military position and continued to assume the country's presidency as well as the army's command. Even after five years, in 2007, despite public pressure for unfettered democracy and free judiciary, Musharraf dismissed the superior judges and imposed severe censorship on print and visual media along with sanctioning military trials of his civilian opponents.

With Benazir Bhutto and Nawaz Sharif both in exile, their parties were not fully allowed to mount electoral campaigns, and eventually splinter groups were cobbled together in 2003 to establish a coalition led by Mir Zafrullah Jamali as the prime minister. He led the cabinet until 2004, when Shaukat Aziz was elected to a parliamentary constituency in Attock and assumed the prime ministership, although in accordance with the Seventeenth Amendment and by virtue of his command over the army, Musharraf remained the de facto ruler until he was challenged by civil society in 2007. This political system might have lacked powers and determination to put the country back on proper democratic tracks through a primacy of the parliamentary institutions, but for five years it provided a needed political defense for Musharraf against his mainstream opponents. Pro-Musharraf politicians were led by Chaudhry Shujaat Husain, an influential Punjabi politician, who for a while headed the cabinet as well. Through him, Musharraf continued to enjoy some political support in the central government and Punjab. Simultaneously, Musharraf was able to forge closer contacts with Altaf Hussain and offered ministerial and gubernatorial positions to the MQM that ensured peace in Karachi.[11]

Musharraf was routinely criticized by U.S. officials for "not doing enough" in the tribal regions to disarm pro-Taliban Pushtuns. Concurrently, after the killing of Nawab Akbar Bugti (1926–2006) in 2006 by Pakistani troops, several anti-Islamabad Baloch dissidents defied official writ in that mineral-rich province. Fallout from the security operations in Federally Administered Tribal Areas (FATA) and Balochistan led to a radical increase in suicide bombings against official installations and public institutions in major cities. Despite suffering a loss of 800 Pakistani troops and incurring alienation among the local Pushtuns and their leaders, Hamid Karzai and his Western supporters routinely and even vociferously accused Pakistan of harboring and tolerating Taliban sanctuaries.[12] Pakistanis, including their president, were deeply annoyed by such allegations against their country. Soon after 9/11, Pakistani authorities handed over hundreds of Taliban and other Al-Qaeda supporters to the CIA, which intensified resentment against the Musharraf regime, especially in the wake of a pronounced anti-Americanism. Many such individuals, irrespective of their nationalities, were given to the CIA for rendition and other such purposes simply to receive quick prize money "totaling millions of dollars."[13] Despite an almost total censorship of ongoing military operations in Waziristan, including coercive treatment of local journalists by the authorities, President Musharraf became sensitive to a growing criticism of his "forward" policy in the tribal belt. After the fracas with the Islamists at the Red Mosque in Islamabad in July 2007 espousing imposition of *Sharia*, the battle lines between Islamabad and the radicals had become clearer and even more volatile.

The anomalous situation in FATA was, in fact, symptomatic of a countrywide malaise, in which the parts of the central government did not share a clear, consensual, and equitable balance of power. The high-handed executive would never tolerate an independent judiciary, vocal media, and transparent politicians fully prepared to take charge of the country. Pakistan's Supreme Court has more often legalized the military coups, impositions of emergency, and the dismissal of political governments since 1953 under euphemisms such as "the doctrine of necessity," although there have been dissenting voices, routinely bypassed by the rulers. As mentioned previously, Musharraf's military coup was not only legitimized by the Supreme Court, the court even significantly and rather dramatically allowed a state employee from the armed services to change the national constitution as well. Emboldened by his de facto position in malaise-ridden governance and irritated by some judicial decisions taken by Iftikhar Mohammad Chaudhry, the chief justice, Chaudhry was called to Musharraf's "camp office" on March 9, 2007 and was dismissed unceremoniously.[14] This mistreatment of the most superior judge, otherwise a Musharraf loyalist, proved to be a rallying point for the country's legal community. "The Black Coats," joined by a vocal media and politicians including Islamists, were soon protesting at a time when the general-president was planning to seek another five-year presidential term for himself from the outgoing National Assembly. Musharraf's own position in 2007 appeared untenable, as the MMA and other groups challenged his concurrent and equally anomalous role as the country's president and army chief. Justice Chaudhry was restored by the Supreme Court on July 20 amid great public enthusiasm, and a vocal civil society, active lawyers, and an alert media sought systemic changes in the country. As domestic challenges multiplied in an atmosphere of resentment and disillusionment, and "faced [with] the gravest threat" to his regime, Musharraf often took recourse to more draconian measures.[15] As seen on May 12, collaboration between the

MQM marauders and several other official bodies caused the brutal murder of 52 people in Karachi in the full glare of television cameras, once again affirming the dictum of the criminalization of politics. In early August, a reawakened judiciary, following the restoration of the chief justice, was not only being proactive on "disappeared Pakistanis" but also sought explanations from the officials on the use of force in Karachi on May 12. Musharraf was eager to seek a second five-year presidential term yet appeared weak and vulnerable, which deterred him from seeking retirement from the army, as was stipulated in the constitution. His personal ambitions seemed to coalesce with those of Benazir Bhutto who wanted to become prime minister for the third time and insisted on the removal of corruption cases against her so that she could return to Pakistan. Altaf Hussain bided for his time, and Nawaz Sharif, based in London after having moved from Saudi Arabia, also sought to restore his niche in Pakistani politics.

On August 23, 2007, the Supreme Court, in another bold decision, allowed Sharif to return to Pakistan by rejecting an official plea to the contrary. When Sharif returned to Pakistan on September 10, however, he was again deported to Saudi Arabia, as Musharraf, banking on Bhutto's indirect support, proceeded to get himself reelected for the next term. In the meantime, all the opposition legislators except for the PPP parliamentarians, chose to resign in protest from the assemblies, which were themselves nearing completion of their tenure. On October 6, 2007, Musharraf was reelected for another term despite serious questions about the Electoral College nearing its own end and also because, by virtue of being the army chief, he was not eligible for a political office. As expected, Musharraf's candidacy and election were challenged through petitions, as well as a debate on private television channels. In the meantime, the return of Benazir Bhutto on October 18 amid a popular reception and numerous fatalities in Karachi resulting from a suicide bombing deeply unnerved Musharraf whose only concern at this stage appeared to be his own survival. Worried about a possible judicial disqualification, Musharraf typically responded with the imposition of emergency on November 3, which singled out the highest judiciary, media, and human rights activists. Musharraf's severe measures were perceived as martial law by a general who wanted to stay in power. Numerous Pakistanis including Justice Chaudhry and other superior judges, were detained by the police, and all the national and international media channels went off the air. As a result, 162 million Pakistanis found themselves in a state of quarantine, causing embarrassment for the Bush Administration and Islamabad's other Western backers. Musharraf's rationale of fighting extremism in the country through detaining moderate forces and suppressing public expression only betrayed his personal insecurity, which had landed the country into an even more precarious situation. Once again, an extraprofessional role by Pakistani generals had pushed the country into another unnecessary crisis, and all subsequent measures such as the formation of a caretaker government and restricted elections failed to provide a structural alternative.

Musharraf finally retired as the army chief on November 28, 2007. The next day, amid grave questions about his election to another five-year term, he was sworn in as president by his newly-appointed chief justice. Musharraf had become quite unpopular due to the increasing frequency of suicide bombings, inflationary food prices, frequent power shut downs and, most of all, the curbing of judiciary and media dialogue in order to centralize power.

On December 27, 2007, Benazir Bhutto was killed by a bomb blast at a political rally in Rawalpindi in the full glare of cameras and Pakistanis. The world at large worried about the scale of violence in the country. Most Pakistanis blamed this on Musharraf's unquestioned support and participation in the U.S.-led war on terror and the related fallout from military operations in Afghanistan, FATA, and elsewhere. Bhutto's traumatic assassination once again alerted Pakistanis to seek alternative policies and systemic changes for their country. Amid intense grief and national mourning, she was buried next to her father in their ancestral village in Sindh and as per her will, her 19-year-old son, Bilawal Bhutto-Zardari, was accepted as the new head of the PPP. Because of Bilawal's tender age and ongoing education at Oxford, his father, Asif Zardari, assumed the party leadership.

National and provincial elections took place on February 18, 2008, registering major victories for the PPP and PML-N, while pro-Musharraf factions and the MMA suffered significant losses. The results were seen as a rejection of Musharraf's one-man rule and his polices as political parties, while uniquely forming coalition governments in the center and provinces, reiterated their promises on parliamentary sovereignty, and independence of judiciary, media, and political dialogue with the radicals in FATA. So far, these elections were the 13th in Pakistan's history through which the electorates reaffirmed their belief in democratic processes to steer the country away from its multiple problems.

On March 25, 2008, Syed Yusuf Raza Gilani, unanimously elected by the nation's representatives, was sworn in as the country's 25th prime minister. This PPP leader from Multan, who had himself faced jail for five years under Musharraf, ordered the immediate release of the senior judges while committing himself to a policy of dialogue, democracy, and reforms. Six days later, his 24-member cabinet took oath to run the government while the nation watched with hope for peace and better future ahead, and also waited for the fate of a marginalized Musharraf. Zardari, Sharif, and Asfandyar Wali Khan, leaders of the main coalition parties, now held the public support whereas the army—the most formidable institution in the country—keenly observed these vital developments from a distance. In March 2008, Pakistan had already begun a new phase in its journey as a young nation.

BACK TO THE FUTURE

Pakistan's simplified rationale as a polity created in the name of Islam—a premise often applied hastily—has only complicated the ambiguous intersection between politics and religion. It is true that "Muslimness" played a crucial role in spawning Jinnah's demand for a separate state out of British and princely India, yet, in most cases, Islam was seen both as an identity marker and a cultural force that would override the ethnodoctrinal differences among south Asian Muslims without assuming any theocratic propensities. Given the open-endedness in both approaches and without a sustained democratic nomenclature in the country, especially after 1958, the official and sectional use of Islam for political purposes gained greater ascendancy until, during the 1980s, General Zia-ul-Haq turned it into the main preoccupation of the state. The discretionary use of Islam, particularly in legal areas, not only circumscribed the civic rights of religious minorities, it also marginalized Pakistani women within an already diminishing public sphere. Another dangerous outcome of bringing in Islam as the mainstay of governance was an increase in Muslim doctrinal and sectarian diversities, resulting in the evolution of militant outfits. The presence of the Afghan refugees and willingness of many of them to become Mujahideen, owing to their own zeal and external encouragement, resulted in the inculcation of a new form of activism in the curricula of several seminaries (*madrassas*) until some of them on the Frontier turned into recruiting grounds.

There have been two views of Musharraf. First, he was genuinely trying to wrest Pakistan from fundamentalist challenges and, despite being a dictator, he was gradually democratizing a country that is otherwise beset with several destabilizing challenges. According to this opinion, largely shared in Western capitals and by several Pakistanis, Musharraf was a bulwark against Islamist and other segmenting forces confronting a nuclear Pakistan.[16] He was credited with having injected a new confidence in Pakistan's economy and in ousting those fundamentalist groups that the intelligence agencies had promoted in the first place. He was also applauded for normalizing thorny relations with India by undertaking bold steps and thus is seen to have accomplished more than a democratic leader could do in a challenging polity like Pakistan. The contrary view has held Musharraf responsible for a crisis in governance by virtue of being part of an establishment that has been indifferent toward Pakistan's democratic imperatives.[17] To such critics, Musharraf was capriciously playing on Western fears of Political Islam and had been successful in projecting himself as the only formidable challenge to an encroaching Islamism in a vital region. Musharraf's high-handedness, targeting judiciary, civil society, and media, and his talks with Benazir Bhutto to safeguard his own political future also revealed growing differences with

U.S. officials about the general and the formation of a broad coalition of "moderate" forces in Pakistan.

By emphasizing its Islamic credentials while being mostly ruled by westernized elite whose own mindset and interests are inextricably linked with the West, Pakistan has often found it difficult to locate a synthesis between some highly contentious realms of tradition and modernity. Certainly, such a dilemma is not merely confined to Pakistan; even countries such as India or Israel, despite their democratic nomenclatures, are often pulled toward specific Hindutva and Zionist agendas. Lack of trust in U.S. leadership has longstanding roots, although Pakistanis would never question the necessity to maintain good relationship with Washington through positive engagement.[18] At another level, there has been grave concern that while one section in the U.S. administration might be appreciative of Islamabad as a close ally, several others concurrently pressure the latter to undertake an even more punitive campaign against Pushtun tribals. Washington and London perceived the Taliban as a major component of Political Islam, which has been at war with the former after having hosted Osama bin Laden and then by undertaking suicide attacks on American and NATO troops. On the contrary, deeper scholarly analyses saw in Taliban a model of Political Islam, which has been predominantly Sunni, puritanical, masculine, and inherently anti-Western. Their use of force and an exclusive view of Islam were seen to coalesce with the tribal Pushtun tradition of resistance, ushering in instability on both sides of the Pakistan-Afghanistan border. Pakistan's critical opinion groups were not totally pleased with the military-led policy of revenge that President Bush unleashed on Afghanistan, although some of them might have felt that a possible day of reckoning had come for the Taliban. Yet there was grave concern about growing sympathy for the former, which was converging with the anti-Americanism in the Pushtun heartland and had begun to prove inimical to civic institutions. Thus Taliban resistance and continuing U.S.-NATO operations increased Pakistani anxieties, especially in view of greater expectations and criticism from its allies, and also because the Taliban's model of Political Islam still had a steady following in the border regions and Swat. Musharraf's hasty and coercive policies directed against democratic forces only seemed to help the extremists while dangerously marginalizing moderate Pakistanis.

Pakistan's ethnic and religious pluralism can be harnessed through a systemic overhaul and corresponding administrative reformism, which may usher a greater sense of belonging underpinning national integration. An empowered judiciary, especially after the ebullient restoration of the chief justice, promulgation of the 1973 constitution without the lateral amendments, a guaranteed and proactive parliamentary form of government, and substantive power devolution at all levels, while pursuing a foreign policy based on noninterference and constructive engagement, can certainly help Pakistan avoid a repetitive cycle of instability.

NOTES

1. For more on his life and ideas, see Pervez Musharraf, *In the Line of Fire: A Memoir* (London: Free Press, 2006).

2. U.S. Department of State, "Transcript: Senior officials briefing on President's Pakistan meetings," *Washington File*, March 25, 2000; Hasan Akhtar, "US shares concerns over south Asia: CE sure talks will improve relations," *Dawn*, March 26, 2000.

3. For a contemporary comment, see "Delicate Diplomacy," *Asiaweek*, March 24, 2000, XXVI vide http://www.asiaweek.com/asiaweek/magazine/2000/0324/ed.diplomacy.html

4. The proposal for this "grassroots democracy" came from the National Reconstruction Bureau (NRB), which was headed by a retired general and sought to bypass mainstream political parties.

5. The Sharifs sought a 10-year exile and remission in their punishment through a written document that caused quite some discussion during August 2007 when they wanted to return to Pakistan. Finally, on August 23, during the hearing on their petition by the Supreme Court, lawyers representing the government presented "Confidentiality and Hold Harmless Agreement" which had been signed by Nawaz Sharif on December 2, 2000. *Dawn* Online, August 23, 2007; *New York Times*, August 27, 2007. Also, Geo TV news report 23 August 2007, monitored in Oxford http://electronicweekly.co.uk/tv/geo_tv_pakistan.html

6. "Musharraf 'forced out' president," BBC Online June 21, 2001 vide http://news.bbc.co.uk/1/hi/world/south_asia/1400383.stm; accessed in Oxford on August 22, 2007.

7. For details see, Iftikhar H. Malik, "Pakistan in 2000: Starting Anew or a stalemate!" *Asian Survey*, 41, January 2001.

8. Musharraf, p. 201.

9. For more on this, see Iftikhar H. Malik, *Jihad, Hindutva and the Taliban: South Asia at the Crossroads* (Karachi: Oxford University Press, 2005).

10. For a pro-Bush account of the events leading to the invasion of Afghanistan and relations with Pakistan and the rest of the Muslim world, see Bob Woodward's *Bush at War* (New York: Simon & Schuster, 2002; also, William Safire, "Let us get on with the war," *The Guardian*, 7 March 2003). Hillary Clinton supported the Bush administration and was quite vocal in her support of Israel. See Hillary R. Clinton, *Living History* (New York: Simon & Schuster, 2003). Certainly, 77 of 100 U.S. senators supported the invasion of Iraq. In the same vein, Tony Blair resolutely reiterated Bush's stance on Iraq and, despite

massive public disapproval, joined the U.S.-led invasion. For a firsthand account on Blair's war efforts, see Peter Stothard, *30 Days: A Month at the Heart of Blair's War* (London: HarperCollins, 2003).

11. After Musharraf's dismissal of the chief justice on March 8, 2007, several peaceful demonstrations by lawyers and civil society were regularly held in Pakistan. The demand for his restoration and an unfettered democracy became the rallying point against the president and his supporters. On May 12, lawyers and their supporters convened a rally in Karachi and headed toward the High Court where Justice Chaudhry was to make a speech. The rally was attacked by some armed men, presumably from the MQM, which was holding its own rally and also was the ruling party in Sindh. As a result of random shooting, 52 protesters were killed and more than 200 were wounded in the full glare of television cameras. The gory events took place at a time when Musharraf, in a special public meeting in Islamabad, traded threats with his opponents.

12. The Pakistani military operation against the Taliban in the border regions first focused on South Waziristan before moving on to North Waziristan with tribal towns such as Miran Shah, Wana, and Alizai, leaving a trail of blood and vendetta on both sides. Apart from both the agencies in Waziristan, the Bajaur Agency farther north also made headlines, with the Pakistani Air Force and militia undertaking punitive campaigns against some seminaries and supposed hideouts of Al-Qaeda supporters. In January 2006, in a similar aerial attack on the town of Damadola, 13 people were killed, and some local press accused the American troops of carrying out this operation. Another missile strike of a seminary at Chingai, however, resulted in the death of more than 80 people, many of them younger pupils. The Pakistani military spokesmen blamed the seminary for housing Al-Qaeda leadership including Ayman Al-Zawahiri, who had been reportedly visiting the area as his wife happened to be a local Pushtun. For details see, *Dawn*, October 30, 2006. A few weeks later, a revenge suicide attack, presumably by the Bajaur dissidents on a Pakistani military training camp in Dargai in Malakand district led to more than two dozen deaths of recruits. In early 2008 three U.S. missiles were dropped on the Pakistan side of the Durand Line, killing 45 people.

13. Musharraf, p. 237. He noted in his book: "We have done more than any other country to capture and kill members of al Qaeda, and to destroy its infrastructure in our cities and mountains. Many of these stories have not been told in full before now." Musharraf, p. 223. For other personal accounts of such illegal transfers, see Moazzam Baig, *Enemy Combatant: A British Muslim's Journey to Guantanamo and Back* (London: Simon & Schuster, 2006); *The Economist*, February 3, 2007.

14. *Dawn*, March 9, 16, 17, 2007. In fact, there was a writ petition awaiting hearing at the Supreme Court against Musharraf's proposed candidacy,

and his advisors learned that the chief justice might disallow the former from extending the Assembly's tenure and thus could debar his second term. The chief justice had recently taken the government to task for selling Karachi Steel Mills rather too cheaply and for allowing Mukhtaran Mai to undertake her publicized visit abroad, which Musharraf had originally banned. In addition, the chief justice, a former supporter of Musharraf, his takeover and referendum, had been proactive on hearing petitions dealing with "the disappeared Pakistanis" who had been taken away from homes by the intelligence agencies soon after 9/11 and have remained unaccounted for. The Human Rights Commission of Pakistan, in a statement on March 9, ruled Musharraf's decision "illegal." See Chairperson, Asma Jahangir's press release on www.hrcp-web.org

15. *The Times*, March 16, 2007.

16. In a speech at the American Enterprise Institute in Washington on February 15, 2007, President George W. Bush reiterated his support for Musharraf by acknowledging his genuine commitment in fighting terrorism. *Dawn*, February 16, 2007. It is a view that one often came across in private meetings with officials in London, Brussels, and Washington, and at times in Delhi. For more details see Zahid Hussain, *Frontline Pakistan: The Struggle with Militant Islam* (London: I. B. Tauris, 2007).

17. "Bankrupt Leadership," (editorial), *The Daily Telegraph*, November 9, 2007. "The talking is over and Musharraf must quit, says Bhutto," *The Daily Telegraph*, November 14, 2007; *The Guardian*, November 13–15, 2007.

18. Stephen Cohen, *The Idea of Pakistan* (Washington, D. C: Brookings Institution Press, 2004).

Notable People in the History of Pakistan

Ali, Chaudhri Muhammad (1905–1980) Senior civil servant in British India and Pakistan. Prime minister of Pakistan from 1955–1956; author of *The Emergence of Pakistan* (New York, 1967).

Ali, Jam Sadiq (1935–1992) A Sindhi landowner and a close associate of Zulfikar Ali Bhutto. Lived in London as an exile during the period of General Zia-ul-Haq and returned to Pakistan to become the chief minister of Sindh from 1990 to 1992. Turned against former Pakistan People's Party colleagues during his tenure.

Ali, Choudhary Rahmat (1895–1951) Cambridge-trained barrister and activist. Wrote books, lobbied for Indian Muslims, and coined the word *Pakistan* in 1933.

Amin, Nurul (1897–1974) A Muslim Leaguer from East Bengal. Chief minister of East Pakistan in 1948 and vice-president of Pakistan from December 1971 until the abolition of this position in 1973.

Aziz, Shaukat (1949–) Born in Karachi and worked as a banker. First served as finance minister under General Musharraf. From June 2004 to November 2007, he was the prime minister with the help from a faction of the Muslim League.

Bhashani, Maulana Abdul Hameed Khan (1885–1976) Leader of East Bengal and the founder of National Awami Party.

Bhutto, Benazir (1953–2007) Leader of Pakistan People's Party, daughter of Zulfikar Ali Bhutto and Prime Minister of Pakistan (1988–1990 and 1993–1996). Published *Daughter of the East* (London, 1988), and *Reconciliation* (London, 2008). She was assassinated at a political rally on December 27, 2007.

Bhutto, Zulfikar Ali (1928–1979) A Sindhi landowner; obtained higher education at University of California, Berkeley and Oxford. Founder of Pakistan People's Party in 1967. Held several cabinet positions under General Ayub Khan and became the president of Pakistan in December 1971. After the implementation of the constitution of 1973, he became the prime minister. Overthrown by General Zia-ul-Haq in July 1977 and subsequently hanged on April 4, 1979 through a judicial verdict.

Bogra, Muhammad Ali (1901–1963) East Bengali diplomat who become prime minister of Pakistan after the dismissal of Nazim-ud-Din Government in 1954.

Gilani, Yusuf Raza (1952–) A parliamentarian from Multan and a PPP supporter. Elected unanimously as the prime minister on March 25, 2008.

Haq, Maulvi Abul Kasem Fazlul (1873–1962) East Bengali leader. Presented the Lahore Resolution in March 1940; chief minister of united Bengal in 1941.

Haq, General Zia-ul- (1922–1988) Army chief under Zulfikar Ali Bhutto. Overthrew the former in July 1977 through martial law. Benefited from the Soviet invasion of Afghanistan in 1979 and promulgated Islamization in Pakistan as a military president.

Hussain, Altaf (1953–) Born in Karachi and a student leader. Founder of Muhajir Qaumi Movement (MQM) and accused of several human rights violations. Fled to London in 1992 and became a British citizen. Has controlled Karachi and MQM from his office in London.

Iqbal, Sir Muhammad (1875–1938) Most prominent Muslim philosopher and poet of the twentieth century. Studied in Lahore, Cambridge, and Munich. Is viewed as the intellectual brain behind Muslim regeneration and the architect of the idea of Pakistan.

Jinnah, Miss Fatima (1894–1967) Sister of Muhammad Ali Jinnah and a philanthropist. Helped her brother during the Pakistan movement and challenged Ayub Khan in the presidential elections of 1965. Is known as *Maadar-i-Millat* or Mother of the Nation.

Jinnah, Muhammad Ali (1876–1948) Karachi-born lawyer known as the Quaid-i-Azam or the Great Leader. Trained at Lincoln's Inn and practiced in Bombay. Became president of the All-India Muslim League and strove for Muslim interests in India. Since 1940 demanded a separate Muslim state—Pakistan—for Indian Muslims and became its founder and first governor-general on August 14, 1947. Known for honesty and integrity and survived by a daughter. Buried in Karachi, the city of his birth.

Junejo, Mohammad Khan (1932–1993) A Sindhi landlord and parliamentarian. Became the prime minister of Pakistan in 1985; dismissed by General Zia-ul-Haq in 1988.

Khan, Abdul Ghaffar (1890–1988) Born in the Frontier and known for his pacifist ideas. Participated in the Khilafat movement and led the Red Shirts movement in the 1930s and 1940s. Demanded greater rights for Pushtuns in Pakistan.

Khan, Ghulam Ishaq (1915–2006) A civil servant from the Frontier. Rose to higher ministerial office to become the president of Pakistan in 1988. Developed differences with Benazir Bhutto and Nawaz Sharif whose governments he dismissed in the 1990s. Forced from office in 1993.

Khan, Imran (1952–) Cricketing hero of Pakistan. Born in Lahore and educated at Oxford. Founder of Shaukat Khanum Memorial Cancer Hospital and leader of his Justice Party.

Khan, Liaquat Ali (1895–1951) A Muslim landlord from the United Province (UP). Educated in Oxford and a follower of Jinnah. Became the secretary-general of the All-India Muslim League and the first prime minister of Pakistan in 1948. Killed in Rawalpindi while addressing a public meeting. Visited North America a few months before his assassination. One of the leading architects of the Muslim nation. Among various speech collections, *Pakistan: the Heart of Asia* (Cambridge, Mass. 1950).

Khan, General Muhammad Ayub (1907–1974) Born in the Frontier and studied at Aligarh. Joined the British army and became the first Pakistani to head the country's army. Took over as the chief martial law administrator in October 1958. Became president through local bodies and developed closer relations with the United States and China. Faced a public movement and surrendered powers to General Yahya Khan in March 1969. Published *Friends not Masters* (Oxford, 1968).

Khan, General Muhammad Yahya (1917–1980) Served British Indian Army. Became the commander of Pakistan army under President Ayub Khan. Imposed martial law in the country in March 1969; pursued a military operation in East Pakistan, which, after a civil war and hostilities with India, became the sovereign state of Bangladesh.

Khan, Sir Syed Ahmed (1817–1898) A Muslim intellectual and educator. Wrote books for Muslim regeneration in India and established modern college at Aligarh, which subsequently became Muslim University.

Leghari, Farooq (1941–) A Punjabi landowner and former leader of Pakistan People's Party. Became president of the country in 1993 and developed differences with Benazir Bhutto and then Nawaz Sharif. Had to leave the office to form his own party and then aligned himself with General Musharraf.

Maudoodi, Syed Abulala (1903–1979) Muslim intellectual and founder of Jamaat-i-Islami in 1941. Opposed military regime of Ayub Khan and sought Islamization of Pakistan.

Mirza, Iskander (1899–1969) A powerful civil servant. Rose to become the governor-general of Pakistan and then President until he was exiled by General Ayub Khan in 1958. Died in London.

Muhammad, Ghulam (1895–1956) Civil servant who became the governor-general of Pakistan. Dismissed the elected government of Nazim-ud-Din, as well as the Constituent Assembly. Involved bureaucracy and army in national affairs and was eased out by Iskander Mirza and General Ayub Khan.

Musharraf, General Pervez, (1943–) Born in Delhi, grew up in Karachi and Ankara. Joined Pakistani army's elite group. Nawaz Sharif appointed him as the army chief. Led the Kargil campaign in Kashmir in 1999 and then overthrew Sharif on October 12, 1999. After 9/11 benefited from close alliance with the United States and faced serious political and constitutional opposition in 2007. Imposed martial law in Pakistan on November 3, 2007 and radically curbed civil liberties, judiciary, and media.

Nazim-ud-Din, Khwaja (1894–1964) Muslim League leader from Bengal. Second prime minister of Pakistan. Dismissed by Ghulam Muhammad and led opposition to Ayub Khan by supporting Miss Fatima Jinnah.

Qureshi, Moeen (1930–) International banker and expatriate Pakistani. Became the caretaker prime minister for three months in 1993 and held elections in the country. Returned to the United States to resume his banking career.

Rahman, Sheikh Mujibur (1920–1975) A former student leader from Bengal. Followed H.S. Suhrawardy in his Awami League and demanded complete autonomy for East Pakistan. His party carried absolute majority in East Pakistan and faced a military operation leading to his arrest. Became the founder-president of Bangladesh in 1972. Killed by military officials along with his family members in Dhaka in 1975.

Sharif, Mian Nawaz (1950–) Born and educated in Lahore in a business family. Became chief minister of Punjab province under General Zia-ul-Haq; became Prime Minister twice (1990–1993 and 1996–1999). Faced a coup on October 12, 1999 led by General Musharraf and sought exile in Saudi Arabia in 2000. Returned to Pakistan on September 10, 2007 but was sent off to Saudi Arabia from the airport. Led the Muslim League (Nawaz Sharif Group) in the elections on February 18, 2008.

Suhrawardy, Huseyn Shaheed (1893–1963) Studied at Oxford. Leader from Bengal and follower of Jinnah. Chief minister of Bengal until Partition. Founded Awami League in 1950 and became the prime minister in 1956. Banned by Ayub Khan after his martial law and died in Beirut in 1963.

Syed, G.M. (1904–1995) Born in a Sindhi Syed family. Demanded separation of Sindh from Gujarat province; supported demand for Pakistan. Developed differences with Pakistani rulers and advocated more rights for Sindhis.

Tarar, Rafiq (1929–) A lawyer and judge. With Sharif's support became the president in 1997 Was eased out by Musharraf in 2000.

Zardari, Asif (1954–) Born in a Sindhi landowning family. Married Benazir Bhutto in 1987 and held ministerial position in her government. Spent many years in jail on corruption charges. After Benazir Bhutto's death, he emerged as the powerful leader of the PPP.

Glossary

Alim: a Muslim religious scholar

Anjuman: cultural or literary association

Ashraaf: genteel or upper castes

Azaan: call for Muslim prayer

Basti: a settlement

Bhadralok: Bengali Hindu moneyed class, usually landowners

Bhikshus: wandering Buddhist priests/monks

Bidaa: innovation in religious beliefs

Biradari: kinship, extended family

Burqa: a traditional veil covering a woman's entire body

Chadar/Chaadar: a loose wraparound for women

Chardiwari/Chaardiwari: within the four walls of the home

Chaudhari: a Punjabi notable

Dasis: slave girls at Hindu temples

Dhimmis: non-Muslims in a Muslim empire

Fiqh/Fiqah: jurisprudence

Ghazi: a holy warrior

Hadith: a saying/tradition of the Prophet.

Hajj: annual Pilgrimage to the Hejaz, Arabia

Hakim: a traditional physician

Hari: a landless farm worker in Sindh

Hawala: private system of transferring foreign exchange

Imam: a religious leader

Jihad: holy struggle

Jirga: assembly of tribal elders

Jizya: a tax on non-Muslims in lieu of military service

Madrassa: an Islamic seminary

Majlis: a cultural association; also, Shia sermon

Mansabdars: Mughal nobility

Maulvi/Mullah: Muslim religious leader

Muhajir: Muslim migrant

Muhajireen: pl. of *Muhajir*

Mujahid: One who undertakes *Jihad*

Mujahideen: pl. of *Mujahid*

Mullah: a less scholarly cleric

Nizam: viceroy

Pir: a Sufi saint

Purdah: veil, also, seclusion

Riba: interest on saving accounts

Sadhu: a Hindu ascetic

Sajjada Nishin: Muslim dynastic Sufi order

Sardar: a Baloch chieftain

Shaheed: a martyr

Shalwar/Shalwaar: loose trousers

Sharia/Shariat: Islamic law; jurisprudence

Shia/shi'ite: a follower of Caliph Ali, a doctrinal Muslim sect

Silsilah: a Sufi order

Sufi: a mystic

Sunnah: Prophet's practices/examples

Sunni: lit. a follower of the Prophetic traditions, a majority doctrinal sect

Tabligh: propagation of Islamic knowledge (also called *Daawa*)

Taliban: pl. of *Taleb/Talib:* students

Ulama: Muslim religious scholars (pl. of *alim*)

Ummah: Transnational Muslimhood

Wadera: a big/feudal landlord in Sindh

Zakat: charity

Zikr: recitation of Allah's names

Bibliography

Reports

Mahbub ul Haq Human Development Centre. *Human Development in South Asia 2006. Poverty in South Asia: Challenged and Responses*. Karachi: Oxford University Press, 2007.

Malik, Iftikhar H. *Religious Minorities in Pakistan*. London: Minority Rights Group, 2002. www.minorityrights.org

Transparency International. *Global Corruption Report 2004*. London: Pluto, 2004.

UNDP, *Pakistan: National Development Report 2003. Poverty, Growth and Governance*, http://www.un.org.pk/nhdr

Books and Articles

Afzal, M. Rafique. *Pakistan: History and Politics. 1947–1971*. Karachi: Oxford University Press, 2001.

Ahmad, Aziz. *Studies in Islamic Culture in the Indian Environment*, Delhi: Oxford University Press, 1999.

Ahmad, Feroz. *Ethnicity and Politics in Pakistan*, Karachi: Oxford University Press, 1998.

Ahsan, Aitzaz. *The Indus Saga and the Making of Pakistan*, Karachi: Oxford University Press, 1996.

Ali, Chaudhri Muhammad, *The Emergence of Pakistan*. Lahore: Research Society of Pakistan, 1973.

Ali, Syed Ameer. *The Spirit of Islam*. London: Christophers, 1922.

———. *A Short History of the Saracens: Being a Concise Account of the Rise and Decline of the Saracenic Power and of the Economic, Social and Intellectual Development of the Arab Nation*. London: Macmillan, 1924.

Allchin, Bridget and Raymond. *The Rise of Civilisation in India and Pakistan*. Cambridge: Cambridge University Press, 1982.

Allen, Charles. *God's Terrorists: The Wahhabi Cult and the Hidden Roots of Modern Jihad*. London: Abacus, 2007.

Armstrong, Karen. *Islam: A Short History*. London: Phoenix, 2001.

Asher, Catherine B. *Architecture of Mughal India*. Cambridge: Cambridge University Press, 1992.

Aziz, K. K. *The Making of Pakistan: A Study in Nationalism*. London: Chatoo and Windus, 1967.

———. *Rahmat Ali: A Life*. Stuttgart: Franz Steiner, 1987.

Basham, A. L. *The Wonder That Was India. A Survey of the Culture of the Indian Subcontinent before the Coming of the Muslims*. New York: Sedgwick, 1954.

Baxter, Craig, (ed.). *Diaries of Field Marshal Mohammad Ayub Khan, 1966–1972*. Karachi: Oxford University Press, 2007.

Bhutto, Benazir. *Daughter of the East*. London: Hamish Hamilton, 1988.

Brown, Judith. *Modern India: The Origins of an Asian Democracy*. Oxford: Oxford University Press, 1994.

Cloughley, Brian. *A History of Pakistan Army: Wars and Insurrections*. Karachi: Oxford University Press, 2006.

Cohen, Stephen P. *The Idea of Pakistan*. Washington, D.C: Brookings Institution, 2004.

Collins, Larry, and Dominique Lapierre. *Freedom at Midnight*. London: HarperCollins, 1997.

Dalrymple, William. *The Last Mughal: The Fall of a Dynasty, Delhi, 1857*. London: Bloomsbury, 2006.

———. *White Mughals: Love and Betrayal in Eighteenth-Century India*. London: HarperCollins, 2002.

Dani, A. H. *The History of Taxila*. Tokyo and Paris: UNESCO, 1986.

Eaton, Richard. *Essays on Islamic and Indian History*. New Delhi: Oxford University Press, 2001.

Early, Abraham. *The Mughal Throne: The Saga of India's Great Emperors*. London: Penguin, 2001.

Feldman, Herbert. *From Crisis to Crisis, Pakistan 1962–1969*. Karachi: Oxford University Press, 2001.

Gascoine, Bamber. *The Great Moghuls*. London: Jonathan Cape, 1971.

Gauhar, Altaf. *Ayub Khan: Pakistan's First Military Ruler*. Lahore: Sang-e-Meel Publications, 1993.

Gilmartin, David, and Bruce Lawrence (eds.). *Beyond Turk and Hindu: Rethinking Religious Identities in Islamicate South Asia*. New Delhi: Research Press, 2002.

Gilmartin, David. *Empire and Islam: Punjab and the Making of Pakistan*. London: I. B. Tauris, 1988.

Hussain, Zahid. *Frontline Pakistan: The Struggle with Militant Islam*. London: I. B. Tauris, 2007.

Ikram, S.M. *Modern Muslim India and the Birth of Pakistan*. Lahore: Research Society, 1995.

Ikramullah, Shaista S. *From Purdah to Parliament*. Karachi: Oxford University Press, 1998.

Iqbal, Muhammad. *Poems from Iqbal*, trans. by Victor Kiernan. Karachi: Oxford University Press, 1999.

———. *The Reconstruction of Religious Thought in Islam*. London: Oxford University Press, 1934.

Jackson, Peter. *The Delhi Sultanate*, Cambridge: Cambridge University Press, 1999.

Jalal, Ayesha. *The Sole Spokesman: Jinnah, the Muslim League and the Demand for Pakistan*. Cambridge: Cambridge University Press, 1985.

Jones, Owen B. *Pakistan: Eye of the Storm*. London/New Haven: Yale University Press, 2002.

Jones, Philip E. *The Pakistan People's Party: Rise to Power*. Karachi: Oxford University Press, 2003.

Keay, John. *A History of India*. London: HarperCollins, 2000.

Keddie, Nikki R. *An Islamic Response to Imperialism: Political and Religious Writings of Sayyid Jamal al-Din al-Afghani*. Berkeley: University of California Press, 1968.

Kennedy, Charles H. (ed.). *Pakistan at the Millennium*. Karachi: Oxford University Press, 2003.

———. *Bureaucracy in Pakistan*, Karachi: Oxford University Press, 1987.

Kenoyer, Mark. *Ancient Cities of the Indus Valley Civilization*. Karachi: Oxford University Press, 1998.

Khan, Muhammad Ayub. *Friends not Masters*. London: Oxford University Press, 1967.

Khan, Liaquat Ali. *Pakistan: The Heart of Asia*. Cambridge: Harvard University Press, 1950.

Khuhro, Hamida. *The Making of Modern Sindh*. Karachi: Oxford University Press, 1999.

Lamb, Alastair. *Birth of a Tragedy: Kashmir 1947*. Hertingfordbury: Roxford, 1994.

———. *Kashmir: A Disputed Legacy, 1846–1990*. Hertingfordbury: Roxford, 1991.

Lamb, Christina. *Waiting for Allah: Pakistan's Struggle for Democracy*. London: Hamish Hamilton, 1991.

MacMahon, Robert J. *The Cold War on the Periphery: The United States, India and Pakistan*. New York: Columbia University Press, 1994.

Malik, Hafeez. *Sir Sayyid Ahmad Khan and Muslim Modernization in India and Pakistan*. New York: Columbia University Press, 1980.

Malik, Iftikhar H. *Crescent Between Cross and Star: Islam and the West after 9/11*. Karachi: Oxford University Press, 2007.

———. *Jihad, Hindutva and the Taliban: South Asia at a Crossroads*. Karachi: Oxford University Press, 2005.

———. *Islam, Nationalism and the West: Issues of Identity in Pakistan*. Oxford: St. Antony's Series, 1999.

———. *State and Civil Society in Pakistan: Politics of Authority, Ideology and Ethnicity*. Oxford: St. Antony's-Macmillan, 1997.

———. *U.S.-South Asia Relations, 1784–1940: A Historical Perspective*. Islamabad: Area Study Centre, 1988.

———. "The Afghan Conflict: Islam, the west and Identity Politics in South Asia." *Indo-British Review*, XXIII, 2, (2002).

———. "Pakistan in 2001: The Afghanistan Crisis and the Rediscovery of the Frontline State." *Asian Survey*, 42 (2002).

Marshall, J. *The Buddhist Art of Gandhara*. Cambridge: Cambridge University Press, 1960.

Matheson, Sylvia. *The Tigers of Baluchistan*. Karachi: Oxford University Press, 1997.

Matinuddin, Kamal. *The Taliban Phenomenon*. Karachi: Oxford University Press, 1999.

Metcalf, Barbara. *Islamic Revival in British India: Deoband, 1860–1900*. Princeton: Princeton University Press, 1988.

Minault, Gail. *The Khilafat Movement: Religious Symbolism and Political Mobilization in India*. New Delhi: Oxford University Press, 1999.

Mumtaz, Khawar, and Farida Shaheed. *Women of Pakistan: Two Steps Forward. One Step Back?* London: Zed, 1987.

Musharraf, Pervez. *In the Line of Fire: A Memoir*. London: Free Press, 2006.

Nasr, Seyyed Vali Reza. *Mawdudi and the Making of Islamic Revolution*. New York: Oxford University Press, 1996.

Qureshi, Ishtiaq H. *Ulema in Politics: A Study Relating to the Political Activities of the Ulema in the South Asian Subcontinent from 1556 to 1947*. Karachi: Maaref, 1972.

———. *The Struggle for Pakistan*. Karachi: University of Karachi, 1969.

Rahman, Tariq. *Language, Education and Culture*. Karachi: Oxford University Press, 1999.

———. *Language and Politics in Pakistan*. Karachi: Oxford University Press, 1996.

Rashid, Ahmed. *Taliban: Islam, Oil and the New Great Game in Central Asia*. London: I. B. Tauris, 2002.

Richards, John F. *The Mughal Empire*. Cambridge: Cambridge University Press, 1996.

Rizvi, Hasan-Askari. *The Military and Politics in Pakistan, 1947–1997*. Lahore: Sang-e-Meel Publications, 2000.

Rose, Leo, and Richard Sisson. *War and Secession: Pakistan, India, and the Creation of Pakistan*. Berkeley: University of California Press, 1990.

Saeed, Ahmad. *Anjuman-i-Islamia Amritsar, 1873–1947* (Urdu). Lahore: Research Society, 1986.

Sayeed, Khalid B. *Politics in Pakistan: The Nature and Direction of Change*. New York: Praeger, 1980.

Schofield, Victoria (ed.). *Old Roads, New Highways*. Karachi: Oxford University Press, 1997.

———. *Kashmir in the Crossfire*. London: I. B. Tauris, 1996.

Shahnawaz, Jahan Ara. *Father and Daughter: A Political Biography*. Karachi: Oxford University Press, 2002.

Shaikh, Farzana. *Community and Consensus in Islam: Muslim Representation in Colonial India, 1860–1947*. Cambridge: Cambridge University Press, 1989.

Sikand, Yoginder. *Sacred Places: Exploring Traditions of Shared Faith in India*. New Delhi: Penguin, 2003.

Singh, Khushwant. *A History of Sikhs*, Volume I. Delhi: Orient Longman, 1992.

Smith-Mackintosh, Tim (ed.). *The Travels of Ibn Battutah*. London: Picador, 2002.

Symonds, Richard. *The Making of Pakistan*. London: Faber and Faber, 1950.

Syed, Anwar H. "Z. A. Bhutto's Self-Characterizations and Pakistani Political Culture." *Asian Survey* XVIII, December 1978.

Talbot, Ian. *Pakistan: A Modern History*. London: Hurst, 1999.

Thapar, Romila. *A History of India*. London: Penguin, 1979.

Titus, Paul (ed.). *Marginality and Modernity: Ethnicity and Change in Post-Colonial Balochistan*. Karachi: Oxford University Press, 1996.

Waseem, Mohammad. *The 1993 Elections in Pakistan*. Lahore: Vanguard Books, 1994.

Wheeler, R.E.M. *Five Thousand Years of Pakistan*. London: Royal India & Pakistan Society, 1950.

Wolpert, Stanley. *Shameful Flight: The Last Years of British Empire in India*. New York: Oxford University Press, 2006.

———. *Zulfi Bhutto of Pakistan*. Karachi: Oxford University Press, 1993.

———. *Jinnah of Pakistan*. Berkeley: University of California Press, 1984.

Woodward, Bob. *Bush at War*. New York: Simon & Schuster, 2002.

Zaheer, Hasan. *The Separation of East Pakistan*. Karachi: Oxford University Press, 1994.

———. *The Time and Trial of the Rawalpindi Conspiracy Case*. Karachi: Oxford University Press, 1998.

Zaidi, Akbar. *Issues in Pakistan's Economy*. Karachi: Oxford University Press, 1999.

Zaman, Muhammad Qasim. *The Ulama in Contemporary Islam: Custodians of Change*. Karachi: Oxford University Press, 2004.

Ziring, Lawrence. *Pakistan: At the Crossroad of History*. Oxford: Oneworld, 2003.

———. *Pakistan: The Enigma of Political Development*. Boulder: Westview, 1980.

Newspapers, Magazines, Web sites, and Television Channels

ARY TV
Asian Age (London)
BBC
Channel 4 TV
CNN
Daily Times (Lahore)
Dawn (Karachi)
Economist (London)
Emel (London)
Financial Times (London)
Friday Times (Lahore)
Guardian (London)
Herald (Karachi)
http://www.aiindex.mnet.fr
http://www.fashionpakistan.co.uk
http://www.hrw.org
http://www.jaring.my/just
http://www.visage.pk.com
Independent (London)
News International (London)
Newsline (Karachi)
Newsweek (New York)
New York Times (New York)

Observer (London)
Sky TV
Sunday Times (London)
Time International (New York)
Times (London)
Washington Post (Washington, D.C.)

Index

About the Author

IFTIKHAR H. MALIK, a Fellow of the Royal Historical Society, is Professor of History at Bath Spa University, England, and is author of *Culture and Customs of Pakistan* (Greenwood, 2005). Professor Malik lives in Oxford, where he is associated with Wolfson College.

Other Titles in the Greenwood Histories of the Modern Nations
Frank W. Thackeray and John E. Findling, Series Editors

The History of Afghanistan
Meredith L. Runion

The History of Argentina
Daniel K. Lewis

The History of Australia
Frank G. Clarke

The History of the Baltic States
Kevin O'Connor

The History of Brazil
Robert M. Levine

The History of Canada
Scott W. See

The History of Central America
Thomas Pearcy

The History of Chile
John L. Rector

The History of China
David C. Wright

The History of Congo
Didier Gondola

The History of Cuba
Clifford L. Staten

The History of Egypt
Glenn E. Perry

The History of Ethiopia
Saheed Adejumobi

The History of Finland
Jason Lavery

The History of France
W. Scott Haine

The History of Germany
Eleanor L. Turk

The History of Ghana
Roger S. Gocking

The History of Great Britain
Anne Baltz Rodrick

The History of Haiti
Steeve Coupeau

The History of Holland
Mark T. Hooker

The History of India
John McLeod

The History of Indonesia
Steven Drakeley

The History of Iran
Elton L. Daniel

The History of Iraq
Courtney Hunt

The History of Ireland
Daniel Webster Hollis III

The History of Israel
Arnold Blumberg

The History of Italy
Charles L. Killinger

The History of Japan
Louis G. Perez

The History of Korea
Djun Kil Kim

The History of Kuwait
Michael S. Casey

The History of Mexico
Burton Kirkwood

The History of New Zealand
Tom Brooking

The History of Nigeria
Toyin Falola

The History of Panama
Robert C. Harding

The History of Poland
M. B. Biskupski

The History of Portugal
James M. Anderson

The History of Russia
Charles E. Ziegler

The History of Saudi Arabia
Wayne H. Bowen

The History of Serbia
John K. Cox

The History of South Africa
Roger B. Beck

The History of Spain
Peter Pierson

The History of Sri Lanka
Patrick Peebles

The History of Sweden
Byron J. Nordstrom

The History of Turkey
Douglas A. Howard

The History of Venezuela
H. Micheal Tarver and Julia C. Frederick

The History of Vietnam
Justin Corfield